Good Gossip

Good Gossip

Edited by Robert F. Goodman
and Aaron Ben-Ze'ev

University Press of Kansas

6011473

© 1994 by the University Press of Kansas

Published by the University Press of Kansas (Lawrence, Kansas 66049), which
was organized by the Kansas Board of Regents and is operated and funded by
Emporia State University, Fort Hays State University, Kansas State University,
Pittsburg State University, the University of Kansas, and Wichita State
University

Library of Congress Cataloging-in-Publication Data

Good gossip / edited by Robert F. Goodman, Aaron Ben-Ze'ev.
    p.   cm.
    Includes bibliographical references and index.
    ISBN 0-7006-0669-6 (alk. paper)   ISBN 0-7006-0670-X
(pbk : alk. paper)
    1. Gossip.   2. Interpersonal communication.   3. Interpersonal
relations.   I. Goodman, Robert F.   II. Ben-Ze'ev, Aharon.
BJ1535.G6G66   1994
177'.2—dc20   93-46229

British Library Cataloguing in Publication Data is available.

Printed in the United States of America

10 9 8 7 6 5 4 3 2 1

The paper used in this publication meets the minimum requirements of the
American National Standard for Permanence of Paper for Printed Library
Materials Z39.48-1984.

Contents

Introduction   1
ROBERT F. GOODMAN

Part 1: Gossip as a Moral Problem

1. The Vindication of Gossip   11
AARON BEN-ZE'EV

2. In Praise of Gossip: Indiscretion as a Saintly Virtue   25
RONALD DE SOUSA

3. Gossip as Moral Talk   34
GABRIELE TAYLOR

4. The Logic of Gossip   47
LAURENCE THOMAS

5. Gossip and Humor   56
JOHN MORREALL

6. The Legal Regulation of Gossip: Backyard Chatter and
the Mass Media   65
ROBERT POST

7. Gossip and Privacy   72
FERDINAND SCHOEMAN

Part 2: Gossip and Knowledge

8. Knowledge Through the Grapevine: Gossip as Inquiry   85
MARYANN AYIM

9. Gossip, or in Praise of Chaos   100
LORRAINE CODE

10. Gossip: A Feminist Defense   106
LOUISE COLLINS

Part 3: Empirical Studies of Gossip

11. Gossip, Reputation, and Social Adaptation   117
NICHOLAS EMLER

12. Used and Abused: Gossip in Medieval Society   139
    SYLVIA SCHEIN

13. Gossip, Gossipers, Gossipees   154
    MARIANNE E. JAEGER, ANNE A. SKLEDER, BRUCE RIND, AND
    RALPH L. ROSNOW

14. Medical Gossip and Rumor: Their Role in the Lay
    Referral System   169
    JERRY M. SULS AND FRANKLIN GOODKIN

15. The Tendency to Gossip as a Psychological Disposition:
    Constructing a Measure and Validating It   180
    OFRA NEVO, BARUCH NEVO, AND ANAT DERECH-ZEHAVI

Notes   193

References   199

About the Contributors   209

Index   211

Introduction
Robert F. Goodman

IN ONE SENSE, this collection of essays on the subject of gossip confirms what most of us probably already know: Traditional moral codes—Christian, Jewish, and no doubt others as well—condemn the practice of gossip and incorporate various forms of punishment that are designed to discourage it. Nicholas Emler, for instance, tells us that in Britain from the fourteenth to the eighteenth centuries ducking stools and stocks were used to chastise gossips. Traditional Jewish law employed punishments such as fines and flogging for persons found guilty of one form or another of gossip. In another sense, this collection is a vigorous attack on the traditional view and identifies many of gossip's virtues. Some of these are not entirely surprising, for any social activity as widespread as gossip must be fulfilling certain important personal and social functions. However, the essays by Aaron Ben-Ze'ev, Ronald de Sousa, and Lorraine Code, among others, provide entirely new insights regarding the phenomenon. The reader will find a number of vital and provocative tensions between tradition and modernity, between a moral view of gossip and the functional one favored by social scientists, and between the informality of gossip and the preference for formalized knowledge that has played such a central role in modern society.

In the modern period, and particularly in this century, many other traditional moral prohibitions and sanctions have undergone fundamental reevaluation, have weakened, or even have disappeared. The moral prohibition against gossip, however, seems by and large to have remained essentially intact, possibly because the prohibition against gossip is actually quite weak. Gossip is proscribed in principle and generally frowned upon, but at the same time it is honored in day-to-day practice.

Until recently, philosophers and social scientists have paid scant attention to gossip, but, as the chapters in this book show, an analysis of gossip can teach us a great deal about social life, knowledge, and the moral implications of complex and subtle forms of human behavior. The chapters consider the circumstances in which gossip occurs and its consequences for society as well as its significance for those people who gossip and for those who are gossiped about. Although a number of contributors conclude that gossip is a positive aspect of social life that ought rather to be encouraged than prohibited, the book as whole is not an unqualified vindication of gossip. Grounds for the moral condemnation of gossip are carefully considered in the essays by Gabriele Taylor and Laurence Thomas, and we all recognize that the reader may be reluctant to make a clean break with the traditional distaste for gossip and people who engage in it, no matter what virtues it may have.

Gossip as a Moral and Social Problem

Its traditional image notwithstanding, gossip might be thought of as a form of what Taylor calls "moral talk." The topics most interesting to gossipers are those, such as infidelity, that have strong moral content. Thus, the subject of gossip is ripe for analysis by moral philosophers. At the same time, as a social practice, it is of intrinsic interest to psychologists, sociologists, and other social scientists. It should be noted, though, that all of the chapters in this book are morally oriented to the extent that each of them, ultimately, is concerned with the question of whether gossip is a good or a bad thing. This concern is no less true of the empirical studies than of the philosophical ones. As a consequence, the book as a whole pulls us into the often-perplexing philosophical difficulties and controversies that arise once an analysis of a moral principle takes social, psychological, economic, and political factors into account.

When we view gossip as a moral problem, we can make an important distinction between circumstantial and consequential forms of moral theory. The consequentialist might argue that gossip ought to be avoided no matter what the circumstances, because gossip causes people a particularly pernicious form of harm, a harm against which they cannot defend themselves and which cannot be undone. A second form of consequentialist argument runs like this: Moral principles lose much of their force when applied on a case-by-case basis. A frequent objection to euthanasia, for instance, is that once the sanctity of life no longer has the status of an absolute principle people may feel free not only to end the extreme suffering of a terminally ill patient or to pull the plug on the machine that is keeping a comatose person alive, but also to take it upon themselves to end the lives of others for financial reasons or because of adverse effects upon their families. By the same token, one might maintain that even if much gossip may be quite trivial, essentially harmless, and even constructive, the prohibition should be sustained in order to protect people in those instances when it can cause serious and irreparable damage. Aaron Ben-Ze'ev objects, however, that some moral prohibitions focus upon and highlight extreme cases, thereby promoting distortion and misunderstanding. This tendency might explain the fact that the positive functions of gossip often are ignored.

The social and psychological analyses of gossip brings to light its richness and complexity. Gossip varies according to the circumstances in which it occurs. It is one thing, for instance, when two old friends and long-time confidantes engage in gossip and quite another when two strangers indiscriminately pass on harmful or malicious information. Furthermore, analysis shows that gossip promotes friendship and group cohesion, helps to sustain group norms, and often serves to effectively communicate important information. Social scientists also emphasize that gossip may be important to the extent that it provides bases for the comparison of an individual's experiences, feelings, and beliefs with those of others; contributes to one's sense of self-esteem by revealing other people's failings; and enhances status among peers. Often, the basic orientation of economists, psychiatrists, sociologists, and political scientists to social behavior emphasizes and brings to light hidden underlying processes, thereby negating our commonsensible judgments. This form of explanation, whether it is employed to account for the deep psychological motives behind someone's antisocial behavior or to justify selfishness in the marketplace, quite often frees us from the sense of moral obligation that is frequently associated with our commonsensible judgments.

The philosopher Ronald de Sousa argues that "though gossip provides fertile ground for the exercise of certain vices, this can no more be held against gossip per se than against love, marriage, or commerce, which afford equally rich opportunities for the deployment of bad motives." He defends the notion of a "utopia of perfect transparency" that serves "to the benefit of realistic expectations about human nature." In other words, good things may result from what might otherwise be seen as bad behaviors. In a similar vein, feminists such as Lorraine Code maintain that gossip is a characteristic form of communication among women and other oppressed groups. To the extent that this is true, the bias against it may reflect the dominance of masculine perceptions in our culture.

As I have suggested, however, some readers may remain very uneasy about the moral status of gossip even after considering these arguments in its defense. Certain instances when I have spoken badly of a friend behind his or her back and felt guilty afterwards remain etched in my memory. Even if the person was not hurt by my gossiping, the act itself left a bad taste in my mouth. Taylor provides an important philosophical grounding for this moral intuition, observing that an "activity's possession of merit does not necessarily indicate any merit in those participating in the activity." Although she grants that gossipers do not necessarily bear the gossipee any ill-will, she nevertheless places significance in the fact that "gossipers trivialize another's experience by ignoring its dimension of being another's experience with the impact of which she will in some way have to cope. In doing so they distort and belittle that person's experience."

An Overview

The book is divided into three parts. Part 1 focuses upon the fundamental nature of gossip and introduces the primary tension between the functional approach, which tends to vindicate it, and the moral perspective, which emphasizes the fact that it remains a morally problematic form of behavior even in this era of moral permissiveness. The moral analysis incorporates the claim that gossip constitutes an unwarranted invasion of privacy. Part 2 considers gossip from a quite different direction: as a form of communication, with particular emphasis upon its role in knowledge acquisition and transmission. The chapters in this part present a number of interesting critiques of modern epistemology. Part 3 includes empirical studies of gossip as it occurs in a variety of settings.

The first task, defining the meaning of the word "gossip" and exploring the fundamental implications of adopting one orientation or another to the phenomena that the term encompasses, is taken up by Ben-Ze'ev, Taylor, and Thomas. They clarify the basic terms by which we analyze the relationship between two gossipers, they examine what occurs in that relationship, and they identify the significance of what occurs therein for the gossipee. Ben-Ze'ev begins the debate by challenging the traditional assumption that what we define as "gossip" is necessarily negative or malicious. He adopts the common dictionary definition of "to gossip" as "to talk (or write) idly about other people, mostly about their personal or intimate affairs"; and maintains further that gossip "typically has its value in the activity itself and not in achieving external ends." Taylor and Thomas object to this way of framing the topic of gossip, though not with a strong defense of the traditional negative conception of the term. Thomas is concerned primarily with the common usage of the term. He writes that "the very idea that purely complimentary remarks about a third party amounts to gossip is very counter-intuitive indeed." After giving examples of negative information that may be passed on with good intentions and positive information that may be communicated to another person with negative intent, he concludes, in contrast to Ben-Ze'ev, that "gossip is conceptually tied to the motives behind the act." Taylor, meanwhile, defines gossip as talk between two or more people about the private life of another, behind that person's back. She emphasizes that the secretive tenor of gossip suggests that it normally contains information that the gossipee would prefer to keep private. Thus, while gossip need not be malicious or potentially harmful, it usually is.

Ben-Ze'ev, as we have seen, disagrees with this claim. By emphasizing the often casual and nonconsequential nature of gossip, he prepares the ground for discussions that underscore gossip's positive functions, and he himself identifies a number of them. He points, for instance, to the claim that gossip is an activity engaged in for its intrinsic worth as opposed to external ends. Even scrupulous people may allow themselves to engage in gossip purely for pleasure; and gossip in the workplace or in other social settings may serve as a refuge from and bulwark against the emphasis upon external goals that increasingly characterizes our interactions with others.

In fact, the theme of resistance or subversion runs powerfully through a number of these chapters. People gossip about the powerful, rich, and famous in order to "cut them down to size." Informal gossip networks flourish in large, bureaucratic organizations as a way of softening, resisting, or subverting their depersonalizing tendencies. Gossip offers passive resistance to many forms of power. Feminists might argue that this aspect of gossip explains why women are more frequent and proficient gossipers than men (a perception that is challenged by Ofra Nevo and her associates). Soldiers gossip about their superiors, prisoners about their jailers, and even slaves manage to find some social space in which to gossip about their masters. The distinctive feature of modern totalitarian regimes, as compared to traditional despotisms, is that they manage to invade even this territory.

John Morreall finds a number of interesting parallels between gossip and humor and discusses the effect that humor has upon gossip. Not only is the subject matter of gossip important, but also the manner. When gossip is in a humorous vein, "we tend not to get hostile toward those we are gossiping about" and, as a consequence, humor "tends to redeem [gossip] from pettiness and viciousness." Morreall's interpretation lends support to Ben-Ze'ev's sanguine view.

Nonetheless, by its very nature gossip constitutes an invasion into the privacy of other people's lives, and Robert Post analyzes the problem of trying to provide protection from this invasion and from its potentially harmful effects by legal means. His discussion of the civil law concludes that its protections are limited to public media and to what can be clearly defined as libel. Similar communication in private, or what he calls "backyard" gossip, is defined as slander and cannot be controlled by civil law. Moreover, the inability to restrain backyard gossip calls into question the utility of trying to control its public manifestations. Post cites a recent case decided by the United States Supreme Court in which this point was deemed crucial.

Ferdinand Schoeman considers the interaction of gossip and privacy from a theoretical rather than legal perspective. He writes that "privacy is a part of an historically conditioned intricate normative matrix with interdependent practices; it is best understood when viewed contextually interacting with other practices in shaping behavior rather than as an independent principle that either succumbs to or overrides other considerations." Once having established this perspective, he then explains that privacy and gossip norms actually work together to protect individuals from overreaching social control. The complex interaction between the two modulates the amount and type of social pressure available to control behavior.

The chapters in Part 2 by Maryann Ayim and Lorraine Code challenge the assumption that the informational content of gossip is highly unreliable. One of the traditional grounds for objecting to gossip is that the emotional content of gossip is far more compelling to gossipers than any information it might contain and that gossipers seldom let the facts get in the way of developing and embellishing a good story. On these grounds gossip is repugnant to the rationalist conception of knowledge that we have inherited from the Greeks and that has dominated Western thought since the seventeenth century. According to this tradition the only knowledge in which we can have confidence is that which is obtained and analyzed by systematic means. One of the most important developments in recent philosophy, however, is an attack, from many quarters, upon the dominance of rationalized, systematic thought. The result is a renewed recognition of the value and virtues of informal knowledge. For instance, the publication of Thomas Kuhn's famous study, *The Structure of Scientific Revolutions* (1970), emphasized the extent to which informal understandings constitute a crucial element even in highly formalized scientific theories. Taking this insight a step further, David Hull (1988) shows that gossip among scientists plays an important role in scientific progress. Nevertheless, Code resists the fusion of formal enquiry and informal gossip within a common framework. She suggests that what is distinct and crucial about gossip is its "unruliness . . . its (self-referential) resistance to paradigmatic summing up, which is at once the locus of its power and its danger. Like the laugh of the medusa, it bursts out unexpectedly."

A second line of attack upon rationalism comes from feminist theory. Collins provides a provocative feminist slant on the nature of knowledge. Like de Sousa, she argues that our understanding of human nature is enhanced by knowledge of the characteristically personal and domestic subjects of gossip. Learning about others helps us to understand our own situation and to develop empathy for other people's predicaments. Indeed, as society becomes increasingly atomized and gossip networks shrink or disappear, people develop other mechanisms, such as self-help groups, to serve these functions.

Insofar as we focus upon gossip as a form of knowledge, the primary moral questions which I introduced earlier may seem to recede into the background. Questions of knowledge and questions of value, we have been taught to believe, inhabit two entirely separate realms. Gossip, however, breaks down this clear division; it is, to use Code's term, a "chaotic" interplay of information and moral judgment.

There are at least two ways to view this interplay. One might argue that the sort of moral judgments made by gossipers cannot be separated from the specifics of particular cases. So enmeshed are such moral determinations in detail that they cannot be fit neatly into a unified moral system or easily generalized to other cases. Others, however, might counter that a primary emphasis of gossip is upon instances of trespass against a community's norms. A primary purpose of gossip is to sustain those norms, not to make fine-tuned judgments of every case. Details, then, serve more to embellish the story than to determine its moral content. This is an interesting empirical question that deserves further consideration by social psychologists.

Part 3 offers several empirical studies of the social and psychological aspects of gossip, beginning with a wide-ranging social analysis by Nicholas Emler. Marianne Jaeger and her associates find gossipers and gossipees alike to be "movers and shakers," the more socially active and central persons in the group that they investigate. This chapter seems to support the claim that gossip does little harm, though I think we should bear in mind that the study investigated a college sorority. Such a group is at least temporarily very close-knit, a condition that may have a moderating effect upon the damage that gossip can cause. Such moderation did not apparently affect the close-knit societies of the medieval world, where, Sylvia Schein tells us, gossip was a practice infused with power and danger. Perhaps, like our traditional concern about "manners," our unreflective judgments about gossip may be a remnant of medieval mores. The chapter by Jerry Suls and Franklin Goodkin on medical gossip and rumor discusses the links between these informal modes of communication and peoples' tendencies to seek medical treatment, to identify symptoms, to be attracted to quack cures, and so on. Ofra Nevo and her associates analyze gossip by means of a twenty-item questionnaire. Their findings suggest that the perception that women gossip more than men is incorrect, that in fact the difference between the sexes lies in the subjects gossiped about, not in the general tendency to gossip.

This book presents a fascinating challenge to our common-sense perceptions and judgments. The contrast between these judgments, which directly incorporate moral concerns and moral intuitions, and functional understanding, in which straightforward moral considerations become far less important or even disappear, is absolutely crucial. By bringing these competing perspectives into direct confrontation, we better understand the pros and cons of both.

Part 1 | Gossip as a Moral Problem

1 | The Vindication of Gossip

Aaron Ben-Ze'ev

GOSSIP IS A VERY POPULAR ACTIVITY, yet its psychological and moral aspects have received little theoretical attention. Consequently, the public image of gossip is often confused and includes features that are neither typical nor common in gossip—in particular, the maliciousness that is commonly attributed to gossip seems to be wrong. The vindication of gossip requires a different characterization of its nature, and two conceptual tools are crucial to this task. The first is the prototypical category, and the second is the distinction between intrinsically valuable activities and extrinsically valuable actions.

A distinction can be made between two major types of cognitive categories: "binary" and "prototypical." Binary categories provide a clear criterion that constitutes the sufficient and necessary conditions for membership. It is an all-or-nothing category with two basic attributes: (a) clear-cut and definite boundaries within which the criterion's conditions are met, and (b) an equal degree of membership for all items. There are no varying degrees of membership in this category because meeting the criterion is not a matter of degree; it is either met or not met. War veterans, eligible voters, and only children are examples of binary categories. One cannot be a partial veteran, semi-eligible voter, or almost an only child. Membership in a prototypical category, on the other hand, is determined by an item's degree of similarity to the best example in the category: the greater the similarity, the higher the degree of membership. The prototypical category has neither clear-cut and definite boundaries nor an equal degree of membership. Some items are so similar to or so different from the prototype that we have no doubt about their inclusion or exclusion; with other items the degree of similarity makes it difficult or impossible to say for sure whether they belong or not (Ben-Ze'ev, 1993b; Lakoff, 1987; Rosch, 1977, 1978).

If, as I believe, various instances of gossip constitute a prototypical category, then there is no single essence that is a necessary and sufficient condition for all instances of gossip and no simple way of describing them. Accordingly, my characterization of gossip concerns typical rather than all cases. The basic features of gossip are fully manifest in typical, or paradigmatic, examples; in less typical examples, these components occur in a less developed form and some may even be absent. I consider the prototypical nature of gossip fundamental to its explanation, and since my characterization refers only to typical examples, the claim that some examples differ from the typical does not contradict my characterization but derives from it.

The use of prototypical categories may draw the criticism that there can be no counterexamples to prototypical characterization, since any such example may be regarded as atypical. True, it is more difficult to confirm membership in a prototypical category than in a binary category, but the characterization is also more complex. A binary category has a clear criterion that constitutes the sufficient and necessary condition for membership; accordingly, there is usually an equal degree of membership for all items. Working with binary categories is easier, but they often do not adequately represent reality. Since in fact there are usually no clear and definite boundaries between phenomena, working with prototypical categories is often more to the point. In light of the prototypical nature of gossip, I will frequently use terms such as "usually," "typically," and "often" while characterizing gossip. A refutation of my characterization of gossip remains possible, but it could not consist of describing an isolated case that seems to be an exception to the suggested characterization; it would have to show that indeed most phenomena differ from the suggested characterization or that the conceptual analysis is inconsistent.

The second basic conceptual tool I employ in characterizing gossip is the distinction between an intrinsically valuable activity and an extrinsically valuable action.[1] An extrinsically valuable action is a means to a certain end; its value lies in achieving this end. The criterion for evaluating this action is efficiency, namely, the ratio of benefits to costs. Time is one resource we try to save in extrinsically valuable actions. Examples of extrinsically valuable actions are cleaning the house, attending job interviews, paying bills, and the like. In an intrinsically valuable activity our interest is directed at the activity itself, not at its results. Such an activity also has results, but it is not performed to achieve these; rather, its performance satisfies our needs. The value of dancing, for instance, is in dancing itself and not in its results (although these may be positive); therefore, we do not try to finish dancing as fast as possible. Another example may be intellectual thinking whose basic motivation is creativity or intellectual curiosity, not the ensuing money or academic publications. Moral activity, which is motivated by a sense of duty without regard for cost-benefit calculations, is another example of an intrinsically valuable activity.

Most human activities have both intrinsic and extrir.
Often the factors underlying each value conflict over how lo
ties should continue or how far other resources should be in ⌐⌐⌐eu in
them. In such cases, we must determine whether the activity in question is an extrinsically valuable action or an intrinsically valuable
activity. De Sousa (1987) cites the examples of sex and tourism. Harried
tourists who consider sightseeing an extrinsically valuable action (or
"achievement") instead of an intrinsically valuable activity want to see
as many possible sights in the shortest possible time: they want "not
to see, but to have seen." Similarly, those many people who construe
sexual activity "as the harried tourist construes sightseeing" are
"taking sex for an achievement instead of an activity" (p. 219). When
people define gossip as an extrinsically valuable action, it loses many
of its important characteristics and often becomes malicious. To understand the nonmalicious nature of gossip, we must, then, consider it
both a prototypical category and an intrinsically valuable activity.
Characterizing gossip as having an intrinsic value does not mean that
it has no practical results. Similarly, one may view chewing gum as an
intrinsically valuable activity but still, chewing gum may have practical, positive results such as reducing the agent's tension or cleaning
the agent's teeth. I do not deny that gossip has practical results or that
it can be used as a means to achieve them. I argue, however, that its use
as a means is parasitic with regard to its intrinsic value.

A common dictionary definition of "to gossip" is "to talk (or
write) idly about other people, mostly about their personal or intimate
affairs." My characterization of gossip is compatible with this definition. Typical gossip is an idle, relaxing activity whose value lies in the
activity itself and not the achievement of external ends. This definition does not imply that gossip has no consequences, but those are
mostly by-products, not ends. Typical gossip is easygoing and enjoyable, with no significant intended practical results. Gossip is usually
relaxing and effortless and, like games, often relieves people of daily
tensions. One reason for the relaxing nature of gossip is being able to
talk about what is really on your mind (Tannen, 1990, p. 98). People
indulging in gossip do not want to ponder deeply the content or consequences of what they say. Sometimes gossip seems to be talk for the
sake of talking. When people are involved in serious, practical, and
purposive talk, they are not gossiping. Thus when two psychiatrists
analyze the love affair of my neighbor, their discussion is not gossip;
however, when my wife and I consider the same information, gossip it
is. The psychiatrists' discussion is not idle talk (or so they claim).

It is important to distinguish between gossip and the spread of unsubstantiated rumors. When recounting a personal affair that one has witnessed, one is engaged in gossip, but the information conveyed is substantiated. Since the typical content of gossip is usually behind-the-scenes, intimate information, it is indeed hard to verify and hence it is sometimes unsubstantiated. Lack of substantiation is not, however, an essential element of gossip, but a by-product of the confidential nature of the information conveyed. The unsubstantiated character is more typical of rumors, indeed it forms part of their definition. Moreover, unlike gossip, spreading rumors is essentially a purposive activity of merely extrinsic value. The difference between these is similar to the difference between harried tourism and an enjoyable sightseeing. The harried tourist, like a person who spreads rumors, wishes to achieve a certain end. The "calm" traveler, like the typical gossip, is engaged in his activity because he enjoys it. Spreading rumors is often a purposive vicious action, whereas gossip is not. Oscar Wilde (in *Lady Windermere's Fan*) said, "Gossip is charming. History is merely gossip. But scandal is gossip made tedious by morality." The derogatory connotation of gossip derives by and large from the failure to distinguish gossiping from the spreading of rumor.

Gossip in fact resembles joking more than rumor-mongering, for both gossip and joking are intrinsically valuable activities. Both are essentially social activities that strengthen interpersonal bonds—we do not tell jokes and gossip to ourselves. As popular activities that evade social restrictions, they often refer to topics that are inaccessible to serious public discussion. Gossip and joking often appear together: when we gossip we usually tell jokes and when we are joking we often gossip as well. Both gossip and telling jokes involve an element of surprise, although this is more important in joking. In gossip the informational content is primary, whereas in joking the crucial element is the form in which this content is presented. The two activities sometimes involve disguised insults, but those are not typically their main focus. Jokes are often about fictional characters, but gossip deals with real people and, accordingly, more often damages reputations. Consequently, though people readily express their pleasure in joking, they are more reluctant to confess pleasure in discussing other people's affairs. Because of its more realistic character, gossip seems to fulfill more complex functions than joking, and yet, jokes have received much greater scientific attention than gossip (see Morreall, Chapter 5).

Heidegger condemns gossip as too trivial to aid genuine understanding of the more profound aspects of human life (1962, pp. 212–13). To be sure, gossip does not address highly sophisticated, profound, and serious issues, but this should not damn it altogether. A great deal of literary fiction concerns issues similar to those discussed in go____, no one takes this as a profound flaw. One cannot and should not wrestle always with serious issues, and gossip is a sort of communication all people can share. Furthermore, I would deny that gossip involves no genuine understanding. Informal talk about trivial and particular issues furnishes an alternative perspective that may in fact shed light on matters that are sometimes misunderstood in serious, abstract discussions. One should not stipulate that human beings must choose between either gossip or the serious discussion of abstract ideas—as if the love of gossip reflected a corresponding hatred of serious matters. Gossip is but one among many kinds of discussion and should be examined against the spectrum of other types. With such comparison, the moral evaluation of gossip becomes more positive.

As an intrinsically valuable activity, gossip satisfies the basic need to acquire information about the personal and intimate aspects of other people's lives. Such knowledge satisfies our curiosity and may be valuable in understanding our own lives (see also Collins, Chapter 10). Although intimacy plays an important role in our lives, we remain quite ignorant of how it works in other people's lives. Gossip is an enjoyable way to gather information that is otherwise hard to obtain. Moreover, intimate and personal aspects often reveal more about the personalities of other people than does their public behavior. This need to acquire knowledge of intimate and personal aspects of other people's lives occupies a central role in gossip because there are very few other ways to satisfy this need. Candid and open self-description is rare and limited to very few close friends. Literature, of course, may partially fulfill such a need, but it does not refer to "real" people who share our surroundings and our lives. Gossip satisfies a personal curiosity concerning people who are of particular interest to us. The results of a statistical survey showing that the incidence of intercourse among average British couples is higher than that of most other Western couples, including, surprisingly, that of French and Italian couples, is not a typical subject of gossip; the number of times each week our neighbor meets with her lover is.

Gossip also satisfies the tribal need, namely, the need to belong to and be accepted by a unique group. (One meaning of "gossip" is indeed "being a friend of.") The sharing of intimate and personal information and the intimate manner of conveying this information contribute to the formation of an exclusive group with intimate and affectionate ties between its members. Gossip functions crucially in establishing intimacy and in this sense satisfies the tribal need. Like friendship, gossip is a kind of sharing (though a quite superficial one). If friendship leads to gossip, gossip also leads to friendship (Heilman, 1973, p. 153). Tannen (1990) agrees that "not only is telling secrets evidence of friendship; it *creates* friendship" (p. 98), and adds that telling secrets is a privilege and even an obligation among friends. People can be deeply hurt when they find out that a friend failed to inform them about confidential intimate events. Moreover, "Small talk is crucial to maintain a sense of camaraderie when there is nothing special to say" (p. 102).

People who are aware of the friendly character of gossip may use it to make new friends. Behaving toward someone the way friends do indicates our wish to consider that person a friend. Similarly, giving someone confidential information conveys our confidence in this person. Such a use of gossip to make friends belies its intrinsically valuable nature, but one can use gossip in making new friends only because gossip typically has intrinsic value as a friendly activity that strengthens social bonds. Perhaps the tribal need is not really satisfied unless intimate information is exchanged; only such information indicates intimate relations.

Like many other kinds of need-satisfying activities, gossip is enjoyable. The teller and the listeners delight in the activity of gossip and not in its results. Really good gossip is usually not just a piece of information but an anecdote, a narrative with a beginning, middle, and end. It is interesting, even to strangers. The pleasure derived is often that of a good story. Most people like to gossip now and then: it is a form of social communication that usually revolves around information not yet widely known and therefore intriguing. The information generally concerns people who are not there to hear it, and includes both description and evaluation of their behavior. Participants appear to share the same standards of right and wrong. And although adherence to such standards is often superficial, even the mere appearance of common moral standards establishes intimacy among the participants. Sometimes gossip becomes a type of commodity exchange: "If you wish to know about other people, tell me what you know about the people of interest to me." Although typical gossip is an exchange of intimate and personal information, it does not require reciprocity. One who loves to gossip does not expect to get an equal amount of information in return (although this person would be glad to hear unknown intimate information about other people). We engage in gossip because we delight in and value the activity itself and not its results.

The suggested characterization of typical gossip as an intrinsically valuable activity accords well with other features of gossip. The two major forms of communication typical of gossip are private conversations and public communication by the media. The former is more typical since gossip is usually intimate not only in the type of information conveyed, but also in the type of communication employed. The limited size of the audience suits the often confidential nature of the information and is compatible with the need to belong to an intimate and exclusive group. This sense of belonging to an exclusive group and of being a source of and one of the few recipients of exclusive information may boost the teller's as well as the listener's ego. And whereas active gossips often convey intimate information to many people, they usually do so not by addressing a large audience but through series of conversations with individuals or small groups. Gossips may indulge their hobby whenever possible and have little concern for the time spent doing so. Gossip has been called verbal chewing gum; Aldous Huxley described a gossip as a professional athlete—of the tongue.

Gossip conveys interesting information about sex, violence, money, vices and virtues, and foibles. These themes, of much concern to us individually, are also the focus of gossip columns (Levin and Arluke, 1987). Those who engage in dissemination of gossip publicly, however, take it as a purposive action of extrinsic value. Gossiping is not an idle and easy activity for columnists whose living depends on it. Professional gossips may enjoy their work in the same way that other people enjoy their extrinsically valuable work, but their enjoyment will usually differ from that of the nonprofessional gossip. Through the public media we learn the intimate and personal details of celebrities' lives. We become familiar with these celebrities and more easily identify with them, as we vicariously share their pleasures and come to believe that our own little world is not much less valuable than theirs. Furthermore, the immoral behavior of famous people, reported in gossip columns, enhances our self-respect. Celebrity gossip also allows us to draw comfort from other people's misfortune; our own small problems pale in comparison to the severe misfortunes of other people. As Levin and Arluke (1987) aptly say: "Misery loves miserable company—especially when the miserable are rich, famous, and apparently successful" (p. 37).

The objects of gossip fall into three major groups: (a) people in our immediate surroundings, (b) famous people, and (c) people whose intimate and personal lives are unique. The common feature of all three groups is our interest, though that interest varies from group to group. Whereas we are usually interested in the ordinary, everyday activities of famous people, we are characteristically interested in the nonordinary activities of ordinary people. Moreover, the more remote an ordinary person is from us, the more unusual their activity must be in order to be of interest to us.

Insofar as gossip does not require intellectual knowledge of the abstract but awareness of specific details of life, it is similar to literary fiction. As Tannen says, "When people talk about the details of daily lives, it is gossip; when they write about them, it is literature." Gossip also resembles anthropology, "the academic discipline that makes a career of documenting the details of people's lives" (Tannen, 1990, p. 97; see also Heilman, 1973; Spacks, 1985). Some gossip develops like folktales that are "told and retold year after year and time after time with all the freshness of a new report" (Heilman, 1973, p. 163). Kierkegaard argues that gossips would be in despair if there were a law "which did not forbid people talking, but simply ordered that everything that was spoken about should be treated as though it had happened fifty years ago" (1962, pp. 71–72). It is true that gossip is mainly concerned with new information about people who are still around. Even so this cannot be used (as it is in Kierkegaard's case) as a weapon to condemn gossip. The curiosity satisfied by gossip differs in important respects from intellectual, scientific curiosity, but this difference in itself is irrelevant to the moral evaluation of gossip.

The enjoyable and interesting elements in gossip stem not merely from acquiring novel information, but also from the content of this information. Like jokes, gossip often includes irony and unexpected features. Thus the sexual life of a priest, or even of our next-door neighbor, makes juicier gossip than the exploits of a prostitute. Likewise, the romance between a very old woman and a very young man is more delectable fare than that between two people of a similar age. This gap between reputation or conventional behavior and actual behavior is what makes gossip interesting.

The claim that gossip satisfies basic human needs is compatible with the observation that most (and probably all) people engage from time to time in gossip and enjoy it. Some people engage in this activity much more than others, however: the gossipmongers. Gossipmongers often have a strong need for repeated evaluation of their own personal and intimate life or for further social relationships. An excessive preoccupation with the intimate and personal affairs of others may be a substitute for "real action"; talk about others may not be as gratifying as interaction with them, but sometimes it is the only available option. Gossipmongers are generally considered tellers, not listeners. But the tellers usually do not invent the information they convey; accordingly, gossipmongers are also listeners who receive novel information about other people that can serve as a basis for their own self-evaluation. Furthermore, in typical gossip sessions many participants respond to novel information by providing other information in return. Gossipmongers may have a stronger need to be accepted by and belong to an exclusive group, for by being a purveyor of novel information, the person not only belongs to the group, but becomes its center of attention. Having exclusive knowledge enhances gossipmongers' status in the group, though in the long run they find that they are no longer trusted with confidential information (Heilman, 1973, p. 16). In addition to the respect gained by conveying interesting behind-the-scenes information, gossipmongers, who often have a low self-image, may gain some respect by conveying information which is slightly damaging to others. Lowering the evaluation of others may seem to them to somehow increase their own. There is indeed some evidence that individuals who are anxious about themselves tend to spread gossip about other people (Rosnow and Fine, 1976; see also Levin and Arluke, 1987).

Society evaluates gossipmongers negatively not because of evil in gossip's essential nature, but because of the excessive preoccupation of gossipmongers with this activity. This preoccupation often distorts the basically harmless and enjoyable character of gossip. If gossip is a constant occupation and harmless or merely embarrassing information not abundantly available, the purveyor can easily slip into hurtful revelations. A quantitative increase in the time one spends on gossip may result in a qualitative difference in the type of activity involved. This possibility underlies the Jewish prohibition against all forms of gossip, including that between husband and wife; the assumption apparently being that loose talk may easily become loose living. Just as sins of the heart may lead to vicious activities, idle talk about sex may turn into loose sexual conduct. To a certain extent this fear is justified, though the same can be said of literature, movies, and most other forms of communication and cultural expression. Furthermore, one may assert this kind of talk in fact substitutes for forbidden activities, thus reducing the likelihood of actually indulging in these activities. Gossip is a safe way to feed on activities in which, for reasons of security or safety, we normally do not engage (Spacks, 1985).

The typical gossipmonger is intelligent, with a good memory and an ability to discern connections between events. Gossips are quite realistic people; their extensive knowledge of embarrassing events prevents them from being naive. Gossips are often quite sensitive, curious, social-minded, and involved. Although incessant gossipers seem to have quite a few positive features, they are wasted on superficial matters and distorted by their excessive occupation with the superficial issues typical of gossip. The opposite of gossipmongers, excessive nongossips, often have little interest in other people, not only concerning their intimate and personal life, but other aspects as well. (Needless to say, there is no clear-cut distinction between excessive nongossips and "normal" nongossips, nor between "normal" gossips and excessive ones.)

Do women gossip more than men? Research indicates that both women and men spend a similar amount of time in idle conversation but that the topics differ: women tend to talk more about other people, whereas men dwell on sports, politics, and weather. In this sense women more often discuss topics typical of gossip. This difference may be explained by traditional cultural expectations: feminine activities were supposed to be confined to family and friendship networks whereas masculine activities were supposed to involve more distant relationships. Indeed, there is evidence that women adapt more to the needs of others and cooperate more than men do (Hochschild, 1983, p. 165; Levin and Arluke, 1987; see also Nevo et al., Chapter 15; Spacks, 1985). Traditionally, many men "have little use for small talk, since they believe talk is designed to convey information" and hence should have "significant content, be interesting and meaningful" (Tannen, 1990, p. 104). Men were supposed to maintain their manhood by not being involved too much in close relations (which are typical of gossip). Just as "real" men should not cry and should be reticent about their emotions, "real" men should not concentrate unduly on their personal and sentimental affairs. Influenced by this traditional image, men often doubt that they can benefit from a candid discussion with their peers; hence the topics of their relaxing, enjoyable conversations are less personal. Nevertheless, these idle conversations provide the benefits typical of gossip: they are relaxing, enjoyable activities that express a form of friendship. Because such conversations do not provide the access to intimate knowledge about others that enables one to understand oneself better, it may also be true that the friendship that evolves from these conversations is less intimate. Perhaps the sex-difference in topics of idle conversations stems not from a lack of masculine interest in issues typical of gossip, but from the pressure on men to eschew personal and sentimental matters. Gossiping about the intimate and personal matters of other people easily leads to discussing these issues in one's own life.

Is gossip a culture-dependent phenomenon? In the same way that there are differences among the sexes concerning the type and extent of gossip, similar differences may exist among cultures. However, since gossip fulfills some basic needs, we might expect to find it in some form in all cultures, although the extent and type of gossip may vary. It seems that the more exclusive and intimate the society is, the more pervasive and important gossip and the more important its role in this society (Gluckman, 1963). However, some form of gossip is to be found in every society. One indication for this is that children (who are supposed to be less influenced by cultures) gossip practically from the time they learn to talk and to recognize other people (Fine, 1977).

The joy of gossip is similar to gloating. Both states are severely condemned on moral grounds as malicious—indeed, their practice often makes us feel uncomfortable. Despite their prevalence, a great deal of confusion characterizes our attitude toward both. A particular significant distortion is perceiving extreme instances as typical and common instances. Owing to this mistaken identification the two states are often perceived to be malicious. (My detailed analysis of gloating appears in Ben-Ze'ev, 1992b, 1993a.)

Gloating usually derives from what we perceive as someone's deserved and usually minor misfortune. This characterization includes two nonproblematic features, namely, the presence of the subject's pleasure and the object's misfortune, and three disputable features, namely, the subject's perception of the object's misfortune as minor and as deserved and the subject's passivity in bringing about the object's misfortune. The two nondisputable features are common and necessary to gloating; the disputable features are typical but not universal. If the misfortune is grave, our gloating often turns into pity. When a person's misfortune seems deserved, we often feel that justice has been done, and the more deserved the misfortune, the more justified the pleasure. Typically, one of the greater contributions to gloating is the feeling that the failure of our competitor is due not to our own wicked behavior, but to inexorable fate. It is as if justice has been done in the spirit of the Talmudic saying: "The tasks of the righteous get done by others."

Do these features—namely, the subject's pleasure, the object's misfortune, the perceived minor and deserved nature of the object's misfortune, and the subject's passivity—typify gossip as well? Although the subject's pleasure is not as essential to gossip as to gloating, it is certainly typical. Whereas in the latter instance the subject cannot be sad, the listener or the teller of gossip may at times be sad, albeit rarely. The subject's passivity is also typical of gossip: we usually do not gossip about our own activities. Less clear is the accuracy of describing the object's situation in gossip as misfortune. Like gloating, gossip often reflects envy;[2] all of them are usually directed at those whose fortune is comparable or better than ours. Those who enjoy better fortune are of more interest to us because we would like to imitate them. Gossip resembles such cases of taking pleasure in others' minor misfortune as people slipping on a banana peel without hurting themselves or fans experiencing the defeat of the rival football team. In gossip the misfortune is more likely a social failure related to embarrassment rather than to shame. The violation of social norms presumably justifies the right of other people to speak about it, and in this sense, the object of gossip (as that of gloating) deserves the misfortune of having his or her intimate life be the topic of other people's conversations.

The similarity of gossip and gloating extends to our attitude toward them. Despite their prevalence, both attitudes are condemned on moral grounds. A major reason for this is the inclination to take extreme cases as typical and common for the whole category. Quite often extreme cases constitute the public image of the category and are mistakenly *perceived* to be both typical and frequent because like other abnormalities, they are more noticeable than the typical or common. For example, the public image of male jealousy includes the picture of a husband killing his wife for her infidelity. Yet it is obvious that murder is neither the common nor the typical behavior in jealousy. Surveys have revealed that between 37 percent and 50 percent of the respondents reported past extramarital affairs. Yet far less than 0.01 percent of the U.S. male population commits murder in response to adultery (Hupka, 1991, pp. 258–59).

The distorted public image that results in confusing extreme with typical cases also surfaces in the identification of gossip with malicious activity. Gloating is not sadistic by nature; nor is gossip inherently malicious. Gossip is engaged in for pleasure, not for the purpose of hurting someone, and though gossip may inflict some damage on its subject's reputation, such damage is usually minor (Jaeger et al., Chapter 13; Levin and Arluke, 1987). Many people cannot really enjoy themselves while explicitly knowing that their activity is very harmful to others. As Kant (1963) observes, "We feel pleasure in gossiping about the minor misadventures of other people." Moreover, the damage sometimes caused by gossip is usually a by-product, not an end. And when gossip does inflict significant damage to other people, the gossipers themselves do not usually consider the damage to be significant. The idle nature of gossip implies not merely the absence of declared purpose, but the lack of concern for such a purpose. Nor is it true that the information conveyed in gossip is totally negative. One study suggests an even distribution of negative and positive information in gossip, and almost half of the information was found to be neither clearly negative nor clearly positive. Furthermore, when the information was negative, it often concerned minor misfortunes (Levin and

Arluke, 1987). Levin and Arluke show that even gossip columnists usually do not convey information meant to harm or destroy a celebrity. In fact, most of the information that appears in gossip columns is favorable. Little wonder that gossip columnists receive much of their information from the celebrities themselves or from their press agents. When these columns include negative information, it almost never refers to the violation of major social norms and is often associated with happy or hopeful conclusions. Thus, criminal activities or a celebrity's connections with criminals are rarely reported in these columns. Similarly, although many stars have been known to be gay, gossip columnists have mostly kept silent, fearing permanent harm to the actor's career. Levin and Arluke argue that these columns have focused on folkway, not moral standards, and on eccentricity rather than on deviations.

Contrary to its popular reputation, then, gossip is not basically concerned with detraction, slander, or character assassination. Negative information may be remembered better, and hence the illusory impression of its dominance. In some cases gossip may indeed involve exaggerated or distorted information, but usually the gossip does not deliberately convey false information. Sometimes gossip is the only way to acquire accurate information, and often gossip is more accurate and more complete than "official" information. Although information conveyed informally may be inaccurate, so too is the news conveyed by the media. Gossip is not essentially an activity of telling lies, and there is no reason that it should be morally condemned on these grounds. If indeed gossip mainly conveyed false information, most people would not find it interesting.[3]

Gossip may also have some positive by-products. It may help to sustain the moral values of a community where people fear becoming a target for gossip. This is especially true of small communities or of famous people. Gossip may also provide lower classes with a socially acceptable outlet for frustration and anger (Spacks, 1985). I do not wish to claim that gossip is a virtue (cf. de Sousa, Chapter 2), but nor are its typical cases malicious. To gossip is to assert the right to be informed about other people's affairs, though one may condemn the way the information is acquired. Gossip seems less immoral if the information about the object is not pejorative, if by relaying the information the subject does not (significantly) hurt the object, and if the telling has some justification. Since the suggested characterization of gossip is compatible with these factors, typical cases of gossip are not strongly negative from a moral viewpoint.

No doubt, gossip has a bad reputation. I believe, however, that this reputation is more in the nature of an unsubstantiated (and even malicious) rumor than of reliable judgment. Although the moral condemnation is not entirely groundless, it applies, for the main part, to nontypical cases of gossip and is not justified with respect to typical gossip, which is mostly harmless. Aristotle's emphasis upon the right proportions is relevant here. Distorting the subtle proportion of typical gossip may indeed be harmful. But the fact that excessive and distorted gossip is harmful does not establish the intrinsic malicious nature of typical gossip, just as the fact that excessive eating is harmful does not imply an intrinsic evil in eating. Much of the negative press gossip has received stems from the confusion of extreme and excessive instances with typical and common instances. I argue that the extreme case, which many people take to be the prototype of gossip, is neither essential to nor common of gossip.

If my claim that typical gossip satisfies basic human needs and is mostly harmless is correct, then gossip cannot be very bad from a moral viewpoint. It may even have some positive moral values. As an old high-school teacher of mine used to say: gossip is not a morally negative activity; after all, it expresses an interest in other people's lives. Indeed, the exchange of relatively insignificant details about daily life sends a message of caring. The noticing of details so typical of gossip "shows caring and creates involvement" (Tannen, 1990, pp. 114–15). Gossip usually does not, however, express a genuine concern for other people's problems. The interest, we may say, is merely focused on the interesting, light aspects of other people's lives. Gossip is not a virtuous activity; I have tried to show that it is not vicious either.

2 | In Praise of Gossip: Indiscretion as a Saintly Virtue

Ronald de Sousa

GOSSIP HAS BEEN THE OBJECT of much malicious talk. But then, so have all forms of power—and gossip is power. It differs from ordinary power as information differs from brute force, but it is power nevertheless. Gossip is typically a subversive form of power: an attempt by the weak, and often, though far from exclusively, by women, to use the power of knowledge independently of those who wield more conventional power. As Patricia Meyer Spacks put it, "The ferocity of several centuries' attack on derogatory conversation about others probably reflects justifiable anxiety of the dominant about the aggressive impulses of the submissive" (Spacks, 1985, p. 30).

This aspect of gossip has motivated a minority of recent writers—including some included in this volume—to come to the defense of gossip. Without conceding that gossip is exclusively a woman's occupation, for example, Maryann Ayim (Chapter 8) and Louise Collins (Chapter 10) point out that gossip is a form of inquiry that remains available to women even when other avenues of inquiry are closed to them by circumstance or convention. Similarly, it is a commonplace that the novel, of all the arts, is the one in which women have been most successful at competing directly with men. This is true of Western culture and even of oriental cultures, where the control and oppression of women have been perhaps even more intense. You can write a novel in snatches, discreetly slipping the paper under the blotter when company comes, without the need for bulky, heavy raw material, without sophisticated tools, and without fear of being given away by the noise of the chisel or the smell of paint. Gossip is inherently democratic, concerned with private life rather than public issues, and "idle" in the sense that it is not instrumental or goal oriented. Yet it can serve to expand our understanding of life in ways that other modes of inquiry cannot.

What, then, are the standard objections to gossip? Gossip, it is said, is often motivated by malice or envy; its enjoyment is often taken at the expense of others, whom it harms by exposing their vices and foibles to ridicule; and worst, it often sacrifices the truth. These objections are, in fact, irrelevant. No doubt malice, envy, prevarication, and other vices often mar the character of those who gossip. But such faults can no more be held against gossip in itself than they can be held against love, marriage, or commerce, all of which notoriously provide opportunities for the deployment of the very same vices. True, if gossip is defined as malicious and harmful talk about the private lives of others, for example, then to discuss its moral worth is superfluous. On the other hand, gossip could be defined simply as conversation about other people's private lives, which would leave open the substantive question of whether such conversations are necessarily, or usually, reprehensible for one reason or another. Clearly, the methodologically superior approach is that which does not prejudge questions of value at the stage of initial definition of the subject matter.

Current discussions of pornography provide a case in point. They frequently get bogged down because some discussants want to define pornography in a morally neutral way, whereas others argue that if a representation can be correctly described in a morally neutral way then that alone is sufficient to establish that it is not pornography. Sometimes, pornography is defined as "depictions of sexual violence degrading to women." In that case, the debate about the worth of pornography will be closed before it can be joined. On the other hand, if pornography is defined as "depictions of sexual activity intended primarily to occasion sexual arousal," we can discuss whether and when that is a bad thing. Perhaps pornography cannot be judged to be bad without appealing to evaluative terms such as "undue exploitation of" or "excessive emphasis on" sex. But in order to begin the discussion we need a morally neutral definition.[1] Similarly, if gossip is defined as malicious, we have gone too far, too fast, and we risk losing sight of that position in conceptual space occupied by uncensored, no-holds-barred—but private—talk about the private lives of others. We do better to endorse a morally neutral characterization of gossip, in order to decide when and whether activities of the type so defined should be condemned.

Of course, someone might claim that the neutrality of the definition in question is only apparent; that a Kantian analysis of its implications would show that it would in fact be incoherent to wish that gossip "become a universal law of nature."[2] Perhaps it is a psychological truth (though not a logical one) that talking about other people's private lives seems interesting only when it is driven by malicious motivation. But if everyone were driven by malicious motivation, it is hard to imagine a world in which this were not generally known. And if everyone knew that when others gossiped they were driven by malice, they would no more be inclined to take them seriously than people could be deceived by liars in a society where everyone lied. I shall give this Kantian form of argument a peculiar twist in a moment, urging that gossip is not only a virtue but, in a very specific sense, a saintly one. But such an argument will not work to attack gossip. For if the listener shares the malicious motivation of the speaker, the latter's gossip is hardly less likely to be credited: on the contrary, it then becomes a shared task of malice, and the argument might even be turned on its head to suggest that gossip is pointless unless it is conducted in a society of malicious participants. That would yield the rather conventional view that gossip is indeed universal because people are universally malicious in fact. This familiar view characterizes some of the more pessimistic satirists in classical literature.

I do not see any reason to grant the psychological speculation that grounds the argument just given. But even if it were sound, it still would not give us a reason to condemn gossip as such. At worst, the attribution of bad motives to those who gossip would condemn the practice as bad de facto because of its association with evil motivation. But suppose that gossip were not merely generally but always, even necessarily, driven by envy, malice, or any other combination of deplorable motives. Would this be sufficient to condemn it? In fact it would not, at least not from a reasonably Utilitarian point of view, for one could not infer from even the most constant association of gossip with bad motives that as a social institution gossiping was worse in its consequences than refraining from gossip. It might have benefits independent of its motivation. Compare, for example, the relation of greed to capitalism. Someone might claim that the success of private enterprise rests entirely on the motivation of greed and thus deplore it. But that person might at the same time grant that the consequences of allowing greed free rein are, on the whole, preferable to the consequences of suppressing it altogether. Similarly, gossip could be a good thing on the whole, even if some of its individual consequences were indisputably deplorable and even if its motivation were invariably malicious.

Yet another defense of gossip might be posited: Gossip is morally defensible even though its actual consequences are not best on the whole. Because I wish to argue in this chapter for a defense of gossip as free speech extended to the private sphere, I must look at a different and more powerful set of objections to gossip that center on issues of privacy. The relevant sense of that somewhat multifarious word carries the suggestion that there exists a right to control information about oneself. Is there such a right?

In the most straightforward terms, what is at question here is simply the right not to be talked about. A friend once suggested that it is an infringement of my personal rights if you use me, without my permission, in your sexual fantasies, be they ever so private. If that were so, then surely, by analogy, would I not have the right not to be discussed or even thought about? In a newspaper article, the Canadian philosopher Tom Hurka recently endorsed this sentiment, claiming that for people to "analyze your deep motivations" is "invasive" (Hurka, 1990). It's not easy to say anything objective about this. Obviously there is nothing literally invasive about merely talking or thinking about someone (that is how information differs from matter!). And I have no idea how the relevant metaphorical sense of "invasive" might be worked out to make sense of Hurka's point. So I don't see what the basis of such a right might be. Nevertheless, some people don't want to be talked about.

But why? Clearly such feelings are sometimes linked to shame or guilt. Indeed gossip not infrequently focuses on aspects of people's lives that are liable to evoke those emotions. But this is not always so: sometimes the feeling of not wanting to be observed is just that and does not depend on the object of observation's being engaged in anything disreputable. Some people, like J. D. Salinger, seem to desire secrecy for its own sake. Living behind high walls of stone and expensive lawyers, they actively repel any inquiry into any facts of their life. Some people do this even while cognizant of the importance to our knowledge of human nature that the whole truth be known about as many people as possible. Freud, for example, surely did more than anyone to break down the barrier between the public and the private, and yet he did his utmost to stop anyone from finding out the private truth about himself. By doing this he undermined the very exploration of human nature that he purported so fearlessly to lead.

This extreme desire for privacy resembles children's feelings that they don't want to be looked at or the "primitive" fear of being photographed. To this is added the characteristically adolescent desire to have "secrets." The difficulty of rationalizing such feelings is that they run rather deep; an appropriate explanation for them belongs properly to depth psychology. Whatever their cause might be, they are no doubt at least partially to blame for the general bad press that gossip has received. But can such feelings justify that bad press? The answer to this question depends on the extent to which justification is linked to general approval. Suppose there is general disapproval of gossip and that people generally claim their disapproval is grounded in the "offensive" nature of gossip to their "feelings of privacy." In a strictly anthropological sense, that would constitute justification enough. But I am interested, perhaps quixotically, in further justification, a justification of the "feeling" itself. And from that perspective, it seems to me that the feelings in question can provide no justification at all.

Consider, first, attitudes to sexual practices. Some people argue that certain practices, while not in themselves wrong, ought nevertheless to be kept in the closet because they are offensive to the sensibilities of others. "I know there's nothing really wrong with homosexuality," we sometimes hear, "but I find it disgusting and I think you should give some weight to my feelings." Using a simplistic interpretation of Utilitarianism, I suppose any feelings of pleasure or unpleasure ought to be taken into consideration. But this supposition is unacceptable. In this case, for example, my own intuition is that the feelings of discomfort themselves are wrong and have no moral weight. Feelings only have moral weight if they reflect some real—that is, objective—value. In the absence of any real superiority of value to heterosexuality, the feelings of discomfort elicited by homosexuality have no moral weight at all.

The rhetorical force of my argument is weakened, I am well aware, by its presupposition of the existence of objective values. Since I don't have the space to defend this presupposition here,[3] let me turn to a second, less controversial analogy. I once met a man who explained to me that he and his wife had no prejudices at all against blacks, but that unfortunately his wife felt sick in close proximity with any African American. Did this strong feeling on her part not constitute a reason, though perhaps not an overriding one, in favor of segregation? No. Surely in this case the simplistic utilitarian view is seen to be without force. Her feelings are not merely overridden by other values; they constitute no reason *at all* for any action whatever, except therapeutic action to eliminate the feeling itself. Accordingly, sensibilities—feelings—can provide no convincing argument against gossip.

There is a second, slightly different, nuance of the putative "right to privacy" that might find an independent justification. The right to privacy in this sense is the right to keep secrets. In his newspaper column, Tom Hurka also articulates this objection. He writes that if we haven't broadcast information about ourselves, this is tantamount to signifying that we want it kept secret. But so what? "When [people] don't [license gossip about themselves,] we should feel more than uneasy" about gossiping. He doesn't say why. Now to claim the right to keep things to ourselves is obviously more reasonable than to claim the right to censor other people's thoughts about you. Nevertheless, the former claim, too, rests on feelings that I have argued can have no moral claim on our respect.

Perhaps, then, there exists a right to keep certain things secret (if one can); but though we must recognize this right, we may deplore its exercise, for to keep some things secret is necessarily to manipulate information in ways that are bound to diminish our understanding of human nature. At the very least, such manipulation is likely to promote self-deception and hypocrisy. And because the things most likely to be kept secret concern areas, like personal relations and sex, about which people know too little and need to know as much as possible, it can significantly lower the capacity of ordinary people to thrive.

Let me put the argument as radically as I can. At question here is the freedom of speech, but applied to private speech about the private sphere: although the dissemination of private information may make some people uncomfortable, its importance must, as a matter of public policy, be deemed to outweigh that discomfort. (This argument has force even if my earlier claim that such feelings have no moral weight at all is rejected.) This is more or less recognized in countries like Canada and the United States that have laws guaranteeing "access to information" or "freedom of information." We might object that this argument applies only to the public sphere, for the private sphere is not important enough to justify a "need to know," and the damage done to private persons by public knowledge of their lives easily outweighs what little gain might still be claimed.

In fact, however, the opposite is true. In the absence of active censorship, public matters are by and large a matter of record. The private sphere is more elusive and quirky, and therefore more difficult to investigate. Indeed, gossip is especially valuable where a strict distinction is made between private and public life. In cultures that emphasize that distinction, the "private" sphere is often a euphemism for the freedom of men to abuse women and children. The concept of a private sphere, by definition, renders a whole domain of people's experience especially difficult to explore by any so-called objective or scientific means. And since that part of life, in terms of the actual quality of our lives, may well be the most important one, accurate knowledge about it is particularly crucial. This is the area that gossip alone can crack.

Here, then, is my radical twist on the Kantian theme:

To refrain from gossip is to be discreet, and according to common prejudice, discretion is a virtue. Certainly discretion is often prudent as well as kind. But this makes it only an ordinary virtue. Indiscretion, by contrast, is a superior virtue, indeed a saintly one.

Unlike ordinary virtue, saintly virtue is not justified by its immediate consequences. On the Kantian schema, what justifies a practice is the consistency and desirability of a possible world in which it were universalized. The practice of saintly virtue, then, does not pretend to be crassly pragmatic. Heroes and saints are not supposed to be utilitarians. Their virtues challenge and enrich our understanding of moral possibilities. Thus it is that heroes and saints, however revered from afar, are detested close up, and generally end up drawn and quartered or burned at the stake. I suggest that the indiscretion of the gossip is, in a small way, a saintly virtue.

La Rochefoucauld taught us that hypocrisy is the tribute that vice pays to virtue. But what is discretion but hypocrisy in the third person? Discretion is the tribute paid in return to vice by virtue. Consider: if your friends had nothing worth keeping secret, there would be no use for discretion. (Remember that I have already set aside the claim based on the sole "feeling" of not wanting to be talked about.) What point would there be to discretion in Paradise? Without the thieves, the Good Samaritan would never have had his chance at memorable virtue. Similarly, the opportunity for discretion about our friends' unusual or not-so-unusual sexual preferences, say, arises only thanks to the society's prejudices.

Among the findings of the Kinsey reports on sexuality—a kind of glorified and systematic gossip—one of the most startling and revealing findings was that most people thought themselves abnormal: Most people, it seems, thought that most other people never did what they themselves mostly did (Kinsey et al., 1948, 1953). This is precious information, which only a great deal of high-quality gossip might have anticipated. People can be harmed by the dissemination of such knowledge only because knowledge of that kind is generally withheld. Consider the harm that used to come from the revelation that someone was a homosexual: If every homosexual could have been "outed" at one fell swoop, the knowledge would most likely have been powerless to harm anyone. If all truths became public, we would approach utopia. We would no longer need to spend so much time on concealment. When petty crimes and mean thoughts can no more be hidden than nuclear warheads, then the deception industries, private and public, will wither away as the state was supposed to do. (Perhaps even the state would wither away, too.) Personal relationships would be far less likely to be poisoned by misunderstandings and disappointments. Love might still be painful, but betrayal would be far less common. No longer would ludicrous and harmful assumptions about human nature be fostered by chronic hypocrisy. Worldwide disarmament would soon follow, and enormous resources would be liberated to the benefit of humankind.

Well, perhaps I exaggerate. Universal knowledge of who was a Jew would not have helped the Jews under Hitler. (But perhaps in my utopia of universal knowledge, Hitler would never have gained power in the first place.) At any rate, it seems likely that a world in which all information were universally available would be preferable to a world where immense power resides in the control of secrets. If so, it is enough to make of indiscretion a saintly if not a pragmatic virtue, and enough to reject the reasons adduced to condemn gossip.

My analysis has a corroborating consequence: if it is at all correct, we can now better understand why in actual practice malice is so often associated with gossip. The reason lies in precisely the fact that makes gossip so necessary in the first place: our appalling ignorance of how people really work, about "what makes them tick." Given our ignorance, all but the more sophisticated among us live in constant fear that their own perverted natures will be exposed for all to see. Malicious gossip reassures them that others are no better than they are. The institutionalized gossip of *People* magazine and other such publications is particularly effective in that regard, because it allows us to believe that the rich and famous are no better than the rest of us. Of course, if information about the intimate lives of real men and women were not jealously hoarded, this would be public knowledge in the first place, and the thirst to expose others as no better than myself could not be slaked by such ordinary revelations.

Gossip is, I have suggested, an assault on the notion of a private sphere of life. Not exactly public, gossip most often occurs within a narrow social sphere.[4] And since the social circle in question is essentially restricted, the resulting judgments, as Spacks points out, are likely to remain conventional and conservative ones: "By generating shame in those who violate social standards, [gossip] helps to enforce agreed-upon values" (Spacks, 1985, p. 141). For anyone who is a strict social constructivist on matters of value, such a conclusion is acceptable; but for those who prize the subversive element in gossip, it is not radical enough. The progress of a culture depends on its mavericks, just as evolution in a species depends on its mutants; thus the extent to which social pressure in a small group enforces conformity should worry us. Here again anthropology offers a parallel damaging to my optimistic thesis. The social pressure to maintain the horrendous practices of ritual genital mutilation where these are traditionally part of the "culture" comes mainly from the women who are both perpetrators and victims. The critical, subversive pressure comes mainly if not entirely from outside the culture (see Boddy, 1989). Even in "pluralistic cultures," like contemporary Canada, small subcultures have a remarkable capacity for retaining and enforcing within the group the most viciously narrow-minded views. My own instinct is always to resist the suggestion that where moral and psychological truths are in question "reality depends on the ultimate decision of the community."[5] Community is a Janus face: though one side wears the smile of social harmony, on the other lurks the scowl of fascism.

We should remember, however, that in the Peircean utopia just mentioned, the "community decision" endowed with criterial power is as Ayim phrases it "the ideal state of complete information" (Chapter 8). And since it is precisely the informational advantages of gossip that I have been insisting on, this Peircan point is one I can endorse in the spirit of what I have called "saintly virtue." In practice, the consensus of any subculture may be a narrow-minded and wrong-headed one, but the conditions under which a broader view might prevail surely include a universalized practice of radical and guiltless indiscretion, a world of transparent gossip such as I have envisaged in my perfectly indiscreet utopia.

Even in the real and imperfect world in which we live, falling far short of complete information, the cultural values articulated by gossip are not necessarily those of the dominant culture. On the contrary, they are at least as likely to be those of a subculture of the oppressed or at least of the less powerful. In this way, then, gossip could serve to articulate an alternative moral psychology as much as it might consolidate the dominant one. No doubt both functions are certainly served; in what proportion, though, is a matter for empirical investigation: I don't know how one could determine a priori which function is better served, the subversive or the conservative. It is up to each of us, as ethically responsible gossips, to find the right mix.

3 | Gossip as Moral Talk
Gabriele Taylor

DELINEATING THE PROMINENT features of gossip helps to pinpoint its morally significant implications and to identify the consequent moral attitudes towards it which one may justifiably adopt. One difficulty is that "gossip" as used in ordinary talk is a complex and fluid notion. Taken in a wide sense, it refers to any easy chat about the trivia of daily life. Often it is thought of as no more than a timefiller for those who have nothing better to do, or as women's talk, unsuitable for the more serious-minded. Gossip in a narrower sense is restricted to talk about private lives and personal relationships. Here the moral significance of gossip will find its place. I shall take typical gossip to be between two or more people about the private life of another, behind her back. Her loves, friendships, marriage, or divorce are the typical subject matter, as well as her public activities insofar as these may throw light on her psychology or character. For gossip to flourish there must be an exchange of information and views, or at the very least a responsive audience. Even within these relatively straightforward limits the range and variety of gossip are still so wide that different samples may have little in common with each other. Definitions of gossip will always be complex and controversial.

The Nature and Range of Gossip

"Gossip," then, in its present context, is restricted to talk about concrete individuals and their concrete situations. It is therefore "easy" or "idle" talk, for it requires no abstract thought or the working out of political, ideological, or moral views. Gossiping is effortless. But not all talk about particular persons and their situations need be gossip. Two contrasting examples should help to clarify the salient features or, at any rate, a central case.

1. "Well, of course, he couldn't be (lecherous) with Sonia there, he would not dare. He has been her young man for years you know." "Don't tell me!" I said, fascinated. That was the heaven of Davey,

he knew everything about everybody, quite unlike my aunts, who, though they had no special objection to our knowing gossip . . . had always forgotten it themselves, being totally uninterested in the doings of people outside their own family. "Davey! How could she?"

"Well, Boy is very good-looking," said Davey, "I should say rather how could he? But as a matter of fact, I think it's a love affair of pure convenience, it suits them both perfectly . . . he's like a wonderful extra butler, and Sonia on her side gives him an interest in life. I quite see it." (Mitford, 1979, p. 66)

2. "I do not know what your opinion may be, Mrs. Weston," said Mr. Knightley, "of this great intimacy between Emma and Harriet Smith, but I think it's a bad thing."

"A bad thing! Do you really think it a bad thing? Why so?"

"I think they will neither of them do the other any good."

"You surprise me! Emma must do Harriet good, and by supplying her with a new object of interest, Harriet may be said to do Emma good. . . . I can imagine your objection to Harriet Smith. She is not the superior young woman which Emma's friend ought to be." (Austen, 1946, p. 36)

It is clear, I think, that Davey and Fanny are gossiping, far less so that Mr. Knightley and Mrs. Weston are similarly engaged. It is not the subject matter that is decisive here, for both love affairs and friendships are proper food for gossip, but the participant's approach to these topics and their respective attitudes to what is under discussion that make the difference. Mr. Knightley and Mrs. Weston exchange views on Emma's intimacy with Harriet because they have her well-being at heart and consider the friendship purely from that point of view. Their primary interest is what is good or bad for Emma; and the topic of discussion, her friendship with Harriet, interests them only derivatively, only because they think it has a bearing on Emma's well-being. Otherwise they would not be discussing it at all. Mr. Knightley has clear aims in introducing the topic, and, by seeking to serve these aims, their talk is, in this sense, not "idle."

By contrast, the discussion in the first example concentrates exclusively on the affair between Boy and Sonia. The participants have no intentions beyond exchanging their views on that topic. They are not particularly concerned with the well-being of the people talked about; for them the interest is in the talk itself. Of course, an interest in the talk implies a certain interest in the people the talk is about: Sonia and

Boy belong to the gossipers' social universe and have an effect on their lives. If Davey's remark had been about some person totally unknown to Fanny she would hardly have been as fascinated. This background interest forms part of the setting of both kinds of talk under scrutiny. But at present Fanny is interested in them precisely and only because they have a particular relationship with each other, as opposed to being interested in the relationship because she is concerned for them. Unlike Knightley and Mrs. Weston, then, Fanny and Davey are detached from the persons they are talking about, but are involved with the talk itself. And because it lacks any further purpose, their interchange can be said to be "idle."

The difference in intention and in the direction of interest is reflected by the emotional coloring of the two conversations. Gossiping is a pleasurable activity and is seen as such by those engaging in it. Their pleasurable interest gives gossip its particular "feel." Fanny and Davey plainly take a kind of pleasure in their talk that is absent from that of Mr. Knightley and Mrs. Weston, who merely express their interest in and concern for Emma.

The distinctions I draw between the two cases hinge on the attitudes of the respective participants, not on the specific subject matter of their conversations. Gossip is therefore best characterized as the talk of gossipers. Fanny and Davey paradigmatically exemplify the type. Paradigmatically, then, a gossiper exhibits the attitudes mentioned: the focus of her attention is the talk itself, and her pleasurable interest in it prompts her to talk as she does. She is therefore detached from the persons discussed, at least in the sense of not being particularly interested in their welfare.

This framework is flexible. The relevant attitudes may be short-lived or long-lasting. They may occur frequently or very rarely, in a variety of circumstances or on very specific occasions only. Further, attitudes may be ambiguous, mixed, and shifting even in the course of one conversation. It is therefore not surprising that the boundaries between what does and what does not constitute gossip are rather fluid. Most importantly, the framework allows for considerable variety in cases of even quite typical sorts of gossip. Not everyone who gossips need be as enthralled by it as Fanny evidently is nor be prompted by her kind of intense curiosity. I spoke of the gossipers' talk as being idle in that it has no aim beyond itself, and is not prompted, it seems, by either malicious or benevolent intentions towards the people discussed. But not all gossip need be idle in quite this sense. It is a feature only of typical gossip in its purest form. In the following passage Grace

Stepney, a poor relation, informs Mrs. Peniston of certain rumours concerning Grace's cousin Lily.

"People always say unpleasant things—and certainly they are a great deal together. A friend of mine met them the other afternoon in the Park—quite late, after the lamps were lit. It's a pity Lily makes herself so conspicuous."

"*Conspicuous*," gasped Mrs. Peniston. . . . "What sort of things do they say? That he means to get a divorce and marry her?" . . .

"Dear me. No! He would hardly do that. It's a flirtation—nothing more. . . . That's the worst of it—people say she isn't wasting her time. Everyone knows that Lily is too handsome . . . and charming to devote herself to a man like Gus Trenot . . . unless there are material advantages to be gained by making herself agreeable to him." (Wharton, 1922, pp. 194–95)

Grace, with the air of merely informing Mrs. Peniston of Lily's conduct and of what is being said about her on the grounds that she ought to know, is both conveying gossip and engaging in that activity herself. Her talk is prompted wholly by ill-will towards Lily, and in talking as she does she means to ruin Lily's reputation with Mrs. Peniston. She therefore has an aim that goes beyond the pleasure of the talk itself. In this respect she resembles Mr. Knightley rather than Fanny. Yet there are also differences that make it more natural to class her but not him as a gossip.

An explanation of these differences is best understood in the context of the overall setting in which gossip occurs. "Gossip" as here understood is restricted in subject matter to the discussion of personal matters concerning particular people, behind their backs. At the least, "talking behind their backs" implies that the persons discussed are not present and not in control of the talk. We may label all such conversations "gossip-talk." If so, then Mr. Knightley and Mrs. Weston are engaged in gossip-talk, as of course are the other two couples in the cases cited. Gossip proper, however, is the gossip-talk of gossipers, to be characterized in terms of certain attitudes towards the people discussed and towards the talk itself. The purest type of gossiper, I have suggested, is wholly absorbed in the talk itself and is detached from the persons under discussion. But the interest and pleasure taken in the conversation may vary in degree and composition. Furthermore, the "idleness" of gossip is more restricted than has so far been indicated. I defined gossip as idle not only in being undemanding but also in being aimless in that the participants engaged in it with no further purpose in mind. But Grace's case seems to provide a counterexample. She has very specific aims that her revelations about Lily are meant to serve. If her attitude is nevertheless that of a gossiper then there must be a distinction between the sorts of aims a gossiper may or may not have and their relation to the talk itself.

Gossip-talk may be gossip proper if either (or both) of the participants has a clear end in mind. A person may, for example, wish to express her feelings and views about the individual under discussion and may wish to present them in a certain light. Such aims are, however, very closely related to gossip-talk; for the talk itself constitutes, or at least partially constitutes, fulfilment of the aim in question. The talk may function to express ill will or goodwill towards those talked about, may, as planned, present them in a poor or flattering light, may constitute, as in the case of Grace, taking one's revenge. Such aims can be accommodated by the characterization of the typical gossip as one whose interest is focused on the topic under discussion. The close connection between aim and talk ensures that an interest in achieving one's aim spills over into an interest in the talk itself, as that which is the essential means towards this end. The case is very different where the interests of the participants are quite contingently related to the talk engaged in and where the gossip-talk is only incidental to the serving of these interests. Here the participants are not involved with the talk as such; their attitude is rather one of scientific detachment. They approach the topic from the point of view of their overall aim and are unconcerned about details that do not serve their extrinsic purpose.[1]

Gossipers take a pleasurable interest in the topic under discussion. At the very least they derive from it that enjoyment that consists in absorbed attention.[2] The more involved they are, the more enjoyable they find the talk. The degree of absorption and the reason for it will again depend on what the participants take pleasure in. Primarily there is the prospect of the pleasures of satisfied curiosity, but in cases where there is a further aim, noncontingently related to the talk, there is also the pleasure of achieving one's ends. And there may also be simple pleasure in the fact that people behave in such a way as to provide food for talk.

One may assume another pleasure, and another reason why Grace Stepney is, and Mr. Knightley is not, plausibly described as a gossiper. She is prompted by malice, he by motives of friendship; and one may assume that gossip is always malicious, or at any rate never benevolent. Malice adds spice to a conversation as benevolence does not.

Moreover, motives of malice explain why talking about a person behind her back is normally understood as having richer implications than merely indicating her physical absence. Gossiping is typically a secretive activity, to be kept from the people discussed, or revealed only to anger or humiliate.

I have tried to indicate some boundary between gossip-talk and gossip proper which allows for the wide variety in cases of typical gossip. The only requirement is that the participants should take a pleasurable interest in the talk itself, for whatever reason. This gives gossip its specific feel or color. To further specify that gossip is always malicious seems arbitrary. But while there is no a priori restriction on a gossiper's motivation, it is nevertheless the case that the derogatory makes a more engaging topic of conversation. Perhaps, as a matter of fact, instances of gossip are more likely to be malicious than benevolent.

The Relationships Involved in Gossip

Those who gossip talk to each other about another person or persons. There are therefore two quite different sorts of relationship to be considered: that between gossiper and gossiper and that between gossiper and gossipee. Given the nature of gossip as "idle" talk and all that this implies, the relation between gossipers would seem a positive one. They should be relaxed with one another, united by a common interest that makes for a happy personal relationship—a good thing, surely. By contrast, the relationship between gossipers and gossipees seems negative. The person concerned, were she to learn that she was being talked about, would very likely react with resentment, even if the talk were not particularly malicious. One does not like to be the subject of gossip.

Perhaps this view is too simple. The relationship between the gossipers will be wholly comfortable only if the pleasure taken in the gossip is "pure" and no thoughts interfere to embarrass one or the other of them and adversely affect their relationship. It may occur to them, for instance, that the piece of information just disclosed should not have been communicated, or that one should not discuss one's friends behind their backs. But setting this aside, they are likely to be at ease with one another not only because the talk itself is undemanding and does not require any particular mental effort but also because by exchanging views on a specific case the participants implicitly rely on certain shared, fixed standards. Not only are the gossipers uninvolved with the fate of the gossipees, their convictions are not at stake, either. They have nothing to lose. For gossip to flourish the participants must also of course share an interest in and information about the topic discussed. Hence they are drawn together further by the consciousness of constituting a special group, membership of which is denied to others, particularly to the gossipee. Gossip, then, is based on a bond between the gossipers, in the form of a common interest and shared assumptions, and will tend to strengthen that bond by creating an intimacy that is dependent on its exclusivity.

The special relationship between gossipers explains some of the attractions of gossiping. It is obviously enjoyable to talk about shared interests and to find oneself in a position to impart relevant information, to give one's opinion, and to be, at least temporarily, on intimate terms with other members of an exclusive group. Such pleasures are not, however, peculiar to gossip. They may also be derived from exchanging views in other contexts, such as, for example, the discussion between academicians of the details of a newly discovered manuscript. How, then, do we account for the specific pleasures of gossiping, or for that which gives it its particular emotional coloring. Perhaps a further pleasure inheres in the gossipers' unconcern for the well-being of the person talked about. Those who are so concerned, like Mr. Knightley and Mrs. Weston, have reason to aim at the truth; only if they can work out correctly the nature and effect of Emma's friendship with Harriet can they hope to offer advice that will be of some use to her. Lacking the relevant concern, gossipers need not be similarly anxious to get at the truth. On the contrary, some exaggeration or some fanciful embroidery will often add to the interest of the talk; gossipers may on those occasions take a creative, though secondary, pleasure in indulging in flights of fancy. There are more central pleasures of creation available to the gossiper, relating to their specific subject matter: human beings, their characteristics, activities, and relationships. The pleasures of creation may be found in imposing order and sense on activities and actors, and thus constructing a bit of another's world.

Because gossip is about the stuff of life, it is relevant to us all. It concerns the events, activities, and reactions in which we can be emotionally involved and interested. Hence, while gossip has the advantage of personal distance, what the gossipers talk about is sufficiently like their own lives to engage their full interest. The attraction here resembles the appeal of soap operas. Gossipers, it is true, deal with real people, and soap operas do not. But the involved soap opera watcher sees the characters as real people leading autonomous lives. Gossipers, conversely, tend to present the real person as a character in a narrative whose activities are offered to an audience to be noticed and commented upon. Essential to both the soap opera watcher and the gossiper is what might be called "the pleasure of recognition," a pleasure derived in some way from being able to identify with the experience of the "actors."[3] Watchers and gossipers contribute to the psychological reality of what they are watching or talking about by imposing their own interpretations. At the same time, the audience remains an audience. It is of course much easier to participate vicariously in another's life than to struggle with one's own. Vicarious living has the added attraction of presenting a story the development of which one can take an interest in and speculate about, secure in the knowledge that it cannot adversely affect oneself. Hence gossipers appear to be in the position of having their cake and eating it.

From the point of view of the relationship between gossipers, their simultaneous interest in the particular activities discussed and detachment from the actors is an important source of their feelings of ease and security. They are engaged in talk that, although closely related to their own lives, no way threatens them and gives rise to no personal anxieties. The consequent feeling of security may be bolstered by the one-sidedness of gossip: whereas gossipers see the gossipee as a suitable object of detached interest and discussion, they do not, while gossiping, consider themselves potential objects of this sort of attention and appraisal; this, too, removes a possible source of unease and discomfort. Hence gossipers are unself-conscious and relaxed in each other's company. They mutually corroborate their sense of security and ease, or at least perceive the other as doing so, by sharing the same focus of attention and the same interested yet detached approach.

Moral Implications

The relation between gossipers can be said to confer some limited but positive moral significance on gossip. Good personal relationships are an important value in our lives, and the circumstances of gossiping clearly foster such relationships, though possibly only for short periods on a relatively superficial level. However, the merit of the activity does not necessarily indicate merit of the participants. Since gossipers have no concern for the gossipee it follows that they are not engaged in an altruistic activity and so certainly are not "moral" in this sense. By the present characterization, their engagement in the discussion need not be prompted by ill-will either, and it seems to follow that there need be nothing immoral in what they are doing. Perhaps, then, the status of the gossipers is morally neutral? Such a conclusion would be premature and ignore the range of attitudes which are expressed in the way they talk about the gossipee.

Very broadly, gossip may be critical or quite noncritical of the doings of the person in question. The gossiping of Fanny and Davey is of the latter type: they neither approve nor disapprove of Boy's and Sonia's behavior, they are simply interested. "Critical gossip," on the other hand, may be approving and even admiring, censorious, or hostile. Such attitudes may add to the pleasures of gossiping; censorious gossip, for example, will tend to make the gossip partners enjoy feelings of superiority over the person discussed. Possibly the critical element may also lessen pleasure—if, for instance, the admiration is tinged with competitive envy. On the other hand, if hostile gossip is prompted by feelings of envy then there may be relief and pleasure in running down the envied person. The critical attitude exhibited will color the type of interest taken in the talk and hence contribute to the "emotional tone" of that particular piece of gossiping.

Those who gossip, critically or not, are curious about and take an interest in the activities and relationships of other human beings. Curiosity is a feature shared by all gossipers. The attitude of the critical gossip has other elements as well. Maybe curiosity so directed is in itself a virtue lacking in those who do not engage in gossip. Fanny and Davey show perhaps a positive quality lacking in the aunts, who care so little about anyone outside their family that other people's doings are deemed unworthy of any attention at all. It would seem, then, that those who never gossip are defective in some way. But no: the aunts' lack of interest in people may well be a bad reason for not gossiping, but it does not follow that there may not be very good reasons for abstention. Interest in others may after all manifest itself otherwise than gossiping. Conceivably, by gathering and discussing information about the personal lives of others, gossipers may come to understand and better control relevant aspects of their own.[4] Although this would certainly be a benefit to be derived from gossip, there is no reason to consider gossip the only route towards such understanding. Nor would this view clarify the moral implications of gossiping.

The question of moral significance connects rather with the attitude of the gossipers towards the gossipee. Noncritical gossipers have no harmful or manipulative intentions. Nevertheless, they do employ their interest in others for their own ends. It is pleasurable activity they seek, and the desires, hopes, and anxieties of others are simply grist to their mill. It may then be that it is always wrong to treat another as an object of gossip, on the grounds that it is to treat lightly what the person herself likely considers a matter of importance and concern. It shows a lack of respect for persons and so infringes the basic categorical imperative: "treat persons never merely as a means but always also treat them as ends in themselves."

Can this Kantian objection be supported? The position of gossipers is evidently very different from that of those who set out to use others for their own ends, to deceive, bribe, or blackmail them, so that their autonomy is threatened. Gossiping offers no such obvious infringement of the imperative, but the gossiper's behavior towards the gossipee may be thought of as a shadowy parallel. The gossiper manipulates, and enjoys manipulating, not the real person, but her counterpart in thought. Gossipers therefore have, in this dimension, a certain power over her, and may well sense that power. But the pleasure they are likely to derive therefrom is, morally speaking, an illegitimate pleasure, contributing no doubt to the entertainment value of gossiping, but only at the expense of a third party.

These objections amount to an argument that the gossipers' attitude is humiliating for the gossipee and that therefore their activity is not after all morally neutral. The interest they show in the activities of others is corrupt. Although there is nothing wrong with curiosity about human affairs as such, it is being exercised in the wrong context. It would be a quite different matter if the person herself chose to make her activities a topic for discussion, for then she would function as an autonomous actor rather than a helpless victim and thus could be expected to be aware of any risk she might be taking. If there is here a feature which makes even noncritical gossip reprehensible, then the situation is worse when the gossip is negative or critical.

The Kantian position assumes that people need to value themselves and have a right to have this value recognized. If we accept this assumption, we may reject the objection to gossip on the grounds that it makes too much of the notion of treating others with respect. Broadly speaking, there are two ways in which this response may be formulated, which I shall label "practical" and "theoretical" respectively. The practical critic holds that this is an altogether too solemn application of the slogan, that to think of gossiping as constituting a failure to recognize another's dignity and value is to take people and gossiping itself far too seriously. It encourages us to be pompous about our status. Further, it is notoriously difficult to be concrete about what treating others with the respect due to them actually amounts to, but it certainly does not include a prohibition to gossip about them.

The theoretical critic agrees with this last point, but for a different reason: the moral implications of the gossipers' attitude may be dismissed as being altogether beside the point. After all, no harm is likely to come to the gossipee. She may never even find out that she is being gossiped about, and there may be no noticeable change in the gossipers' behavior towards her. It is absurd to put so much weight on attitudes that may have no practical effect, particularly when we consider the concrete social benefits of gossiping in the form of generating comfortable relationships. The Kantian objection need therefore not be taken seriously.

A full discussion of the theoretical points would take us too far afield. This is not the place to try and settle whether for some activity or happening to constitute an evil to a person she must be aware of it.[5] Nor need the outcome of such a debate affect what I have labeled the 'Kantian' position. For its thrust is to point to a defect in the gossipers, and their attitudes may be indicative of this, whatever its effect on the gossipee. More relevant is the question whether attitudes, as opposed to intentions and actions, should be taken as morally serious. Again, this is not the place to defend the view that attitudes and feelings matter in themselves.[6] Against the theoretical critic it can however be said that to ignore them, to isolate feeling and attitude from intention and action, is to operate with a wholly unrealistic and distorted picture of human motivation. Intentions are not formulated in isolation but are dependent on a person's relevant feelings and attitudes. Without this context we could not make much sense of our lives. The manner in which a person is represented in thought, whether justly or generously, in terms of clichés or caricatures, is bound to affect at least to some degree one's behavior towards her, if not necessarily what one does, at least how one does it. Treating someone justly or lovingly is rooted in certain attitudes towards her. The "shadowy" dimension is clearly related to the actual one. The theoretical criticism seems to me therefore unsuccessful, and I shall set it aside.

There is more to be said for the practical point. True, a discrepancy exists between gossipers and gossipee, and, probably, the attitude of the former is not conducive to the self-esteem of the latter. But this by itself may not be enough for moral censure. Self-esteem is after all often foolishly based, and it is surely unreasonable to demand that others take a person as seriously as she, apparently, takes herself. Why should we respect her own misguided sense of her dignity? In any case, self-esteem is for her to look after herself. Moreover, the relative position of the parties involved has been distorted by not allowing for the fact that we are all both potential gossipers and potential gossipees, and hence the "balance of power" may be quite evenly distributed. The practical critic's point is that in the context of gossiping talk of the dignity of human beings is far too heavy-handed.

It is difficult to see how to settle the issue between the two parties. Both parties seem to have a point, but both arguments seem rather sweeping. An attempt to modify the position of the practical critic, though not solving the problem, should at least serve to indicate the circumstances in which gossiping is most likely to constitute lack of respect. Attention should at any rate be paid to whom is being gossiped about, and how. Talking about a person behind her back may not in general be degrading of her status, but it would surely be degrading of the status of a friend. To gossip about a friend, who has a right to expect concern, may be a violation of trust. Similar considerations apply to those who have spoken of their affairs in confidence. And whether the gossipee is a friend or not, gossiping maliciously can be said to be wrong on the grounds that the malicious gossiper presents the other's activities as showing them up as being weak or foolish, and hence expresses contempt for them. Similarly, the censorious gossip may be seen as intolerant or arrogant in presenting the gossipee as not abiding by acceptable standards.

Suppose we agree that there is something reprehensible in an attitude that expresses contempt or arrogance towards another. Still, some gossipers are prompted simply by the fascination of human behavior in situations with which they can identify. They want to know how people manage their lives, how they cope in different situations, how they solve the problems generated by personal relationships. These are the noncritical gossipers, and the question is whether they, too, may be subject to a Kantian objection.

I think there is some justification for the unease sometimes felt about even these sorts of cases. Crucial to the objection to gossiping is the gossipers' position as curious and detached observers and their consequent handling of the material. Gossipers picture the activities of another for their own purposes. They discuss her personal affairs without concern for her well-being. To have concern for another does not necessarily mean having deep personal feelings for her, but consists in thinking (and, when appropriate, acting) on behalf of that person. It is to put oneself aside and consider the impact and consequences of the experiences on her whose experiences they are. This in turn implies that concern requires us to seek an understanding of how the world appears to the other and to react appropriately. Gossipers, though they may or may not attempt to see the world through the gossipee's eyes, do not respond appropriately because they do not set the self aside; on the contrary, they relate all information to themselves.

Consequently, gossipers' attitudes towards these doings are very different from those of the agent herself. They may understand and be interested in her own assessment of her experiences, but their understanding will remain a wholly cognitive one; there is no sharing of such feelings, no sympathy or compassion. Gossip is often thought of as "trivial talk" and maybe it can be said to be trivial in this sense: it is not its subject matter that is trivial, but the manner in which it is handled. Gossipers trivialize experience by ignoring the impact with which the author of the experience will in some way have to cope. Thus they distort and belittle that person's experience.

The basis for unease about gossiping is twofold and rests on two dimensions of gossip isolated earlier, the detached attitude and the fact that the talk occurs behind the gossipee's back. The attitude of the gossipers puts the gossipee outside their moral concern, and does so in relation to personal matters that the gossipee is likely to want to reveal, if at all, only to those she knows or hopes to have concern for her.[7] The gossipee's potential dislike and resentment at being gossiped about is a consequence of finding herself in a position where she is exposed, helpless, and vulnerable. Gossipers enjoy a position of relative power, and she is at their mercy. In this sense, gossiping may be seen to infringe a person's autonomy.

I do not claim that these points against gossiping are conclusive. Nor have I questioned the assumption that autonomy and right to privacy are basic values. I have asked merely whether the attitude of gossipers constitutes a threat to such values. Even within the given framework, the issue of the moral implications of gossiping is not settled. We might for example argue that the defects mentioned are too slight to weigh against the pleasure derived from the activity, and, perhaps more persuasively, to weigh against its social benefit. But it must be borne in mind that the benefits I have pointed out have been narrowly confined to the gossipers themselves. There will be other points to consider that may not always work in gossip's favor.[8]

4 | The Logic of Gossip

Laurence Thomas

GOSSIP IS BEST THOUGHT of as conversational embroidery. A small or large pattern can be embroidered on a piece of cloth. The extent to which the pattern on the cloth stands out depends on a number of things: its location, the character of the design, the color of the design, and so forth. A small pattern can be absolutely eye-catching or easily missed. On the other hand, a pattern that covers the entire cloth can be subtle or eye-catching, depending on color and design. Then, of course, there are the intricacies of the design. If gossip is like embroidery, then it is false to think of it as a sustained mode of conversation. By way of examples and analysis, I hope to offer an account of gossip that is true to this general way of framing the subject.

Though neither a bodily function nor a fulfillment of a basic human need, gossiping is an activity that just about everyone engages in to some extent, including many who disapprove of it. Gossiping is clearly a matter of two or more people talking about someone who is not a party to the conversation, though gossip does not occur every time two people talk about someone who is not a party to the conversation. Consider:

(1) Austin: Is Cohen going to the presidential address? I would like to talk to her about her recent paper on particle physics. Lee: I don't think so, since she will be accepting the Nobel Prize then.

Certainly we have no gossip here. The conversation is factual and without innuendo. But suppose the conversation continues:

(2) Austin: I can't believe that they are awarding her the Nobel Prize in physics. Must be because she is a woman. Lee: To tell you the truth, I have been thinking the same thing myself.

This is surely gossip—perhaps even malicious gossip. The move from nongossip to gossip can happen ever so swiftly. Do we have gossip, however, if instead of (2), the conversation continues as follows:

(3) Austin: Wonderful. They could not have picked a more deserving person!
Lee: Absolutely. Everyone thinks that Cohen's work on the origins of the universe is just first-rate.

I doubt if many would call this gossip. But suppose the conversation began as follows:

(1') Smith: Hey Lee, guess who is getting the Nobel Prize in physics?—Cohen.
Lee: Are you serious?
Smith: No kidding! I overheard the decision makers as they were leaving the room. They obviously did not think anyone was around. I wonder when they will go public with the announcement.

Professional gossip, as we have here, is not necessarily negative or malicious; for nothing about the context of (1') reveals malice on the part of either Lee or Smith. On the contrary, we can imagine that both are good friends of Cohen and are absolutely delighted that she is being honored in this way. But if we have benign professional gossip in (1'), then what do we have in the following example:

(4) Austin: Hey Paul, I just witnessed a most wonderful event: Just as a shark was being let into the pool at the museum, a three year old fell into the water. Without thinking, Cruz jumped into the water and saved the infant. The jaws of the shark missing them both by mere seconds.
Jones: Incredible. If there are any saints in this profession, surely Cruz numbers among them. I don't know anyone who is as giving as he is.

This does not sound like gossip; indeed, the very idea that purely complimentary remarks about a third party amounts to gossip is counterintuitive. But how can it be that (1') is gossip, but (4) is not? Any satisfactory account of gossip must explain this seeming difference between (1') and (4).

Although conveying information can constitute gossiping, not every exchange of information does so, nor is it necessary to convey new information in order to be gossiping. Suppose long-time friends Baldwin and Gilbert are about to part for their separate offices when they see Johnson driving by in a new car with, apparently, a new lover. Baldwin and Gilbert meet later as is customary, and the conversation begins:

(5) Baldwin: Well man, what do you think. With Johnson the pattern seems to be new car, new lover.
Gilbert: I have never seen such rash behavior. Every lover is easily half Johnson's age.

There can be no doubt that we have gossip here, although the point of the conversation is not to convey new information about Johnson, since in fact both know much the same things about Johnson.

I imagine that for most of us (5) is what most readily comes to mind when we think of gossip. This is malicious gossip, though not as malicious as it can get. Now suppose a conversation similar to (5) takes place between a married couple:

(5*) Husband: Johnson worries me. He has been going through cars and loves like people go through handkerchiefs.
Wife: I know what you mean. I never would have suspected that inheriting $100 million would have affected him in this way. I wonder if we should speak to him, since we are perhaps his closest friends?

I believe that (5*) falls short of being gossip, although both (5) and (5*) are occasioned by Johnson's recent behavior.

Through examples of conversation, I have tried to indicate in an intuitive way when a conversation constitutes gossip and when it does not. The question now is whether any satisfactory account of when we do and do not judge a conversation to be gossip can be constructed. I propose the following:

(G) Gossip exists between A and B if and only if
(i) A's motive in talking to B about (some aspect of) C's behavior is simply to comment on C's behavior; A neither intends to express admiration of C's behavior nor to elicit admiration from B regarding C's behavior, and there is no socially legitimate reason for commenting about C's behavior;

(ii) A's purpose is to ventilate A's negative feelings about C, where the presumption on A's part is both that C's behavior does not, in and of itself, constitute morally admirable behavior and this is more or less evident to B.

(iii) the information conveyed fails to be in keeping with the norms of social protocol when it comes to offering information concerning the well-being of another.

A gloss on (G)(ii) is in order. Usually a person gossips to another in the hopes that the other person will also gossip in return, either about the same individual or another individual. And that hope is realized often enough. It is certainly possible, however, that a person's gossiping will meet silence. (G)(i) captures the reality that gossip can be either benign or malicious. Plenty of conceptual space separates admiring and disparaging speech about someone else. Clearly, (iii) rules out as gossip "Did you hear, Jones just had a heart attack last night" or "Rubin gave birth this morning." The latter is not to be confused with "Rubin is pregnant," which is not covered by (iii). Only Rubin or her lover can make this announcement, unless the pregnancy is public knowledge or Rubin has indicated that she does not care who knows about her pregnancy.

According to (G), gossip does not exist when the point of a conversation is to find a way to cope with an individual's unacceptable behavior. If Johnson of (5) and (5*) above lives in an apartment building and has taken to having wild parties nightly the neighbors need not be gossiping if they gather to develop a strategy for dealing with him. It might be difficult to imagine that no one at the gathering would gossip about Johnson, but certainly it need not be that everyone does, including those who give evidence about Johnson's unruly behavior by offering a few sordid details. Some will be moved to embellish what they have to say; others will try as best they can to stick to the facts.

Now, (G) does not rule out the possibility that one can gossip about morally admirable behavior. A may call B to talk about C's saving a life, knowing full well that B will speak disparagingly of C's deed. After all, there are people who can find something negative to say about just about anything, including morally admirable behavior. The wording of (G), however, is meant to emphasize that A is not gossiping about C's morally admirable behavior if A draws B's attention to it simply as a way of expressing A's own admiration for C and eliciting B's. A's point is not at all to excite a negative reaction or to vent feelings, but to engage in a bit of mutual moral admiration. One way to show our admiration for the deeds of others is by speaking about them with the aim of expressing our own approval and eliciting approval from others.

Yet (G) allows for the unfortunate reality that people can gossip about what is in fact morally admirable behavior on the part of others. We have malicious gossip when A draws B's attention to C's behavior just to engage in demeaning it. But one need not do that; and in this regard so-called professional gossip comes readily to mind. Of course, professional gossip can be quite malicious, but it need not be so, and that it need not be malicious is no accident. Information about who is moving up the ladder of professional success, or just plain moving, can be conveyed without discussing personal aspects of a person's life. One can extrapolate without denigrating. Professional acquaintances are often interested in such information for its own sake, having no desire whatsoever to offer any assessment of the character of the individual involved.

This distinction between professional and nonprofessional gossip—personal gossip, let us call it—is rather illuminating. Both can avoid character assessment based on a person's behavior. Cases of admiration aside, however, it is generally very difficult to say much about a person's life that does not constitute a violation of the individual's privacy or that is not in some way malicious. It is difficult—but not impossible. We sometimes consider a person's behavior rather eccentric. We neither admire the behavior nor regard it as having any redeeming qualities. Nor, however, do we deem it inappropriate. For example, suppose Wong is compulsive about his teeth. He owns five or six toothbrushes, which he is constantly replacing, and he brushes his teeth four or five times a day. Or suppose Ahn is "crazy" about peanut-butter sandwiches, consuming at least five or six of them a day. To be sure, these things can be commented upon in a malicious way, but surely they need not be, and rarely would such comments about a person constitute a violation of privacy. Here we have paradigm examples of benign gossip.

By contrast what often is called professional gossip in no way comments on a person's private life. Moreover, the behavior in question generally counts as amoral, in the way that drinking a glass of water does; accordingly, the gossip does not involve an explicit or implicit moral assessment of the behavior. That "Briggs is accepting an offer at such-and-such" can be noted without any assessment of Briggs's character or any invitation to make such an assessment. Obviously, there can be borderline cases, as when upon being informed that Briggs accepted the offer, the auditor remarks, "Briggs is moving again!"

Sometimes what is called gossip is not that at all; for example, conveying public information does not constitute gossip. Something can be made public without, at the same time, being generally known. Thus, when Susan Briggs posted on her door at 9 p.m. a note that she had accepted the offer from Chemistry for Everyone, she made that fact public, though not generally known. If a late-working colleague sees the note and calls across the country to tell a friend and professional acquaintance, the colleague is not gossiping about Briggs, any more than he would be if Briggs had taken out a very small back-page advertisement to the effect that she was accepting the offer and the colleague happened to have seen it and called the friend. The claim here, needless to say, is not that one cannot gossip about public information, but that the mere conveying of such information does not constitute gossip. Otherwise, a person would be gossiping if he merely conveyed the contents of a newspaper to someone who had not read it.

Consider a private marriage between two people who had a secret ceremony. Marriage is a public relationship in that a document of marriage must be filed with the state, and the fact that one is married is a matter of public record. Suppose, then, that the official recording the marriage for the state happens to be someone who knows the husband and wife. According to our analysis, for the official simply to inform yet another person of the couple's marriage does not constitute gossip. The official is at a party, and someone remarks, "What a wonderful wife so-and-so would make. She is so incredibly brilliant." To this, the official responds, "Well, I think you had better look elsewhere. She is legally spoken for." Given the distinction between information being public and its being publicly known, it follows that, strictly speaking, what often passes for professional gossip is not that at all, for quite often the content of so-called gossip is merely public information that is not yet widely known. Perhaps, then, one reason why professional gossip seems so benign is that it is not gossip at all.

I do not deny that people slip into gossip in the course of conveying information, though there are people able to convey appropriate information without engaging in editorial comment. They also refrain from remarking upon the editorial comments of others; in fact, some will make it clear that they are not interested in such comments. When Jones asks whether Cohen is accepting the Institute's offer, and Martin says that according to the Professional Physicists Bulletin she is, Martin is hardly gossiping. Perhaps Martin has quite an opinion on the matter but, characteristically, keeps it to himself.

Let us return to (5*) and the claim that this conversation, unlike its counterpart (5), falls short of being gossip. No doubt gossip often constitutes an exchange of useful information or offers speculation about a person's life. Not every exchange of useful information or bit of speculation about a person's life, however, constitutes gossip. Friends often have reason to discuss a person's behavior precisely in order to determine whether they should confront the person about it, and if so for what reasons and in what way. Consider a conversation that seems perhaps to be gossip, but which I maintain is not:

(6) Baldwin: What's wrong? You have seemed so down lately.
    Gilbert: I still can't get over Jones's behavior. He is the very last person in the world I would have expected to make such a crass sexist remark.
    Baldwin: Well, no one is perfect.
    Gilbert: We are not talking about perfection here, but a gross form of immoral behavior. There is just no excuse for him calling woman after woman at the reception "a cute whore." It is not just sexist, but indecent sexist behavior even among self-avowed male chauvinists. Have I been friends with such a dyed-in-the-wool sexist? What does that say about me?
    Baldwin: Don't you think that you are being a little too hard on yourself? It is not as if you became friends with Jones knowing full well that he was given to uttering such remarks. Everyone at the party was taken by surprise.
    Gilbert: True. But you know that he did not apologize either then or later. I have sensed no shame on his part at all.

Clearly, we have the beginning of what could easily be a very long conversation that speculates about Jones's personality, motives, and behavior in all sorts of ways. Yet the conversation between Gilbert and Baldwin is not gossip.

There can be significant self-disclosure among friends and lovers. Indeed, this is a defining feature of deep friendships.[1] The point of the conversation is not to discuss Jones as such, but for Gilbert to achieve a measure of self-understanding and direction concerning his relationship with Jones. Baldwin is the vehicle through which this is being achieved. Baldwin and Gilbert are rather like the wife and husband scenario of (5*) above. In this regard, we suggest that deep friends are more like lovers or spouses than many are inclined to suppose.

Gossip is an extremely difficult notion to grasp, partly, I believe, because it is a mistake to think of any given conversation as either constituting gossip (in its entirety) or not. Gossip is not an all or nothing proposition. A conversation can be entirely free of gossip, except for a single remark limited to a single sentence. Or a conversation may be peppered with gossip. Or gossip may be the point of a conversation where little or no information alone is conveyed, as with (5) above. In just about any conversation, one can easily move from simply conveying information to a remark that constitutes gossip, or vice versa, for gossip lacks the conventional markers promises and introductions offer.

If my analysis is correct, gossip is tied conceptually to the motives behind the remarks being made. Given one motive, we have gossip; given another, we do not. Recall (5) and (6). Since we often do not know another person's motive, we can be quite mistaken about whether a person is engaging in gossip. What may sound like gossip may not in fact be gossip at all. Some light falls, then, on the stereotype that women gossip far more than men. For what may seem to the ears of men to be gossip may not be that at all. The interests of men are not the only measure of things worthy of discussion.

Tying gossip to motives is important in another way. It is sometimes important to convey negative information about another to prevent a person from being harmed. Thus, a female graduate student might inform other females that if they work with a certain distinguished male professor they can expect to be propositioned by him. To be sure, the woman may simply be conveying this true information in order to damage the professor's reputation. But I take as obvious that conveying this information need not constitute gossip. Naturally, it is possible for a person to be mistaken or confused about why they are conveying such information. More than one motive may in fact be operating. I merely have to underline the reality that a negative comment about another person, if inspired by the right motives, does not constitute gossip.

Significantly, my analysis reveals that gossip need not in any way constitute an invasion of privacy. Gossip can be about what is widely known, although much gossip has to do with conveying private information about a third party—information which one has come by illegitimately, as a result of carelessness on the part of the possessor of the information, or by some structural inadequacy or foul-up of information control. The distinction between benign and malicious gossip helps us to understand why gossip that involves violations of privacy is often malicious. If nothing else, there can be little moral justification in conveying information about a person that she does not want revealed. And although I have claimed that gossip about private information is generally malicious; I did not mean to suggest that gossip about public information is not likely to be. Conversations about public information regarding the personal lives of public figures will in all likelihood be largely gossip unless it is a genuine expression of admiration. The fact that such gossip can be extremely malicious shows that the public status of information is no bar to malicious gossip about it.

I should like to emphasize, finally, that just about any conversation is likely to be a mixture of gossip and nongossip. Fortunately, though, not all gossip is malicious, and even better, we can talk about others with admiration in a way that does not constitute gossip at all. Recall the adage: "If you can't say anything good about a person, then don't say anything at all."

5 | Gossip and Humor
John Morreall

HUMOR AND GOSSIP were traditionally neglected by academics, and for many of the same reasons. In the last fifteen years, fortunately, humor has come into its own as an academic topic; there may well be hope for gossip. Two of the most important traditional objections to humor are that it is frivolous and that it is mean-spirited or even hostile. These objections apply also to gossip. A third objection to humor, that it is irrational—more precisely, that it is cognitively irresponsible—has a counterpart in objections to gossip. In gossiping we spread stories without caring about the evidence for their truth, and this epistemic irresponsibility can be seen as a kind of irrationality.

I have argued in several places (Morreall, 1983b, 1984, 1989b) that traditional objections to humor do not stand up as general objections. Even if they did, of course, objections to humor are not by themselves objections to research on humor. Suppose humor turned out to be as evil as slavery. It might for all that, indeed because of that, be a good topic for research. And I would say the same about gossip. Traditional objections do not apply to all gossip, and even if they did, gossip might still be a respectable object of research.

The formal features of humor, such as its use of surprise, its hypothetical exploration of topics, and its social features, particularly its playfulness and its fostering of intimacy, make the comparison of humor and gossip especially interesting. Indeed, I will argue that when gossip is dominated by the spirit of humor, it tends to transcend the pettiness and viciousness that have given gossip such a bad name for so long.

Many similarities link gossip and conversational humor. Aaron Ben-Ze'ev (Chapter 1) points out, for example, that gossip and joking are intrinsically valuable social activities, they allow us to refer to taboo topics, they sometimes involve disguised insults, and in both surprise is important. We can add three more similarities here. One of the pleasures of gossip that Ben-Ze'ev notes is being the source of information. Likewise one of the pleasures of joking is being the source of humor. To make a witty comment and have others laugh at it is an accomplishment that is socially valued.

A second similarity between gossip and conversational humor is that both usually take narrative form. As Ben-Ze'ev observes, the pleasure of gossip is often that of a good story; the same is true of conversational humor. In both we present entertaining narratives, and in both the basic skills are those of storytelling—knowing how to organize the material, which details to include and which to leave out, how to mimic voices and facial expressions, when to pause. Both are performances that can be evaluated. Just as people have reputations as good or poor tellers of jokes and funny stories, people can be known as good or poor gossips.

The third similarity between conversational humor and gossip is that both primarily please the imagination, making humor and gossip candidates for aesthetic experience.[1] Not truth value, but entertainment value—their ability to delight, shock, amuse, or move us—is paramount. People love a good story—a funny narrative or a juicy bit of gossip—whether or not it happens to be true. The same holds true, I think, for gossipy newspapers such as the *American Weekly World News*, the *National Enquirer*, the *National Examiner*, and the *Star*. People read these publications not so much to acquire information as to be titillated by exciting ideas. Articles like "I Sold My Baby to UFO Aliens!" "Preacher Explodes During Sermon," and "Gigantic Elvis Statue Found on Moon" aren't so much journalism as fiction in a journalistic style. Their purpose is to entertain, not inform, readers.

In much humor, of course, especially fictional jokes, the issue of truth doesn't even arise. But in any case the distinction between fiction and reality offers no hard distinction between humor and gossip. Much humor is based on real, not fictional events, and even when funny stories are fictional they are often presented as real, like in most stand-up comedy. Humor, then, can be based on either fictional or real events. And so can gossip. Some gossip, of course, is fictional but thought to be real by its tellers, but not all gossip is even presented as real. Suppose we are discussing our friend Bob's secret affair with his boss, Rhonda. One of us says, "What if Bob accidentally ran into his wife at the ski lodge some weekend when he's there with Rhonda?" And off our gossip goes with possible scenarios. We're not saying that he did or will do any of the things we are imagining—we're simply entertaining these ideas for the pleasure they bring.[2] Given all these similarities between humor and gossip, it's no surprise that they often overlap. There is humorous gossip and gossipy humor.

Gossip as Conversation

Some treatments of gossip include newspaper columns and television programs about the personal affairs of celebrities as instances of gossip; I don't, because these noninteractive, impersonal forms of communication are significantly different from what has traditionally been called gossip. So in what follows I'll limit "gossip" to certain kinds of personal, interactive communication and leave aside these other phenomena.

I'm treating gossip, that is, as a kind of conversation. Conversation in general serves several purposes, all of which are served by gossip.

1. There is the pleasure simply of talking with other people.
2. Conversation promotes solidarity—we feel close to those with whom we converse.
3. We receive new information.
4. We reveal new information to others.
5. We hear other people's opinions and evaluations of people, things, and events.
6. We express our own opinions and evaluations.

Gossip can be distinguished from others kinds of conversation, I suggest, if we consider ten characteristics of gossip, seven having to do with its subject matter and three with the manner in which it treats that subject matter.

1. Gossip is about people—we can't gossip about carburetors or the weather.
2. Gossip is primarily about people not involved in the conversation. You and I can't gossip by simply talking about ourselves and each other.
3. Gossip is not abstract, like science or history, but is focused on individuals in their concreteness.
4. Gossip is focused on the personal details of people's lives, like their sexual relationships and their virtues and vices. A discussion of whether Marcia plays trumpet or trombone in the band is not gossip.
5. The details of people's lives discussed in gossip are private and behind-the-scenes, or at least are thought to be so by those gossiping. That's why gossip has a short "shelf-life," and why "gossip columns" in newspapers are misnamed.
6. Gossip is concerned with aspects of people's lives that can be

morally evaluated. The evaluation in gossip, furthermore, is usually negative and can be mean-spirited. We often gossip about people having sex with other people's spouses; we almost never gossip about their putting away money each week to give to UNICEF. Even when gossip is about good news, as when we note that Ted is probably going to get the promotion he wants so badly, that good news is usually followed by negative comments—his promotion isn't fully deserved, it will cost him his marriage. In gossip we seldom speculate on someone else's achieving some success or happiness and then magnanimously express our good wishes for that person.

7. There is a Hobbesian reason why in gossip we tend to evaluate other people negatively and why we tend to express envy, jealousy, and indignation. In gossip we often relate what other people do, have, and experience to ourselves. Indeed, in much gossip we not only compare others with ourselves, but express our reactions to how they have treated us. We may gossip about the way a friend broke a promise to us, for instance, as a way of expressing our bad feelings over that incident. An overall function of gossip is to allow us to arrange in our own minds, and express to others, how we stand in relation to those we are gossiping about. The last three characteristics of gossip have to do with the way in which the content of gossip is expressed.

8. The attitude toward the people talked about in gossip is one of presumed familiarity. The original meaning of the noun "gossip" is instructive here: a godparent (God's sib), one intimate with the family.

9. Gossip is idle, light conversation—small talk that does not delve deeply into issues but emphasizes their most attention-grabbing aspects.

10. Gossip is idle and light in another way, too—it does not have a rigorous standard of evidence, thus its close association with rumor.

Humor in Gossip

Many studies of humor, especially humor in conversation, concern themselves primarily or exclusively with prepared jokes—fictional stories or riddles with punch lines, not created by the person reciting them. Since jokes are relatively fixed texts, this focus makes the research easier. Studying jokes, however, is not studying humor in general, for humor is wider than humor in conversation, and conversation contains more kinds of humor than prepared jokes. There are, for instance, funny anecdotes about people's lives and wisecracks about events within and outside the conversation.

To understand the full nature of humor, we can analyze the experience that humor evokes, humorous amusement (henceforth called simply "amusement"). To amuse is to delight, bring pleasure, in a certain way. The most comprehensive theory of humor is the incongruity theory. Amusement, in this theory, is the enjoyment of experiencing or thinking about something that somehow clashes with our conceptual patterns and their attendant expectations (see Morreall, 1983a, ch. 5–6; 1983b; 1987, ch. 20; 1989a). If the doorbell rings and I get up to answer it, for instance, I expect there to be at least one person on the other side of the door who wants to speak to me. If I open it to find no one there, or a goat, or a person who stands there silent, those experiences are incongruous; and if I enjoy that incongruity, that enjoyment is amusement. Jokes, it has often been observed, work by leading us along one mental track and then at the punchline forcing us onto another.

Not all incongruity is enjoyable, of course. Whereas a goat at my door might make me laugh, finding no one there could make me puzzled or angry. For me to enjoy having my conceptual patterns and expectations violated, the setting has to be right—most importantly, the incongruity should not present a serious threat to me nor evoke other major practical concerns. That's why it's easier to laugh at incongruous events in other people's lives, or in our own lives since they are safely in the past, than to laugh at them in our current experience. As the American humorist Will Rogers put it, "Everything is funny if it's happening to the other guy." And as Steve Allen said, "Tragedy plus time equals comedy."

We will use the idea of amusement as an enjoyment of incongruity to explain the special usefulness of humor in gossip. But before doing that, we should consider the more general topic of gossip in language, especially in conversation. Humor is possible in language wherever there are patterns and expectations to be violated in an enjoyable way (see Morreall, 1983a, ch. 6). And so there is linguistic humor based on phonological, morphological, syntactic, semantic, and pragmatic patterns. Things as simple as excessive alliteration can be funny, as can spoonerisms and puns. Most humor in conversation, however, is based not on these simpler features of language, but on the semantic content of language and on its pragmatics.

There are two standard humorous moves in a conversation, which we might label "saying funny things" and "saying things funny." The first and easier move is to describe something incongruous, as when we tell an anecdote about spilling the bowl of soup on the mayor's tuxedo. The second, and more properly linguistic, move is to violate a rule of semantics or pragmatics, as when we exaggerate or understate a truth. This is the domain of wit, where the enjoyable incongruity lies largely in the way things are said. U.S. President Calvin Coolidge had the reputation of not saying or doing much, for example, but it wouldn't have been funny to simply report that Coolidge was passive. When someone told Dorothy Parker that Coolidge had died, however, her response—"How can they tell?"—was funny. Parker's wit was based on an exaggerated representation of Coolidge's passivity, and more importantly, on her not asserting that exaggeration—as president, Coolidge seemed dead—but instead saying something that presupposed it. Almost anyone can do a passable job of recounting funny events, but it is much harder to be funny through such clever presupposition, irony, sarcasm, and other semantic and pragmatic incongruities. Many conversations include funny stories, few include much wit.

When we look at gossip as a kind of conversation, we find the full range of humorous linguistic devices. And we also find that humorous conversational moves are ideally suited to gossip. For example, Ben-Ze'ev (Chapter 1) notes that gossiping and joking involve an element of surprise. A central aim of both gossip and conversational humor is to present to our listeners novel ideas or arrangements of ideas that will cause a pleasurable mental jolt. The best gossip and the best humor catch us off guard; they violate our ordinary trains of thought by presenting things we hadn't considered. The weakest gossip and humor are conversely, easy to process cognitively, familiar, stale, unimaginative, and boring.

To put all this in terms of the incongruity theory of humor, causing a mental jolt in our listeners—an experience of incongruity—is central in both conversational humor and gossip. Suppose, for example, that our neighbor Lydia was just arrested for shoplifting, and we are going to describe this event in a conversation. The funniest and probably the most conversationally successful way to present it is to make the event, and Lydia's general situation, as incongruous as we can. We might, for instance, emphasize the incongruity of her trying to seem innocent when it was clear to everyone that she was guilty, or the incongruity between her shoplifting and the moral principles she preaches to her children. In gossiping about Lydia, in short, it's only natural to make her and what she did seem funny. Similarly, in gossip consisting of speculations—the kind beginning "What would happen if . . ."—humor is a natural technique. We naturally try to make the hypothetical events unexpected, out of the ordinary, funny, much as a stand-up comic would do.

In gossip it is natural not only to say funny things, but also to say things funny—to get laughs through semantic and pragmatic incongruities. A standard conversational device of this kind is sarcasm, which typically involves understatements, exaggeration, or saying the opposite of what we believe. While gossiping about how Richard will soon be indicted for mail fraud, for instance, we might bring up the fact that he just won an award as "Entrepreneur of the Year," and then say facetiously, "He's a businessman's businessman."

There are other ways, too, in which humor is natural in gossip. One of the pleasures of gossip is to entertain and delight people. Making people laugh is one of the greatest delights we can bring them, judging from the millions of dollars people spend annually to hear stand-up comics. (In the United States there is now even a cable television channel devoted exclusively to comedy.) In gossip, the anecdote or wisecrack that makes people laugh, shake their heads in agreement, and then make a funny quip of their own, is a high point of the conversation.

A good part of the pleasure here is based on the community of feeling produced by humor.[3] Laughter, as Bergson pointed out, is essentially social. When we are alone we seldom laugh aloud in the way we laugh with others, and on enjoying a funny thought, we automatically want to share it with someone. When we want to get to know someone quickly, we usually try to make the other person laugh; and when we want to keep our distance from someone, say a spouse with whom we are quarreling, we refuse to laugh together about anything. Conversation that makes us laugh together, in short, creates a special kind of solidarity. As Victor Borge once said, laughter is the shortest distance between two people.

Both gossip and humor foster intimacy and solidarity. Creating humor and gossiping both presuppose and strengthen shared attitudes. For you and me to laugh together at a wisecrack about someone's duplicity, for instance, we have to have similar suspicions about that person. Similarly, to gossip about where Sandra *really* went last weekend when she claimed to be on a business trip, we have to share a certain attitude toward her. Sandra's best friend would probably not participate in such gossip.

As these two examples indicate, the community of feeling fostered by humor and gossip often has an outside as well as an inside. In any conversation, when a funny comment is made, there are insiders who understand it and have the beliefs and attitudes needed to enjoy it, and there are outsiders who lack one of these ingredients. The same is true of a bit of gossip in a conversation: there are those who are in on the gossip and those who aren't, perhaps because they don't know the background or understand the significance of the story, or simply because they don't share the necessary attitudes toward those being gossiped about.

Still another similarity between humor and gossip is the playfulness that we find in both. Each emphasizes the entertainment value of the ideas being considered, but humor emphasizes it more and is more playful. In a play mode, our ordinary cognitive and moral responsibilities about using language are not in force. We are allowed to think and say almost anything in a bantering conversation, just as the traditional court jester could say almost anything to the monarch. We can engage in fanciful fictions as if they were real, can explore far-fetched analogies, impute preposterous motives to people, and so on. Indeed, Freud (1959) held that in humor we revert to the pleasure principle of our childhood. This playful, speculative, exploratory approach of humor is nonthreatening and provides a good way to make comments in gossip that would otherwise seem heavy-handed. When we criticize someone with a touch of humor, for example, we are saying that we can see the problem in perspective and thus appreciate that it is not the end of the world. In this respect humor in gossip is like kidding friends in face-to-face interaction. When said jocularly, almost any criticism of a friend can be made to his or her face. Indeed, kidding is a sign of affection; we kid only people to whom we feel close. And although gossiping about someone in a humorous way does not guarantee that we are close to that person, closeness is certainly less likely if we gossip in a nonhumorous way.

Gossip With and Without Humor

In this last benefit of humor and gossip—its playfulness—we find an answer to traditional attacks on gossip as mean-spirited. From the start we should admit that there are cases of small-minded, nasty gossip that gloats over the faults and mistakes of other people and may even try to ruin people's reputations. But a notable feature of such cases is their lack of humor. Where humor prevails, gossip rises above pettiness and viciousness. This redemptive power of humor comes partly from the incompatibility of humor with strong negative emotions.[4] People cannot anger us or make us indignant, for instance, at the same time as they make us laugh. When we gossip with a sense of humor, similarly, we tend not to feel hostile toward those we are gossiping about.

The best kind of humor in gossip, it seems to me—best in the sense of conversationally most interesting, and in the sense of morally best—has four aspects. First, it is playful. Those gossiping are in the conversation for the surprising news and ideas that will emerge, for the witty banter, for the entertainment. Second, this humor is self-reflective: those gossiping are aware of the lightness, superficiality, and sensationalism of the conversation, of the lack of evidence for much of what they are saying, and of the fact that self-awareness contributes to the fun. Part of what is funny to those gossiping is precisely that they are having a superficial, sensationalistic conversation (much as it can be funny to display kitsch in our homes knowing that it is kitsch). When, for example, we are engaging in wild speculation about why Jamie has been out of town for over a week, and we're exploring the fantasy that he is having an affair with his former lover in Reykjavik, our preservation of a sense of humor about what we're doing reminds us that our banter is basically for our own entertainment and not an objective assessment of anyone's character. We might, for example, work the groundlessness of the rumors we've been hearing and spreading into the conversation in order to make a joke about it. Third, the best kind of humor in gossip is universalizing—it sees the faults and problems of the people being gossiped about as faults and problems any of us might fall into. This week it is funny that Ada got caught lying to the boss in the same way that last week it was funny when I got caught doing the same thing, and it will be funny when the next one of us gets caught. In the best humorous gossip about people's folly lies the implicit acknowledgment that folly is part of the human condition. Last, because this kind of humor sees mistakes and problems as universal, it is gentle and relatively unjudgmental in its treatment of individuals, even when they have major shortcomings. The laughter does not express moral castigation or pettiness.

The kind of playful, self-reflective, universalizing, gentle humor that I have in mind here is not found in all or perhaps even in most gossip, but it occurs often enough to show that there is nothing inherently vicious about gossip. Gossip can express some of our most valuable human traits, especially the interest we take in each other's lives and the delight we take in entertaining one another.

6 | The Legal Regulation of Gossip: Backyard Chatter and the Mass Media

Robert Post

I SHALL BEGIN by distinguishing gossip as a noun, a particular subject matter, from gossip as a verb, a form of activity. *Webster's Third New International Dictionary* defines gossip as a noun in this way: "4a. rumor, report, tattle, or behind-the-scenes information esp. of an intimate or personal nature," a definition that quite properly evokes Erving Goffman's distinction between "front-stage" and "back-stage" (Goffman, 1959, pp. 106–40). When we act in full view of the public, when we must exercise politeness and decorum for the sake of our audience, we are front-stage; we obey the standards of proper behavior. But when we can let our hair down and act ourselves, we are backstage. The distinction between the two is made by reference to social conventions. Normally the distinction is policed by considerations of privacy. The noun "gossip," in at least one of its meanings, concerns the revelation of the backstage.

Gossip in this sense implies an intimate knowledge of the social norms distinguishing the public from nonpublic aspects of the self; it points beyond itself toward a particular conception of community structure. But gossip has a two-edged relationship to that structure. On the one hand, gossip threatens to subvert community norms by exposing back-stage behavior and revealing the pretensions, faults, peccadillos, and scandal of community actors. On the other hand, gossip reaffirms community norms by bringing social pressure to bear on their enforcement. As Thomas Starkie remarks in his 1826 treatise on defamation law, "The dread of public censure and disgrace is not only the most effectual, and therefore the most important, but in numberless instances the only security which society possesses for the preservation of decency and the performance of the private duties of life" (Starkie, 1826, pp. xx–xxi).

Webster's is far less helpful in its definition of gossip as a verb, which it defines largely in terms that recapitulate its definition of the noun: "to retail facts, rumors, or behind-the-scenes information about other persons." A finer sense of the verb emerges from the work of anthropologists like Max Gluckman. Gluckman suggests that gossip and the scandal it offers about back-stage life "maintain the unity, morals and values of social groups."

> The important things about gossip and scandal are that generally these are enjoyed by people about others with whom they are in a close social relationship. Hence when we try to understand why it is that people in all places and at all times have been so interested in gossip and scandal about each other, we have also to look at those whom they exclude from joining in the gossiping or scandalizing. That is, the right to gossip about certain people is a privilege which is only extended to a person when he or she is accepted as a member of a group or set. It is a hallmark of membership. Hence rights to gossip serve to mark off a particular group from other groups. (Gluckman, 1963, p. 313)

Gluckman allows us to see how gossip as a noun and gossip as a verb complement each other. If the content of gossip is always two-edged, always both reenforcing community norms and threatening to blow communities apart, the activity of gossip supports the first of these tendencies. By carefully choosing the audience for our gossip, we maintain the boundaries of the very community that the content of our gossip potentially endangers. When we confine our gossip to "insiders," to those who share our interest in community as a whole, we establish that, in Gluckman's words, our scandal is "virtuous" in that "its aim [is] to demonstrate some kind of unity." Thus gossip as a noun and gossip as a verb fuse into a single communicative act in which the community-affirming aspects of gossip are emphasized and its potential social divisiveness muted. In this sense, gossip, as Gluckman observes, "does not have isolated roles in community life, but is part of the very blood and tissue of that life" (1959, p. 308).

The primary point about the contemporary mass media—both print and broadcast—is that they separate gossip as noun from gossip as a verb. In the gossip columns and tabloids we can read the substance of gossip—the backstage whispers, the tantalizing revelations—but we cannot partake of the activity of gossip. The mass media are indiscriminate; they are available to anyone who can read or see or hear. They thus do not reinforce community boundaries, but threaten to dissolve groups into the larger public. We can expect, therefore, that gossip in the media will be perceived as decidedly more threatening to community values.

We can, I think, trace this effect in the legal regulation of gossip. Since the seventeenth century, for example, the law of defamation has treated slander, defamation conveyed by oral conversation, much more leniently than libel, defamation conveyed by writing or broadcasting. Libel was crime; slander was not. A plaintiff suing for libel could receive general and presumed damages not available to a plaintiff suing for slander (unless he could demonstrate one of four specific and especially egregious categories of slander). These differences were always justified in terms of libel's greater potential for injury than slander. But this explanation is hard to credit. As the example of Iago illustrates, a well-placed slander can be far more devastating than a piece of writing directed to an indifferent public. The general approach of the common law, moreover, would ordinarily determine the amount of injury on a case-by-case basis. Why, then, was the law making a categorical distinction between libel and slander?

The whole purpose of defamation law is to uphold community norms of civil speech, and by so doing to maintain for the community, in Kai Erikson's words, "its distinctive shape, its unique identity" (Erikson, 1966, p. 11).[1] Defamation conveyed by slander, because of its contextualization in oral conversation, can serve these very purposes in ways that libel, defamation conveyed by writing, cannot. Writing always threatens to pass beyond the boundaries of the community's control. Thus if the activity of slander is "part of the very blood and tissue of community life," written libel exposes community faults in a manner not softened by a virtuous concern for the "unity" of the community. Hence writing was to be more severely regulated than slander.

The tort of invasion of privacy, like that of defamation, is also intended to maintain community identity and norms. (Post, 1989, p. 957). It is thus natural that when in 1890 Samuel Warren and Louis Brandeis came to write their famous article "The Right to Privacy," which virtually invented the tort, they retained the same distinction between oral and written communication. In their opinion, the law should "not grant any redress for the invasion of privacy by oral publication in the absence of special damage" (Warren and Brandeis, 1890, p. 217). Almost half a century later, when the California Supreme Court issued its significant opinion in *Melvin v. Reid*, it ruled that "the right of privacy can only be violated by printings, writings, pictures, or other permanent publications or reproductions, and not by word of mouth" (*Melvin v. Reid*, 1931).

A similar distinction continues in the modern tort, which allows liability only if a defendant "gives publicity" to the "private life of another." Thus it "is not an invasion of the right of privacy . . . to communicate a fact concerning the plaintiff's private life to a single person or even to a small group of persons. On the other hand, any publication in a newspaper or a magazine, even of small circulation, or in a handbill distributed to a large number of persons, or any broadcast over the radio . . . is sufficient to give publicity" (Restatement of Torts, 1977). One final example will suffice to make the point. Florida Statutes Section 794.03 (1987) provides that "no person shall print, publish, or broadcast . . . in any instrument of mass communication the name, address, or other identifying fact or information of the victim of any sexual offense." The statute in effect prohibits the mass media from conveying a certain kind of gossip, but it places no such restrictions on gossip that is embodied in conversation.

In 1989, Section 794.03 was declared unconstitutional as a violation of the First Amendment. The United States Supreme Court purported to weigh the value of privacy against the "public interest . . . in the dissemination of truth" (*Florida Star v. B.J.F.*, 1989). At least one of the reasons offered by the Court for its conclusion is that the statute did not punish "backyard gossip":

Section 794.03 prohibits the publication of identifying information only if this information appears in an "instrument of mass communication," a term the statute does not define. Section 794.03 does not prohibit the spread by other means of the identities of victims of sexual offenses. An individual who maliciously spreads word of the identity of a rape victim is thus not covered, despite the fact that the communication of such information to persons who live near, or work with, the victim may have consequences equally devastating as the exposure of her name to large numbers of strangers. See Tr. of Oral Arg. 49-50 (appellee acknowledges that Section 794.03 would not apply to "the backyard gossip who tells 50 people that don't have to know").

When a State attempts the extraordinary measure of punishing truthful publication in the name of privacy, it must demonstrate its commitment to advancing this interest by applying its prohibition evenhandedly, to the smalltime disseminator as well as the media giant. Where important First Amendment interests are at stake, the mass scope of disclosure is not an acceptable surrogate for injury. A ban on disclosures effected by "instrument[s] of mass communication" simply cannot be defended on the ground that partial prohibitions may effect partial relief.[2]

The considerations we have been discussing throw a fascinating light on the Court's opinion. The Court is of course absolutely correct that the distinction between mass media and backyard gossip cannot be sustained on the basis of any objective or measurable concept of individual damage. What is striking, however, is the Court's assumption that such a concept of damage is the only acceptable justification for the statute. The Court does not even consider the possibility that backyard gossip may be performing an important community-defining function that the mass media cannot serve. This function is consistent with the general thrust of the Court's First Amendment jurisprudence, which is to prohibit states from regulating public discourse for community-sustaining reasons—but this is a complex subject that I have elsewhere discussed in some detail.[3]

I shall conclude, then, by briefly focusing on the role of the mass media as purveyors of gossip. This role is by no means trivial, and it is increasing all the time. As *Time* put it in a recent cover story, "Gossip is booming on television, in magazines, in nonfiction books, in docudrama TV movies and mini-series" (*Time*, March 5, 1990, pp. 47–52). *Time* poses the appropriate question of how we ought to understand this "alchemy," in which "the private doings of public figures" is "taken seriously by millions of bystanders."

It is clear enough that media gossip often carries for its audience the same revelation of backstage conduct, the same *frisson* of transgressing privacy conventions, the same glimpse of scandal and pretension, as does backyard gossip. Gossip in the media, then, also points toward a larger structure of community standards, from the violation of which it draws interest and fascination. But whereas the behavioral context of backyard gossip affirms that structure, it is quite otherwise with media gossip, as E. L. Godkin, the editor of *Scribner's*, noted in 1890:

As long as gossip was oral, it spread, as regarded any one individual, over a very small area, and was confined to the immediate circle of his acquaintances. It did not reach, or but rarely reached, those who knew nothing of him. It did not make his name, or his walk, or his conversation familiar to strangers. . . .

In all this the advent of the newspapers . . . has made a great change. It has converted curiosity into what economists call an effectual demand, and gossip into a marketable commodity. The old Paul Pry whom our fathers despised and caricatured, and who was roundly kicked and cuffed on the stage for his indiscretions, has become a great wholesale dealer in an article of merchandise for which he finds a ready sale, and by which he frequently makes a fortune. (Godkin, 1890)

Bluntly, gossip in the media commodifies violations of community norms. One cannot imagine an activity more destructive of community standards, which implies that media gossip is drawing on an exhaustible resource. Community norms cannot continue to function as commodities, because their power to sustain our interest in gossip will diminish as we progressively consume them. This effect accounts, I believe, for the escalating sense of exposure in contemporary media gossip. The subject matter of today's gossip, according to *Time*, concerns "items that were once unthinkable."

The function of media gossip is not, however, merely negative. Media gossip is constitutive not of community, but of what the sociologist Alvin Gouldner defines as a "public," which "emerges"

> when there is an attenuation between culture, on the one side, and patterns of social interaction, on the other. Traditional "groups" are characterized by the association and mutual support of both elements; by the fact that their members have patterned social interactions with one another which, in turn, fosters among them common understandings and shared interests, which, again in turn, facilitates their mutual interaction, and so on. A "public" "refers to a number of people exposed to the same social stimuli," and having something in common even without being in persisting interaction with one another. . . . "Publics" are persons who need not be "co-present," in the "sight and hearing of one another. (Gouldner, 1976, p. 95)

A public, in short, is a social formation united by common access to the same stimuli. In our society these stimuli are provided by the mass media, so that, as Gouldner points out, the "emergence of the mass media and of the 'public' are mutually constructive developments" (Gouldner, 1976, pp. 95–96).

In this sense, media gossip sustains a public of millions of people who are united in their interest in the doings of the rich and famous. The legal protection of that public has in this century become a central object of constitutional law, because in a heterogenous nation the public, rather than any particular community, must fulfill the function of democratic decision making. Thus the Supreme Court's use of the First Amendment to strike down the statute at issue in the *Florida Star* decision, which was an attempt to use the norm of privacy of a particular community to limit the discourse necessary for an entire public.

There is a tension, then, between community and public, and gossip plays a special role in that tension. When it is situated within a certain kind of normative conversation, gossip supports community. But when it is liberated from that conversation and located instead within the mass media, gossip destroys community. Yet it is at the same time constitutive of a public. One can trace this tension in the widely contradictory attitudes of courts toward the press. If a court wishes to defend community values (like privacy), it characterizes the press as a commercializing, self-interested entity. When it wishes to uphold the public, it praises the press as an agent of the public's right to know.[4] Thus in the evolution of gossip, and in the varying forms of its legal regulation, lie tantalizing clues to the sociology of our culture.

ɔssip and Privacy
ˍˍˍdinand Schoeman

PRIVACY, IN ONE of its important and characteristic roles, insulates us from inappropriate manifestations of social pressure. Gossip involves bothering with parts of another person's life that are characteristically none of our business, and introduces an indirect form of social pressure that privacy norms would seem designed to exclude. Although not directed to the individual discussed, gossip does precisely what it would be rude to do to the person herself: discuss that which is none of our business. Furthermore, gossip gives access to information about an individual in apparent violation of her private domain. In a culture where people know that others gossip, the very social pressure from which privacy presumably insulates us is unleashed, albeit in an attenuated form.

The apparent conflict between the role of privacy and the role of gossip rests in the exclusion of concern for another person's business, in the case of privacy norms, and in its invitation, in the case of gossip. This apparent conflict, notwithstanding, gossip actually presupposes privacy norms and in so doing works with them to protect individuals from overreaching social control. My claim is that privacy and gossip norms together modulate the amount and type of social pressure available to control behavior.

Privacy is part of a historically conditioned, intricate normative matrix with interdependent practices; it is best understood in context, interacting with other practices in shaping behavior, rather than as an independent principle that either succumbs to or overrides other considerations. Thus we appreciate that privacy is central to social life, not in opposition to it. Private behavior and behavior in private contexts, even when most liberated and expressive, is subject to an array of social norms and controls. Likewise, gossip is at once structured by social norms and is itself a primary means of maintaining and enforcing them.

Privacy and Disclosure

The public-private distinction is not especially edifying.[1] There are many private realms; disclosures made in some private settings seem consistent with privacy norms, whereas disclosure in other private settings seems inconsistent with the same norms. If I tell you, someone I know only casually, out of earshot of anyone else, that you should lose weight, there is a sense in which this is not public communication. Others in general have no access to this criticism. This case is very different from placing an ad in a personals column and declaring my thoughts both to my subject and the rest of the interested world. Alternatively, if I say to my local lodge, whose members are sworn to secrecy, what I think about your shape or romantic habits, this communication should be considered private and not public for our purposes. Public disclosure typically involves a communicative act normatively open to anyone. Similarly, there are legal proceedings, like family court hearings, in which further communication of information disclosed is prohibited, but where much that is intimate and personal is exposed to strangers acting in official capacities who have no stake in the outcome. Here an innermost sphere is exposed to a wider audience but is nevertheless restricted once so exposed. For these situations, it seems more fitting to contrast levels of privacy than to contrast the private with the public. Nor does talk about restricted audiences form part of a strict definition of what counts as private and what as public, for it just suggests that disclosure of information to groups, even potentially large groups, might still be considered private provided still larger groups were excluded.

It is important to appreciate how fluid and relative the distinction between public and private really is. A person can be active in the gay pride movement in San Francisco, but be private about her sexual preference vis-à-vis her family and coworkers in Sacramento. A professor may be highly visible to other gays at the gay bar but discreet about sexual orientation at the university. Surely the streets and newspapers of San Francisco are public places as are the gay bars in the quiet university town. Does appearing in some public settings as a gay activist mean that the person concerned has waived her rights to civil inattention, to feeling violated if confronted in another setting? (see also Zimmerman, 1983).

Another distinction that can be usefully interjected here is that between normative and descriptive privacy (see Gavison, 1984). The disclosure of a rape victim's name to a public at large does not make the information itself less private in a normative sense, though it does in a descriptive sense. Even if the law requires public disclosure of rape victims' names, as long as we have social norms that adjudge such disclosure inappropriate, we can continue to regard information of this sort as (normatively) private, however widely and legally disseminated.

For instance, even if rape victims are not treated as guilty for acting provocatively, or for not resisting enough, and even if it helps to bring public attention to the plight of rape victims by publicizing them as identifiable people, there is something intrusive about, and thus there is a cost to, the publication of their names. People who have been raped, like people who have accidentally killed someone or who have lost a loved one, face emotional trauma and are shrouded in a varying set of protective societal norms.

Privacy is affected by common social practices. For instance, it is impolite for me to say to a work associate who is not a friend that she should lose weight or restrict her dating of men. These matters, most would agree, are none of my business, because according to our cultural rules my coworker is not answerable to me for those aspects of her life that are not germane to our business relationship. Likewise, there are parts of every person's life to which others should not have access without the consent of the individual concerned, assuming no relationship that warrants or legitimizes such access. In contrast to a person's coworker, a person's doctor, responsible for advising her on health matters, may and should discuss weight with her. Her close friends, able to judge whether discussion or advice would be constructive, may also perhaps raise the topic with her. On the other hand, complete strangers, a person she casually talks with on the ski lift or a seatmate on a train trip, might get away with intimate discussion simply because they play such an insignificant role in her everyday life. Social pressure from a stranger counts less than pressure from people with whom a person has some significant connection and to whom she is vulnerable.

To understand the role of privacy, it is useful to differentiate between two overlapping types of social norms that protect privacy. First, social norms exist that restrict access to an individual in a certain domain where the individual is accorded wide discretion concerning how to behave. These norms promote private life, individuality, and the integrity of various spheres of life. A second type of social norms restricts access in a domain where the behavior carried on in private is rigidly defined and affords little discretion. Though this sort of behavior is performed in private and is guarded by privacy norms, the point of the norms is not the enhancement of individual choice or expression. For instance, although defecation is a paradigmatically private activity for an adult in our society, there are many ways of managing this activity in private that would violate social taboos. The privacy afforded a person for such an activity does not serve the purpose of self-expression; instead, it manifests a rigid and internalized form of social control. (Thus parents of small children tend to discourage displays of fecal art that might tempt the child who has not yet internalized our taboos.) The fact that there is little opportunity for directly enforcing the norms should not obscure the point that much socialization is directed to erecting internal barriers to norm violations (Douglas, 1966). To take another example, there is ample historical evidence that families have functioned and still do function largely as social control mechanisms rather than as refuges from social control.[2] The privacy accorded them enhances the controlling rather than the liberating forces.

One way to gauge this distinction between the two sorts of privacy norms in the context of the family is to consider whether spouses define themselves primarily by reference to a role or in reference to a relationship. Roles imply patterns of outlook and behavior that are internalized and enforced independently of how the other partner behaves.[3] The term "relationship" emphasizes how the way one behaves is largely a function of the behavior of the other. Suppose a husband both disregards and mistreats his wife. In some contexts, this would be seen by the wife as a burden but not as a reason to forgo her domestic role or think differently about her responsibilities. These responsibilities are, from her perspective, unconditional. To a large extent, we relate to our children this way. Even if they are unresponsive to supportive overtures and nonreciprocating in love and communication, parents feel they should continue to love and emotionally nurture their children.

Both sorts of norms relate to our practices of showing respect for people and reflect social structure and symbolism. But their function is often distinct. Whether our norms lead us to avert our gaze from others' genitals or feet may well be a matter of convention. But as a way of promoting private life and freedom from social control, the means are not as arbitrary. Relaxing the norms that restrict exposure to someone's diary would be more violative of private life than would a relaxation of norms that restrict exposure of activity on the toilet. The privacy restrictions related to elimination are not designed to afford or facilitate intimate or personal opportunities otherwise not available. The practice of writing a diary aims directly at such opportunities.

Granted, some people may find it more upsetting and debilitating to be exposed in their bathroom behavior than to be exposed in their diaries; this can be conceded without altering the point about the different roles of these norms in promoting private life. Hannah Arendt (1958) observes that many widely shared privacy norms relate to bodily functions that we share with other animals. Stanley Benn (1984) has reminded us that these norms often involve notions of shame and impose upon us not to present certain facets of ourselves in public. Some of our privacy norms, then, would seem to express respect for human dignity by protecting us from public association with the beastly, the unclean. Such norms do not protect individual expression or limit social regimentation. Privacy norms that enable private life to transpire by freeing people from social control represent an additional component of human dignity—a component that emerges in certain cultural settings.

One type of privacy can evolve into the other. We can think of marital relations as private in the sense that limited exposure norms apply to them even when the behavior in these relations is completely ritualized and allows for no self-expression. Over time, this same institution could evolve into the primary locus of self-expression, still protected by limited exposure norms. Failing to draw this distinction between privacy norms has hampered our understanding of central cultural dimensions of privacy.

Max Scheler draws a helpful distinction between two sorts of roles by differentiating between those in which individuality is central and those in which it is out of place.[4] Scheler points out how shame can arise when one thinks of himself impersonally in a role but others treat him as personally involved: being noticed by a painter not as a nude model, for example, but as something fuller. Being treated as an individual rather than as a fungible abstraction leads to a loss of anonymity and, in some contexts, to a loss of self-respect.

This distinction suggests that the way rules operate in impersonal and in personal roles differ dramatically. We can concede that all roles are rule governed, both by local practice (i.e., rules governing painters painting models) and by more global moral and social principles (i.e., people should not be murdered or exploited). Nevertheless, most roles are sufficiently flexible to allow for individual expressiveness and emotional engagement, because external scrutiny and regulation tend to be focused only on the most objective aspects of such roles. Otherwise, inhibitions to fulfillment would abound, as would temptations to redirect the point of the practice to serve public ends. Most significantly, roles that involve an individual distinctively and personally are ones in which an individual is emotionally most exposed and vulnerable. This exposure presupposes trust and acceptance of vulnerability. Roles that embrace this trust and vulnerability, and thus permit certain forms of expression and personal development, cannot flourish without privacy of the sort that promotes self-expression.

The two sorts of privacy, one restricting access to areas that are nevertheless highly regulated, and the other restricting access in order to allow individual expression, have some parallels to the distinction in roles that Schcler articulates. The privacy norms that promote self-expression are those that involve people as fully engaged: expressive-roles. Expressive-roles are to be contrasted with more functional roles on the one hand and with restrictions on access that are not aimed at role performance of any sort, but reflect social taboos, on the other.

The Scope of Privacy Norms

Some scholars limit privacy to informational or physical access to a person; others regard privacy as encompassing nearly all dimensions of private, personal life. The association of privacy norms that enable personal expression with dimensions of personal life seems to legitimize more inclusive interpretations of the scope of privacy. Whether a woman may use a contraceptive or have access to abortion services is so intimately tied to her expressive-role dimension that we may say it is encompassed in her right to privacy.

We might ask how innately personal or expressive is an activity like childbearing.[5] There are many contexts in which women are held accountable for becoming pregnant or for not becoming pregnant, but where they experience this domain of their lives as private and intimate. In many cases we can point to other features of the environment that encourage intimacy and expressive-role privacy. Control over pregnancy cannot be experienced as fully or rightfully public when intimacy and individuality are sanctioned in ways that affect people's overall outlook.

This broad interpretation of privacy can be challenged. Forcing persons into a labor camp or killing them precludes their being able to engage in expressive-roles. It does not, however, follow that assignment to a labor camp or condemnation to death are infringements of privacy. The difference between death and access to contraceptives, vis-à-vis privacy, is that while life is a necessary condition for expressive-role activity, it is also a necessary condition for all activity. Access to contraceptives is necessary primarily and specifically for an activity that is peculiarly expressive-role related. It qualifies as falling within the domain of privacy; prohibitions on killing do not. When we look at the political and social debate over the scope of privacy, we will find that this characterization is the one that fits.

Someone can still complain that, as used here, privacy has been conflated with autonomy, the issue of who has authority to govern a domain of life, whether public or private. But we need not deny that a measure of autonomy is relevant to expressive-role domains of life. If we are discussing the borders of privacy and autonomy, it is premature to say that if one category, autonomy, applies, the other does not. Moreover, assuming that privacy and autonomy do overlap, and because autonomy is the broader concept, it is more informative and therefore more appropriate to describe a situation in terms of privacy than in terms of autonomy.[6]

But I think a richer answer to the complaint is possible. Clearly, people need some autonomy in order to engage role-expressive aspects of self. The point of such autonomy, however, is not to disengage the person from the web of relations, but to enhance a feature of these relations to make a deeper or more variable relationship possible. Notions of privacy and intimacy imply this possibility. Notions of autonomy, as usually elaborated, are oblivious to it, and emphasize instead other less social dimensions of moral personality. Privacy, not autonomy, is the appropriate category for conceptualizing expressive-role domains because it situates the domain ultimately in relational ties and not in individualistic boundaries. Both privacy and autonomy suggest that some people have no business crossing a threshold. In addition, privacy suggests that on the other side of that threshold there may be something still interpersonal. The point of the restrictions on access is in large part not to isolate people but to enable them to relate intimately.

The privacy norms that promote self-expression involve people in creative roles and are categorized as expressive-role norms. Such norms are significant because they facilitate deeper and more variable relationships. Notions of privacy and intimacy suggest this possibility. Expressive-role privacy norms enhance prospects for relational ties in which, within a domain, people erase some of the boundaries that separate them from others. Privacy norms, particularly of the expressive-norm sort, are important because of the dimensions of self, both relational and individualistic, people can generate in supportive social contexts. Because behavior is expressive of the self, it tends to evoke and engage what become our deepest commitments.

In suggesting that privacy is properly attributed to the domains of personal life, I do not make any claims about whether the United States Constitution affords protection for these domains. My discussion is limited to the issue of whether in ordinary parlance privacy norms appropriately govern certain domains of personal life and personal choice. My conclusion is that they do.

Gossip and Privacy

It is important to distinguish between public and private disclosure. If I know that a friend has been raped, I might tell other people who could be sources of support to this person. Mass communication media would result in notifying these same people of the victim's need for assistance, but it would simultaneously notify people who could not be expected to extend support. Worse, as in the case of a recently published rape victim, she might receive calls threatening further sexual violence. Besides, there typically would be plenty of people she does know whom she would not like to have access to this information about her. For instance, a middle-school teacher might well hope that her students were not privy to this information. By no means is all gossip designed to help victims by selectively directing resources to those in need. Presumably only a small percentage of gossip is so directed. But it is an important function of social life, and were privacy norms really to preclude all dissemination, such prospects of expression of support would be lost to those in need.

Some years ago (Schoeman, 1984), I drew attention to an aspect of sharing information about oneself that is germane here. Information that is very emotionally charged for an individual, information that makes or shows an individual particularly vulnerable, is experienced as violating one's innermost self if treated as commonplace. I used the analogy of a sacred object, which is treated as sacred only if understood as such. Reflections like this help us see some difference between the effects of private and mass communication, though the difference is insufficient to establish a realistic view of gossip. For gossip is not restricted by norms of privacy, or any other relevant norms, to pieces of information and situations that treat people as vulnerable let alone sacred beings. For instance, if I find out that trouble exists in a relationship between people I do not care for, I do not feel constrained to convey this information only to people who will show them support. More likely, I would tell people who would take some delight in hearing about other people's, particularly enemies', troubles. If I convey this in the manner suggested, I do not feel like a violator of social norms. (Saints, looking to different norms, might well regard such communication as wrong.)

When my mother calls me and tells me about the private lives of her neighbors, people I knew growing up, I do not feel that she violates their privacy even though I am neither situated nor motivated to help them. Nor would the neighbors think my mother should not say such things to me, even if they would prefer that I not know. I think we all fully expect to be discussed by others who know us, with no sense of impropriety. We might think our friends in whom we confided should hold confidences. But this is different from thinking that people in whom we have not confided are restricted in their range of interests in our lives. Those of us who think that privacy norms are important, even in private life, have to address the question of how gossip fits into this picture. Maybe privacy as a normative institution is restricted to instruments of mass communication.

Gossip can concern almost anything. As Max Gluckman (1963) pointed out in an early discussion of gossip, the practice is highly organized by principles of social inclusion and exclusion. Social cohesion, social identity, social norms, social pressure—these dynamic factors of social life are all maintained and managed through the agency of gossip rules. Gossip is structured and strictured by norms. People can go too far, or not far enough, in terms of playing by the rules of the game. Several standard treatments of gossip focus on its positive contribution to social association and norm maintenance (Sabini and Silver, 1982, ch. 5). As Gluckman put it, people who gossip may be idle, but gossip itself is anything but idle. It is a primary means of maintaining and reinforcing social norms and of holding those in high status to the same standards that govern those not so situated. It also provides people with information about the social world, revealing both the norms and the extent of noncompliance. Even if the knowledge that one's actions are discussed behind one's back functions as a means to enforce society norms, the actor knows that she will not be confronted about the transgression. So long as information remains in the realm of gossip and is not treated as public information, the pressure is attenuated. One is aware of the sanctions but is not held accountable to those who know of one's behavior.

What differentiates gossip norms from social news? Much that we gossip about we would not think right to reveal "publicly." We may gossip about things we may not broadcast to the world at large. We surely invade a colleague's privacy if we announce at a meeting that she and our secretary are having an affair. Norms of privacy make this sort of disclosure unconscionable. Norms of privacy, however, do not make it seem as serious, or even at all serious, if we simply privately relate the same information to each person in the department. What we mean by privacy, then, or invading a person's privacy, is not the fact of disclosing the personal information to a variety of people without the consent of the object of discourse, but the means by which the private information is distributed. Thus, characterizations of gossip as revelation are incomplete or misleading. We must differentiate dissemination from publication. Publication means dissemination plus the conversion of a matter that is personal into a matter that is "open" or acknowledged as a "public fact."

A public fact is governed by its own set of norms. Just because something happens in public does not mean it becomes a public fact: the Central Park rape occurred in public, as did the trial of the accused, but the victim maintains a measure of privacy as to her identity. In less dramatic cases, the notion of civil inattention directs us to the same realization. We protect the dignity and public persona of a person by not discussing or publicly acknowledging, in a way unconstrained by certain considerations, what is apparent to all. A colleague's ex-wife, for instance, can be heard down the hall hollering at him that he is not paying child support and is a rotten father. Everyone hears this, but it is still not a matter for open discussion. People may discuss it outside the presence of the colleague, but deference toward the colleague precludes us from acknowledging our awareness of this incident and treating it as a public fact.

Gossip therefore permits a person to maintain a public face. The person presents himself as professionally responsible and emotionally collected despite being domestically irresponsible. Can we afford to tolerate this hypocrisy? Wouldn't exposure be better? Wouldn't we understand more about people and perhaps enable people to realize more about what they share with others without the restrictions on open or unrestricted disclosure, especially of what is known anyway? Clearly, I believe that the pseudoprivacy afforded someone should be viewed in a positive light. Rules governing gossip, like rules governing privacy, are designed to respect different spheres of life, according each a degree of autonomy. There is a presumption that what a person does in one domain is functionally irrelevant to what she does in another domain. This restriction in use of information is respected as long as from a social perspective the amount of social control available within the domain is adequate to maintain the practice. When forms of local pressure are inadequate and if the practice or domain is treated as important enough, then limited sorts of publication, domain crossing, are arguably permissible.

Privacy norms and gossip norms seem to allow us to have it both ways. Gossip norms permit or advance social knowledge as well as serve other social ends. They insulate the potential gossipee from direct and decontextualized social pressure. Privacy norms, in turn, define the presumptive boundaries within which it is permissible to apply direct social pressure of accountability and of threatened social disgrace. We need privacy to understand and engage in gossip, because we need the domains of life so demarcated in order to properly gossip. Rather than it being the case that privacy and gossip work at cross purposes, we see that privacy norms are a precondition of gossip norms. The person is left to maintain her relations and private resources, but at the same time other people are informed about norm deviation. Thereby, the norm transgressed is reinforced and reaffirmed communitywide. Moreover, other people can continue to relate to the individual without raising the specter of what might be a highly charged emotional unraveling. Insulated from full public disclosure, the individual is able to maintain control over what she will have to address, thus retaining resources for managing her own psychic economy.

Part 2 | Gossip and Knowledge

8 | Knowledge Through the Grapevine: Gossip as Inquiry

Maryann Ayim

THE SEARCH FOR KNOWLEDGE is part of what it means to be human. One of the most powerful myths of our civilization has us squandering a place in paradise because of our insatiable thirst for knowledge of good and evil. In knowledge lies power, and perhaps what the myth is really telling us is that as a species our lust for power is more compelling than our dreams of paradise.

The avenues we follow in our pursuit of knowledge are remarkably similar from person to person. This similarity is partly internal, attributable to our human nature: that is, we are limited to the sorts of perceptual and rational faculties with which we are equipped, although high technology has expanded these faculties far beyond what we would have dreamed possible a century ago. Social and political structures, however, impose external limits on our access to knowledge. That venerable institution designed specifically to promote the promulgation of higher knowledge, the university, was also designed to place strict limits on access to this knowledge. For centuries, women, among many other groups, remained well beyond the periphery of the chosen. There have always been other avenues to knowledge, less revered, but often more efficient. Gossip is one such avenue.[1]

In *The Murder at the Vicarage*, Agatha Christie's Miss Marple responds spiritedly to an attempt to undermine the qualifications of gossip to get at the truth.

> "Don't you think, Miss Marple," I said, "that we're all inclined to let our tongues run away with us too much? Charity thinketh no evil, you know. Inestimable harm may be done by the foolish wagging of tongues in ill-natured gossip."
>
> "Dear Vicar," said Miss Marple, "you are so unworldly. I'm afraid that, observing human nature for as long as I have done, one gets not to expect very much from it. I daresay idle tittle-tattle is very wrong and unkind, but it is so often true, isn't it?" (Christie, 1930, p. 14)

Much of this chapter will be devoted to supporting Miss Marple's claim that gossip is "so often true." Contrary to what people may say about gossip, there is in fact widespread agreement with Miss Marple's claim that those at the heart of the most powerful institutions, including the university, the corporate world, and the political arena, frequently rely upon gossip as a source of crucial information inaccessible by other means. Although the examples here tend to focus on the university since that context is most familiar to me, the use of gossip in acquiring knowledge is by no means limited to the academy; Neustadt (1990) provides a fascinating account of the critical role of gossip in politics. Those who are excluded from gossip circles will be hardpressed to maintain power and control, for they will not be privy to crucial inside information.

The precise sense of "gossip" to be analyzed is gossip as a form of inquiry used to elicit information or knowledge. I shall not defend a particular definition of gossip here; to do so would be a chapter in itself. Instead, I shall provide a loose characterization of the concept that I believe is widely accepted. First, a number of necessary conditions: (1) gossip is informal talk, (2) conducted within very small groups of participants, (3) who know one another fairly well, and (4) trust one another not to violate each other's confidence. (5) The subject matter is highly personal, focused on knowledge of other people, and (6) the person or people who form the subject matter are not among those doing the discussing. Another set of features, though not necessary, is frequently associated with gossip: (1) There is a sense of illicitness connected with the activity of gossip, and, hence, participants often engage in it covertly; (2) gossip is conversational (rather than lecture-style, for example), depending upon real interchange among the participants. Other characteristics of gossip are subject to much debate: (1) whether gossip endorses or undermines social norms, (2) whether its content is trivial or highly significant, (3) whether it is limited to women or extends to men as well, (4) whether it occurs only in private domiciles, or extends to shoptalk as well, and (5) whether it is unreliable and unsubstantiated, or highly accurate and worthy of belief. Many items in these three lists (necessary conditions, features frequently associated with gossip, and the commonly debated items) pertain to gossip as a peculiarly female form of discourse.

My interest is not so much with gossip as imparting information, but as eliciting it, that is, conversations directed towards acquiring facts or information. Once acquired, the knowledge can be put to various uses—it can be used to defame others, to establish bonding within a group, or provide a forum for self-expression and expression of those intimate others within the gossip circle. All of these applications of gossip are documented in the literature (see Spacks, 1985, pp. 4–5 and Medini and Rosenberg, 1976, p. 458). I examine here the acquisition of knowledge through gossip, rather than either the application or the dissemination of that knowledge. In what follows, I shall frequently use the term "investigative gossip" to make it clear that I am referring to gossip's role in eliciting information rather than imparting or applying information.[2]

My interest in gossip is as a mode of inquiry, and, like other modes of inquiry, it will be important to determine the nature of the standards of truth and canons of evidence with which those who undertake the inquiry operate. Investigative gossip is not dissimilar to science as depicted by Charles Sanders Peirce. Peirce describes science as "the pursuit of those who are devoured by a desire to find things out" (1:8),[3] and this is very much the sense in which I have experienced investigative gossip operating.

Gossip's model captures several aspects of Peirce's notion of a community of investigators. Describing what he sees as the causes of "the triumph of modern science," Peirce speaks specifically of the scientists' "unreserved discussions with one another, . . . each being fully informed about the work of his neighbour, and availing himself of that neighbour's results; and thus in storming the stronghold of truth one mounts upon the shoulders of another who has to ordinary apprehension failed, but has in truth succeeded by virtue of the lessons of his failure. This is the veritable essence of science" (7:51). The notion of a community of investigators, working and discussing freely with one another, is a theme that runs throughout Peirce's discussion of scientific inquiry (see also 5:413, 7:54, 7:55, 8:136). Even apparent failures may be important components of the process that, one hopes, leads ultimately to the truth. The value of a particular scientist's work can never be measured in isolation from the overall scientific picture. Most scientists contribute only minuscule pieces to that ultimate true depiction of reality, but the compounding of the minuscule pieces is exactly what is needed to get us to that picture. One of the most important functions of scientific progress is to keep the conversation going, to ensure that no blocks get placed on the road to inquiry. Peirce adds, "Next after the passion to learn there is no quality so indispensable to the successful prosecution of science as imagination" (1:47). If Peirce is right that unreserved discussions with one another are a cornerstone in the triumph of modern science, then gossip, by its very nature, would appear to be an ideal vehicle for the acquisition of knowledge. Gossips certainly avail themselves of their neighbors' results; discussing unreservedly and sharing results constitute the very essence of gossip. I suspect that precisely because investigative gossip does share these critical features with scientific investigation it is recognized as a very efficient means of acquiring knowledge. We fear the gossip not because we believe her tales are totally without foundation but because we know they are too close to the truth for comfort. It is inconvenient to admit this, however, so we leap upon what the gossip does not know, the missing parts of her picture, and declare her to be a creator and disseminator of falsehood and malicious slander. No particular scientist is expected to produce the full picture; minuscule contributions and even outright error are readily accepted as part of the scientific enterprise. Not only is this tolerance of error not extended to particular instances of investigative gossip, but gossip, as a very form of inquiry, is deemed to be undermined by the presence of error in its results.

According to Peirce, the first rule of reason is that we ought "not block the way of inquiry" (1:135). There can be no doubt that gossip satisfies this first rule of reason. Far from blocking inquiry, gossip promotes inquiry. Gossip involves unreserved discussion; it is not surprising, therefore, that gossip is conducted in informal styles. Some studies in anthropology indicate that when formal and informal dialects are available, the informal dialect will be selected for gossip (Brenneis, 1984, p. 493). Gossip is not the style of speech one would use in a public address, a televised broadcast, or a lecture. Gossip is dialogue in the true sense rather than monologue or soliloquy. It does not work in the manner of a public speech or lecture, in which one person, an authority, passes on knowledge to large masses of relative strangers. It takes place instead within small intimate groups of two or three close friends, relatives, or neighbors, with all participants working together as a group to achieve knowledge. In this respect, it more closely resembles small class discussions or seminars than lecture formats.

Seminars and small class discussions share vital features with gossip—namely, such classes involve a genuine interaction among the students through a pooling of ideas and perspectives. The students will, at least after a few classes, know one another on a level not possible in a large lecture hall and thus will feel much freer to present their own perspectives and to press for details of the perspectives of the other students. There will tend to be fewer marks of formality than in a lecture situation—for example, the instructor will often be seated, together with the students, and students will tend to speak up as ideas occur to them, much as they would in an interaction outside the classroom, rather than raising their hands prior to speaking. In other words, the classroom interchanges will be, like gossip, much more real conversations than commonly occur in the lecture hall. Also, like a gossip interchange, the small classroom interactions will characteristically have some participants who are more eager to contribute and elucidate their own point of view than they are to listen to other points of view.

It is not just the prevalence of "unreserved discussion" that links gossip to Peirce's notion of scientific inquiry. The nature of the initial hypothesis and the role of evidence in determining the ultimate status of the hypothesis are also analogous. The good scientist, as described in the work of Charles Sanders Peirce, will be likely to start with a hunch, or retroduction, as Peirce calls it, a tentative hypothesis appealing because of its great explanatory capacity. The scientist's retroduction will be no more able to stand alone than the gossip's hunch, however, and so the scientist too will seek the support of hard corroborating evidence, which will lead to the more commonly recognized procedures of science, deduction and induction. Peirce calls upon scientists to "look through the known facts and scrutinize them carefully to see how far they agree with the hypothesis and how far they call for modifications of it. This is a very proper and needful inquiry" (7:114). Peirce adds:

> The Deductions which we base upon the hypothesis which has resulted from Abduction produce conditional predictions concerning our future experience. That is to say, we infer by Deduction that if the hypothesis be true, any future phenomena of certain descriptions must present such and such characters. We now institute a course of quasi-experimentation in order to bring these predictions to the test, and thus to form our final estimate of the value of the hypothesis. (7:115 n. 27)

The competent scientist, like the good investigative gossiper, will sift through the plethora of data generated in this listening stance and amend, embrace, or reject the hypothesis accordingly. Thomas Pavel provides the following characterization of good gossip:

> [that the speaker must] stay within the limits of the subject matter and . . . tell the truth . . . that gossip-hypotheses be as specific as possible and that the evidence for them be a matter of common knowledge. . . . Thus gossip (good gossip) is an informal exercise in hypothesis devising and evidence finding. . . . Its purpose is the

understanding of the person or the situation discussed. . . . Basic gossip . . . is limited to the report of facts together with some explicit or implicit simple explanatory hypotheses, [whereas] . . . sophisticated gossip . . . is involved with the divising [sic] of elaborate, unexpected hypotheses, often supported only by tenuous evidence. (Pavel, 1978, p. 147, and cited in Spacks, 1985, p. 105)

In this passage, Pavel is drawing what he perceives to be strong similarities between literary criticism and gossip. If we accept Pavel's characterization of gossip, then the similarities between investigative gossip and scientific investigation as envisaged by Peirce are no less remarkable. Some theorists are less sanguine than Peirce that scientists strive to submit their own hypotheses to the severest of tests, preferring instead to amass a watertight case in support of such hypotheses. David Hull, for example, claims that scientists are far more willing to refute their fellow scientists' hypotheses than they are to expose their own hypotheses to severe testing (1988, p. 4). According to Hull, "one of the strengths of science is that it does not require that scientists be unbiased, only that different scientists have different biases" (1988, p. 22). On this analysis of the scientific process, gossip may appear to be even more analogous to science in its procedure for arriving at the truth, with gossipers, ever ready to attribute no security whatever (6:470) to the beliefs and claims of *others*, subjecting them to the harshest of critical analyses, adopting such claims and beliefs "only . . . on probation" (7:202), insisting on the stringent tests that Peirce saw as a vital component of scientific progress, and standing "ready to abandon one or all as soon as experience opposes them" (1:635). The difference between science and gossip lies not in their procedure, then, but in the type of subject matter that will characteristically interest them.

The good investigative gossiper will similarly refuse to rest happy with a theory, no matter how attractive on the surface, until she has tested it out against the real world and found it to pass the test of evidence. A large part of the good gossiper's method is to keep her ear to the grapevine as it were, to listen very carefully to the village talk as a means of gleaning information about events that she may be precluded from directly observing herself. There is a certain sense in which this sort of gossip, careful listening to the right sorts of conversation, could be characterized as passive. In an important sense, however, even the listening gossiper actively manipulates the information thus received; one selects when to listen and whom to listen to.

The most skillful gossipers will manipulate the discourse even more directly, by making carefully selected contributions to it, so as to steer it in the desired direction, and then, switching momentarily back to the more passive role of listener, watching the other participants' reactions carefully. Those who limit their contribution to talking are unlikely to learn much; such gossip may provide them with enjoyment, but it is unlikely to lead to knowledge. On the other hand, those who listen exclusively will learn more, but much of what they learn will be of little relevance to their own particular interests. The epistemological winner here will be the person who plays both roles strategically, maintaining the desired focus on the conversation by contributing judiciously to the discourse and then recording responses with a phonographic ear.

In this interactive process, more is going on than speaking and listening, of course. In addition, the gossiper is constantly sifting through the information, evaluating the talk, comparing component parts to one another, and judging what is truth, what is falsehood, and what needs further investigation before judgment can be passed. Some gossipers will leap to conclusions on the basis of insufficient evidence, but the investigative gossiper at her best will not attach her confidence to any judgment that has been arrived at by a sloppy procedure.

On occasion, the investigative gossiper may have no particular focus of interest; in this case, the gossiper will simply keep an ear to the ground, hoping as much for insight in selecting a particular focus as in acquiring specific information. This approach resembles that of the researcher who scans the journals in search of an interesting topic to investigate rather than to acquaint herself with the latest literature on a particular topic; it also resembles that of the corporate leader who scans conversational tidbits for a sense of anything new among the employees. This scanning method, while it has its place in both gossip and standard academic research, is certainly not the common stance.

The investigative gossiper usually begins with a particular exploration in mind, just as the academic more usually scans journals with a particular topic already uppermost, and the corporate leader with a particular question—such as whether the employees are considering forming a union—looming large. The investigative gossiper may, and often does, start with a hunch, but the hunch must be followed up with the support of hard evidence. Notice, however, that the investigative gossiper listens rather than eavesdrops. This difference underlines the interactive role of the gossiper who combines conversational input with keen listening skills so as to maximize the amount of knowledge generated by the gossip.

There is one further important similarity between gossip and Peirce's notion of scientific inquiry. The test for truth in investigative gossip is inherently social. That is, the investigators will use community consensus as a primary indication of their proximity to the truth. The similarity with the Peircean view of science is remarkable. Peirce says, "The very origin of the conception of reality shows that this conception essentially involves the notion of a COMMUNITY" (5:311). Again, "as what anything really is, is what it may finally come to be known to be in the ideal state of complete information, so that reality depends on the ultimate decision of the community" (5:316). Human beings, in their individuality, are mired in "ignorance and error" (5:317); to achieve knowledge, we must enter into cooperation and dialogue with the community, for "reality consists in the agreement that the whole community would eventually come to" (5:331). If we are cut off from that community, we have no hope of acquiring knowledge. According to Peirce, "the social principle is rooted intrinsically in logic" (5:354). "Logicality inexorably requires that our interests shall *not* be limited. They must not stop at our own fate, but must embrace the whole community" (2:654, Peirce's italics.) Peirce offers us this social test for truth as a safeguard from the quirks or idiosyncrasies of particular practicing scientists. The requirement of community agreement allows us to move beyond the ignorance and error of individualism in our pursuit of knowledge.

I do not want to suggest that there are no differences between the Peircean community and the investigative gossip community. One big difference has to do with size. Peirce envisages the scientific community as worldwide, encompassing all serious researchers in the area, past, present, and future. I suggest that the traditional subject matter of the two investigating forums has a great deal to do with dictating size differences here. When the object of inquiry is the shape of a planetary orbit, it is easy to envisage a community whose parameters extend as widely as Peirce suggested. When the object of inquiry is whether Mary is having an affair with Peter, or whether Doris's children are doing drugs, or whether Sally is in trouble with the IRS, or whether Sandra is reliable enough to be short-listed for the position of chairperson, the boundaries of the relevant community of investigators shrink drastically. The subject matter of gossip is generally characterized by a high degree of particularity, and hence the community of investigators is likely to be a relatively small one. This is not to say that discussion is limited to the particular. Universal judgments about truth, morality, fidelity, and other concepts may form an important part of the conversation; nevertheless, much of the focus will be decidedly particular.

Whether or not Sandra would make a good chairperson is not likely to survive, as a subject of inquiry, more than one search committee, let alone more than one generation of investigators. Furthermore, the community of relevant investigators, those qualified to contribute to the investigation of whether Doris's children are into drugs, will be limited to those with fairly direct acquaintance with the family, normally a community whose members are small in number. (Gossip about a famous person, such as a movie star, may provide an exception to this rule, as the media may have disseminated details of the movie star's life so widely that the relevant community exceeds even that attributed to science by Peirce.)

A second difference may be more apparent than real. The agreement among members of a scientific community legitimates particular claims because we assume that individual scientists or groups of scientists have arrived at these same claims independently of one another. The claims of investigative gossip do not enjoy this confidence. They are more likely to be perceived as emanating from a single incestuous group rather than being replicated by separate teams of independent researchers.

I believe that this assumption begs questions about standards. There may indeed be gossipers who leap to conclusions on the basis of inadequate evidence; the good gossiper, however, will not do so. She will check her sources carefully, and one of her criteria for placing confidence in a belief will be the replication of the findings among the pool of qualified investigators. Furthermore, to suggest that scientists or academic researchers reach the same results totally independently of one another is foolishness. One has only to examine mutual citations in the published work of academics to put this theory to rest forever. These two so-called differences notwithstanding, the similarities between the community of investigative gossipers and the community of scientists envisaged by Peirce are compelling. The literature on gossip actually contains very little that directly addresses the standard distribution of knowledge, the relationship between gossip, gender, and speech style, and the subject matter of gossip.[4] Hence, my remarks will be largely speculative, drawing obliquely upon the literature where it is applicable. I shall provide tentative answers to these questions, attempting to be true to both the general consensus of what gossip is and of what it is to know something.

In the past and still to some extent today, even in this society, women have been excluded (either totally or partially, and in various ways) from access to the prestigious forms of knowledge, particularly as these are disseminated through the professions and institutions of higher learning. In the past, of course, women were blatantly denied the right to attend universities; at a later period, they were allowed to attend classes but not to receive degrees. Today even when degrees are within reach, women are not always welcomed by the programs sponsoring the degree. Therefore, women have either remained outside the confines of academia or slipped unnoticed into the academy in some form of gender disguise. We are all familiar with the high-ranking woman in politics or administration who is indistinguishable from her male counterpart in any way except appearance, and who may even mimic the navy blue suit "uniform" of the successful and upwardly mobile executive. It is safe to say that the "chilly climate" still discourages women from moving up many corporate ladders and from undertaking advanced study in particular disciplines, insofar as it undercuts their sense of legitimacy and belonging within the worlds of business and academia.[5]

The forum provided by gossip generates sets of conditions for belonging and thus creates its own group of insiders and outsiders. The gossipers admitted to the group become insiders, with clearly understood entitlement and privilege within the gossip circle; this sense of belonging undoubtedly accounts for much of the testified-to pleasure of gossip. According to one popular view of gossip, those who engage in it endorse and perpetuate social norms (Fine, 1977, p. 182; Rysman, 1977, p. 179) often by formulating negative and perhaps malicious judgments about particular people who eschew these social norms, thus maintaining the very fences that block their entry to sources of power. There is, of course, always the danger that gossip participants will come to question, criticize, and eventually reject the principles and values of the powerful. Viewed in this way, gossip is a clear threat to the social order, and one would expect social sanctions against it.[6] This is one reason for the sense of uneasiness or anxiety that society might harbour towards gossip.[7] Jones maintains that this view of gossip explains the secretive or furtive air with which it is frequently engaged in (1980, p. 195).

I do not believe these two views are incompatible; in fact, I believe they are both true, and although consistent, there is nevertheless considerable tension between them. I believe that women frequently do use gossip, as well as other vehicles, to perpetuate the very norms that disadvantage them. Given the obvious danger posed to those in positions of power by powerless people grouping and talking together, the uneasiness surrounding such talk is readily understandable. Far from being paranoid, such uneasiness is very sensible, for the line between talk that sustains and talk that subverts oppressive norms is an easy one to cross for those who are heavily penalized by such norms. Furthermore, talk that tells the truth about people may be very damaging indeed. Black slaves were not permitted to converse in their own African languages by American slave owners. Women have, in one sense, always spoken the same language as men, so outlawing mother tongues was never a possible vehicle for controlling women's speech. Social sanctions against women's speech, such as Aristotle's admonition for silence as a peculiarly female virtue (1941, Becker Reference 1260b18–19), and against gossiping in particular (Rysman, 1977, pp. 179–80; Jones, 1980, p. 195) are as close as the patriarchy could come to outlawing women's language.

As a form of discourse engaged in by very small groups of people, typically two or three, gossip is consistent with the contexts in which women have historically done their talking—around the kitchen table over a cup of tea in the presence of one to three female neighbors or relatives. An equally important feature shared by gossip and women's speech styles is the tendency for both to be "interpreted small." The literature on gossip sometimes refers to it specifically in these terms as "small talk" (Levin and Kimmel, 1977, pp. 167, 172; Rosnow and Fine, 1976, pp. 4, 81, 84; Rosnow, 1977, p. 158). Even where the actual phrase "small talk" is not used, near synonyms are in abundance. Daniel Dennett describes gossip as "biologically trivial" (1984, p. 48), a quality he attributes to poetry and philosophy as well; the OED introduces "idle" as part of its definition of gossip. This characterization does not mean, however, that gossip cannot provide access to knowledge of large or important issues; the details of people's lives revealed by investigative gossip are often sufficiently important to make the average person very nervous about the content of gossip centering on oneself. Furthermore, knowledge of more public matters may also be made available through gossip. Gossip may be used, for example, to acquire knowledge of the political leanings of new faculty members, the personal circumstances of employees potentially promotable to middle management, the "real" research interests of applicants for a teaching position, the sexual orientation of a political candidate, the perceived competence of professors from students' perspectives, the sympathy (or lack of it) within a community for a strong antiracist political stance, and the alliances and networks among academics. Such knowledge is of crucial importance in launching political campaigns, making decisions within the corporate world, and running the university; anyone denied access to the sorts of gossip that would augment such knowledge is severely handicapped. It is difficult to imagine a selection process for tenure or grant applications that does not utilize knowledge obtained by means of gossip.

It is interesting to speculate on whether gossip, as a style of speech, might have achieved popularity due to the almost constant presence of small children in women's lives. Women might indeed have felt reluctant to openly discuss important personal/moral matters concerning other people in the presence of small ears; it would make sense, in this context, to allude to the topic of the conversation, rather than to name the party, to speak obliquely rather than directly, to say nothing that could not be reinterpreted in a favorable or at least a different light if brought back to one's doorstep by little tongues. Anyone who has tried to hold a serious personal conversation in the presence of young children will see in this mode of talking the potential for a survival strategy and recognize in it perhaps the only possible alternative to silence. It is important to also point out, however, that although gossip may be oblique, it need not be so; in fact, the context of gossip (a small group of known and trusted participants, together with the absence of the subject) often promises the safety in which people feel free to speak directly.

The literature on gender differences in language is filled with allusions to the speech patterns of women as weak, uncertain, tentative, and trivial (Lakoff, 1975, pp. 15–17; Key, 1975, p. 76; Newcombe and Arnkoff, 1979; Gleason and Greif, 1983, p. 148; Pearson, 1985, p. 188). Shakespeare captures this perception of women's speech beautifully when he describes Ann Page in *The Merry Wives of Windsor*, as one who "speaks small like a woman" (1.2.48). Gossiping people were not always characteristically identified as women (the "gossip" was at one time a truly generic term [Rysman, 1977; OED], but the gossip who "talked small" was definitely a woman, and the bulk of her verbal behavior dismissable as "small talk." This categorizing is ironical, flying in the face, as it does, of a widespread fear of gossip and a widespread recognition of the damage that gossip can wreak. Sir Oliver, in *School for Scandal*, captures this notion when he speaks of "gossips . . . who murder characters to kill time" (Sheridan, 1966, 38; 2.3.19–20). This general unease about gossip is inconsistent with its being, in fact, small talk. Those who fear gossip understand all too well that far from being small, it is the kind of talk capable of wrecking reputations, undermining relationships, radically shifting the balance of power, and even in some cases bringing down venerable institutions.

When we use gossip to acquire information (or knowledge), what if any are the peculiar features of such knowledge? We do not engage in gossip to acquire knowledge of the laws of nature, chemical interactions, or the nature of igneous rock. Gossip is stereotypically identified with the acquisition of knowledge of personal things or intimate details often (but not always) specifically about relationships. Gossip is in fact used to acquire knowledge of many of the realms in between these two extremes; for example, whether Jones's teaching is really good enough to put her forward for promotion, whether Mary, if promoted to a middle management position, will be sympathetic to the employees' desire to unionize, or whether Lee, if elected chair of the department, will fight to get tenure for the two new faculty members. I think the characteristic relegation of gossip to the extremely personal private realm has been more a matter of historical accident than logical necessity. That is, there is no reason why gossip could not be used to procure knowledge of igneous rocks, for example, but for such topics the more traditional academic approaches of reading journal articles or listening to lectures will lead us to what we want to know more surely and more quickly. There would seem to be little point in employing gossip in such a context.

Conversely, for acquiring knowledge of personal intimate details of people's lives, gossip may well be the only form of inquiry that could possibly work. Information of such a highly personal nature is not likely to be accessible to the modes of inquiry more standardly perceived as legitimate. Thus, in cases where the information or knowledge is extremely sensitive (and frequently importance is concomitant with sensitivity here), gossip will be the only form of inquiry available. Several factors account for the unique eligibility of gossip in such cases. Such information is likely to be missing from the standard literature or the public storehouse of received knowledge. One of the reasons for this is that, traditionally, the subject matter of gossip has been dubbed too trivial and too subjective to merit rigorous investigation by the academic disciplines. But the subject matter of gossip is frequently far from trivial; how else can we explain society's intense nervousness surrounding gossip? I believe that the subject matter of gossip is not accessible through the academically respectable modes of inquiry in part because it is too important and potentially too dangerous to the disseminator. Gossip allows the indirectness and innuendo that make it safe to talk about certain things.

Hiring committees at universities (especially for high-ranking jobs) frequently totally disregard formal letters of support for applicants, assuming that such documents, becoming as they do part of the file, are always liable to the possibility of falling into the hands of the candidate. Consequently, the committees often believe that such a format is not conducive to receiving either substantive or even reliable information about the candidate. In such cases, a committee member is likely to telephone the referee and informally report the conversation to the rest of the committee. Such conversations, though they will form an important part of the decision procedure, do not become part of the official record. They remain, like gossip, "off the record," offering the referees a margin of safety conducive to speaking their minds freely and honestly. Most committees will attach more credibility to such an informal chat than to a formal letter. This is not to say that the telephone conversation consisted essentially of gossip, although it may well have. My claim is that it is an informal and unofficial conversation, both features shared with gossip and features that, in this case, render the contents of the conversation more rather than less reliable in the minds of the committee members.

Vulnerable people, for example political candidates who have not yet won their big election or those without job security in the university system, may also shrink from speaking the truth as they know it within an official format; tenure protects the academic freedom only of those who have it. Perhaps we should be as worried about not getting the whole truth or even the significant truth from those who speak for the record as we are about not necessarily getting the literal truth from those who speak off the record.

Those vulnerable in another sense, those in power, but not secure in terms of either their right to be there or their confidence in remaining, will naturally be wary of the kind of talk that could undermine their position. They will see in the gossip of those around them sinister allusions to themselves even when this is not the case. This attitude is captured by the character Teddy in Joan Barfoot's *Family News* (1989). When he thinks about his ex-lover, Susannah, talking to her long-time friend, Frannie, he is "uneasy; he is unnerved by how many hours the two of them must have spent, over how many years, using how many words, discussing him. . . . He feels them dissecting his affairs, his talents—himself, really" (p. 111). Further reflection makes it clear to Teddy that they can't have spent the better part of twenty years discussing him exclusively. When he attempts to visualize other possible focuses of their conversation, the list he comes up with reflects an amazing combination of male derision of perceived female concerns and an uneasy recognition of several major feminist grievances. They might have talked about "other men, he supposes, small ups and downs in their careers. Makeup, clothes, families, their little causes, child care, choice, and equal pay—whatever women like that talk about" (p. 111).

If gossip were used by women to talk only about makeup and clothes, it would be of no concern to men; it is because we know very well that gossip spills over into the topics of choice and equality that the patriarchy has good reason to worry about women's gossip.

Like that ill-fabled tree in the Garden of Eden, gossip promises us knowledge of good and evil. Like that same tree, it threatens us with expulsion if we are caught. The more vital the information exchanged through gossip, the more potentially damaging such gossip is both to those who are the topic of the conversation and to those who do the conversing. If Peter's wife learns that her best friends have conversed among themselves about Peter's affair with Mary, she will probably be less than pleased with those friends, who thus risk Mary's anger if she catches them in this gossip. The upwardly mobile employee who divulges spicy tidbits about the vice-president's life to the corporation president in the hope of ingratiating herself with that president risks losing her job if the president decides to leak this information, together with its source, to others. Hence, the astute gossiper will ensure that the other members of the gossip circle are trustworthy in this regard. The danger of being caught enhances the excitement of the endeavor, for all gossipers have something at stake; it also strengthens the sense of bonding among the members of the gossip circle, for gossipers render themselves vulnerable to the other members of the group. Gossip is therefore mutually empowering to its participants. Not only do the gossipers achieve access to knowledge of the person discussed, but simply by being privy to who engaged in the discussion, they are put in a position of power with respect to one another should they choose to betray the unwritten rules of confidentiality within the gossip circle. The notions of power, community, and belonging itself are redefined by gossip in ways which may pose a serious threat to the status quo.

Those who remain shut off from the bastions of commonly recognized social and political power will continue to look to gossip as one form of inquiry, knowing, and power available to them as other forms are not. Meanwhile, those in privileged decision-making positions will continue to rely on gossip for the acquisition of certain sorts of information or knowledge simply not amenable to other forms of inquiry. We would be well advised, therefore, to underestimate neither the enormous appeal, nor the importance, nor the veracity of gossip. If, like Peirce, we want to keep the road to inquiry open, we are obliged not just to condone gossip but to encourage it; for gossip is virtually ubiquitous, providing avenues of access to inquiry in terrains too steep, too marshy, too eroded, and far too dangerous for science to operate.

9 | Gossip, or in Praise of Chaos

Lorraine Code

IN A RECENT PAPER, John Shotter argues that "humanly *adequate* social orders . . . can only be created, sustained, and transformed . . . by . . . drawing upon the resources made available . . . in the zones of relatively disorderly activities surrounding them—activities such as play and gossip . . . and a myriad other . . . activities, all usually dismissed as a waste of time" (1989, p. 150). His observation suggests why an analysis of gossip is peculiarly pertinent to feminist inquiry. At the same time, it recalls an example that demonstrates the effectiveness of gossip as an emancipatory tool challenging moral and epistemological assumptions.

The example I refer to is the film "A Jury of Her Peers," based on the 1917 story "Trifles" by Susan Glaspell. The story, very briefly, goes as follows: a farmer is found dead in his bed one bleak morning in the midwestern United States. No evidence can be found either of an intruder or of a struggle so his wife is detained for questioning. Two men—one the sheriff—return to the empty house to search for clues, a motive, a weapon. Their wives go along to collect some things that the woman in prison has asked for and to keep each other company. While the men search the second story and the outbuildings, the women (who do not know each other well and are plainly wary of one another) move about the kitchen preoccupied with women's things: putting the place in order, collecting what they have come for, chatting about how it must have been to live there with him. Gossiping. Out of "trifles" that a formal investigation would have passed over without notice, they read a story of systematic brutality and coldness that leaves them in little doubt about the events that culminated in murder.

Three features of this example connect with the aspects of gossip that I want to explore here. One, the details that the women piece together, in a frankly interested, engaged process, yield knowledge more plausible than the formal, objective search is likely to produce. Two, out of their idle, seemingly cursory involvement with the domestic details that they read both affectively and "empirically," realistically, the women achieve a solidarity, a community, that is at once strong, vulnerable, and committed to a course of action that contests the adequacy of the social order. Three, the randomness of their activity, its disorderliness (cf. Shotter), contrasts markedly with the men's orderly search that follows "normal" procedures of inquiry into "cases of this sort." Yet that randomness, that lack of methodological constraint, proves peculiarly effective in establishing what happened in the farmhouse.

There is no doubt that it is knowledge that the women construct out of their activities—knowledge that neither one of them could have produced alone. The process of reciprocal prompting, imagining, picking out and integrating details (conversational moves that check for truth: "Did she really?" "Are you sure?"[1]—the dispersed, informal interplay—is essential, sine qua non, to their conclusions. All the while they are otherwise engaged; the gossip accompanies, grows out of, and embellishes (cognitively) their practical preoccupations. It locates them—and the dead man's wife—vis-à-vis the death and the social order. They want to know about her, empathetically; theirs is no disinterested inquiry. The conclusion therefore suggests itself that if knowing other people were acknowledged as knowledge without which it would be virtually impossible to negotiate the world successfully, it would not be so difficult to demonstrate the epistemic worth of gossip. Neither—and this is a separate, larger point—would social scientific practice (at least of the postpositivist, empiricist mainstream) be so inadequate to the people who are its subject matter if gossip were acknowledged as an epistemic, knowledge-producing practice.[2] The processes of mutual, speculative, engaged critique and correction inherent in gossip suggest a more plausible experiential picture of the production of knowledge than mainstream epistemologies can offer. Moreover, these processes yield "results" that bear more directly on the location of knowledge in human lives than does the standard picture of disinterested observation. Because it is always specifically located, attuned to nuance and minutiae ("Did you pick up the hesitation in her voice?"), gossip is a finely tuned instrument for establishing truths about people. This is my first point.

The initially fragile, tentative move toward community and solidarity between the two women opens a space where the sheriff's wife is, unintentionally, caught in an urgent conflict of loyalties. (The power of gossip to change moral and political views, to instruct in empathy, is apparent here.) This woman has to choose whether, in the interests of formal morality and justice, she will present her husband with incriminating details, or whether she can act from her newfound empathetic solidarity with the two women: her companion and the accused. Her decision to withhold the evidence attests to a struggle and conversion that shifts the terms of moral debate onto different ground. The debate moves into an area that has become central to feminist moral and legal discourse. There, contextual reconstructions and judgments are displacing the formal, "objective," principled judgments from on high that attest to persistent liberal assumptions that people are all, really, alike and interchangeable. In an implicit assertion of the inadequacy of that social order, contexts, differences, and specificities are constructed in gossip out of the "trivia" and disorder for which philosophy has little time in its self-presentation as an orderly, controlled project.

These newfound moral and political positions are no longer the monologic stances of the self-sufficient principled agent, for whom neutrality, impartiality, and freedom from context are the guiding ideals. They are moves into specifically located, dialogic stances that subvert and disrupt the order of "received" discourse with the chaos, the unruliness of lives where things do not fit so neatly. These disruptions of the moral-social order are effected in disorder. Unity and community of inquiry and purposes are accomplished unexpectedly, both morally and epistemically: indeed, morally because epistemically—a community sustained around a truth that requires the women to act, to declare their loyalties. This is my second point.

There is an epistemological subtext at work in assessments of the moral-political effectiveness of gossip. Here, as I note above, knowing other people is knowledge that matters and that demands epistemological analysis. Indeed, I would suggest that moral and political theories always have an—often unaddressed—epistemological subtext, in the sense that their adequacy is crucially dependent upon the knowledge of people and circumstances that they often collaborate in constructing. Thus, for example, in "A Jury of Her Peers" an explicitly noninstrumental, disorderly event becomes a site for the production of knowledge that contests liberal-empirical theories that portray knowledge acquisition as an elaborate yet neutral process of fact finding. The knowledge produced here is knowledge of intimate details, of particularities; it comes to inform a nuanced, complex set of moral judgments. I now want to consider the issue of instrumentality as it bears on the construction of such knowledge.

In Chapter 8, Maryann Ayim analyzes certain instances of gossip that are instrumental rather than random. They intend explicitly to elicit the range of information that theories of knowledge commonly seek to explicate. She likens these kinds of gossip to the practices of communal inquiry that she discerns in a (Peircean) scientific community, and she illustrates the effectiveness of gossip as a method of inquiry with the example of Miss Marple's investigative practices. I suggest that Ayim risks overemphasizing the instrumentality of gossip and, in so doing, translates its randomness into an orderly exercise that would control its inchoate ubiquity, collect its dispersals, and finally disarm its political efficacy.

It is not, I think, necessary to legitimate gossip by appealing to a mode (albeit a divergent mode) of scientific inquiry. Although I agree with Ayim that gossip is worthy of heightened esteem, this is not primarily because, after all, it is a process of inquiry not so different from the concealed underside (contrasted with the public surface) of scientific inquiry. Attempting to ensure the respectability of gossip with a scientific model—even a model with its own subversive possibilities—prevents feminist inquiry from departing as radically from mainstream epistemology as an analysis of gossip could, potentially, allow.

Nor is it clear that a Peircean scientific community is as communal as a community of "co-gossips," or that it lends itself to a fundamentally interactive, mutually engaged and interested characterization. Conversation and consultation are not simple equivalents of gossip, however loosely all three are understood. Gossip is both more, and less, and other, than either of these, even though the boundaries that differentiate them are fluid. A Peircean scientific community is large, professionally structured, and consistent. It aspires to be methodical, logical; to provide assurances against deception and error. This is its role as arbiter. Yet as I understand it, nothing in Peirce's description precludes the community's being one to which each member brings his own results, singly and self-sufficiently, with little interest in or engagement with his fellow inquirers. His results are often gained in an imaginative (retroductive) leap to a conclusion, rather than inductively and deductively corroborated. But because individual imagination is at once so central to the process, and so individual, this is a community that need not be more than the sum of its parts. It need neither interrelate nor be held together in solidarity or suspicion.

Appealing to Miss Marple's investigative method as paradigmatic of gossip reinforces the impression that gossip, like science, is a form of inquiry directed toward instrumental ends. But I want to argue that the similarity is generated out of the appeal to this particular example: this is not gossip in its everyday ubiquity. Gossip-as-inquiry, as I see it, is an atypical, controlled, no longer random activity. Miss Marple has to simulate gossip, exploit its power, work her way onto the grapevine. Hers is no longer gossip in its ordinary randomness, even though, admittedly, gossiplike techniques can sometimes be adapted to these instrumental purposes. I would therefore resist representing the practices of a community of scientific inquirers as a paradigm under whose aegis it would be possible to move gossip into the realm of respectable argumentation. My resistance is prompted by the fact that abandoning the model—any model—of "received" scientific inquiry has been one of the most radical feminist contributions to reconstructing epistemology, and with it, moral analysis. Although it would be foolish to deny that gossip can be turned to instrumental ends, it is important to note that characterizing it as inquiry, as instrumental, amounts to reclaiming it for respectable discourse cast in a traditionally disinterested mold. Such a reclamation obscures its power as a located, committed, and therefore peculiarly perceptive activity.

On the other hand, it would equally constrain the scope of gossip and minimize its political effectiveness to deny it any instrumental— and therefore public—role. Characterizing gossip as a practice that is confined to a "private" domain constituted by close friends requires postulating an enclosed group, for whom gossip often functions to affirm commonality. The "Jury of Her Peers" leaves no doubt that this affirmation is one of gossip's principal achievements. But analyses that overemphasize its "private" dimension fail to capitalize on the political power of this practice—this art—whose efficacy extends far beyond "the private." Consider the power of gossip in the workplace and in politics of the macrocosmic variety. Egalitarian analyses that represent it as essentially private and cooperative gloss over the places where gossip manipulates and creates power structures within groups, fragmenting community as readily as it cements it. I am, therefore, maintaining that neither the benign nor the malign manifestations of gossip are paradigmatic: both characterize it equally and offer sites for specific analysis in particular circumstances. In short, it is crucial for feminist readings neither to make too much of the instrumentality of gossip, nor to make too little of its instrumental potential. To put the point differently: knowledge by any other name informs as well, yet naming it locates it—whether at the center, or on the margins. For feminist inquiry there is something at stake in "naming" gossip-knowledge connections well, so as neither to contain them within received epistemological paradigms, nor to domesticate them within an invisible and powerless space "down among the women."

My argument is an appeal, then, to the unruliness of gossip, its (self-referential) resistance to paradigmatic summing up, which is at once the locus of its power and its danger. Like the laugh of the medusa, it bursts out unexpectedly. Its eruptions depend for their success on exact, interested specificity—on an attunement with the historical moment and the circumstances that comprise it. This is no ahistorical practice. Gossip about Gary Hart ends his political career; "the same" gossip about JFK touches his not at all. Gossip is located, situated discourse, yet never stable nor fixed. For this reason, above all, it has a peculiar appeal to feminists, working both in epistemology and in moral theory, who are striving to produce humanly adequate social orders.

10 | Gossip: A Feminist Defense
Louise Collins

THIS CHAPTER presents a picture of the practice of gossip and its significance in relation to a certain philosophical anthropology and a correlative view of moral philosophy. Much of what follows is suggestive rather than tightly argued; much verges on armchair sociology like gossip itself. My challenge to those left unconvinced is to generate a better account, not just of the pleasures of gossip but also of its endless interest.

Distinguishing gossip from other forms of discourse with which it may be interwoven in practice yields a set of characteristic conceptual and pragmatic features that reveal nothing intrinsically morally disreputable about gossip, although like most social practices it may in fact degenerate into vice. Critics of gossip rely on a paradigm of reputable discourse that rests in turn on a masculinist philosophical anthropology. In my terminology, a masculinist position is one that posits one set of features as typically or peculiarly masculine and thus as more valuable than those features correlatively identified as "typically feminine." Gossip's characteristic features make it a suitable context for moral development where selves are seen in terms of a non-masculinist model.

Various kinds of talk are referred to as "gossip." This chapter takes as central the social practice of chatting with friendly acquaintances about third parties known to us and about aspects of their private lives. In practice, gossip in this narrow sense is interwoven with other kinds of talk: advice-giving, teasing, talking about the weather, speculating about the love lives of movie stars and soap-opera characters. I might also call a conversation woven out of these strands "a really good gossip," as we call chatting with intimates about ourselves, or defaming someone we have never met, "gossip." What, then, are the characteristic features of gossip in the narrow sense whereby it differs from other discourses?

Gossip requires more than one active participant. In this it differs from soliloquoy, monologue, or lecturing. To count as an active gossip one must have an independent contribution to make to the talk. Hence there must be some overlap in the circle of co-gossips' acquaintances. For although one may be able to sustain some interest in gossip about nonacquaintances by appeal to parallel cases in one's own experience, after a while such impersonal gossip gets boring.

Gossip is not an instrumental discourse, that is, one structured to achieve a prespecified aim extrinsic to the talk. In this it differs from legal cross-examination or flattery, for example. These discourses can succeed or fail partly as a result of the participants' skill in facilitating an aim. We speak of someone as "a skilled lawyer," when her talk is efficacious in promoting the defense of her client. Nor has gossip a constitutive end internal to the talk that would support a distinction between gossiping well or badly. Moreover, though we sometimes gossip for a further reason (to pass the time, to catch up on the news, whatever), we often "just gossip" as we "just doodle." This "aimlessness" allows the inadvertent emergence or deliberate achievement of more specific particular ends—setting up a joke, telling a tale, identifying a problem to be solved—all in the framework of "just gossiping" together.[1]

Gossip is an informal discourse in contrast to a business meeting, for example. It has tacit norms, an etiquette, but it has no explicit formal rules governing who speaks when, the order of business, and so on. In particular, no participant is recognized as having special authority by virtue of a formal role. In this sense, gossip is an egalitarian form of discourse. There are no theoretically based rules of entitlement to speak: there is no prespecified level of back-up evidence required, in contrast to scientific discourse; no fixed criteria of relevance, in contrast to legal discourse; no rules of proper sequence, unlike the construction of a deductive argument in philosophy. Indeed, the style of gossip is characteristically anecdotal, containing reported speech or embedded narratives, and oblique, relying on conversational implicature rather than assertion, on suggestion rather than logically rigorous argumentation. It cheerfully elides evaluative and descriptive language, in contrast to the utterances of positivist social scientists.

Gossip deals in the private, personal aspects of individual lives. It may appeal to generalizations, for example, about "what men like him usually do," but these rest on a range of explanatory factors and styles—what I had for lunch, my upbringing, my having struck the match, my aim of burning the place down. Gossip also pays attention to the individual as eluding generalization, to the details of a person's life and speech: "Of course she wore white, but how long was the dress?" "He's not what you'd think from the look of him," "Anyone would be angry in those circumstances, but what exactly did she say?" Thus, gossip is informal, dispersed talk about other people and their lifestyles, directed to no specific end.

But what of its pragmatic features? We do not gossip with just anyone. The presumptuous or promiscuous gossip soon finds herself isolated, partly because gossip is the sharing of information, both what you know and that you know, and hence of power. Thus gossip makes us a mutually vulnerable group.[2] One key feature in determining with whom we gossip is agreement in values. First, we must share the meta-value that engagement in gossip is worthwhile. Second, we must agree with most of the evaluative judgments of the group with respect to the range of subjects discussed. This is crucial. It is manifest in the language of gossip and it gives gestures their significance, gives jokes their point, and impregnates silences. Tied to these shared evaluations is a shared outlook in a broader sense—witness the expressions "of course," "needless to say," "you'll never believe," which presuppose consensus on what is obvious, inevitable, or incredible, what normally happens, what people usually do. Offering more than just a shared judgment about what is the case, these expressions often invite us to ratify the unspoken evaluation of what is then reported, "Needless to say, he ate the last pickle." In this role of shared evaluation, gossip differs from any discourse that purports to appeal to the objective bystander.

Given the above characterization of gossip, why might one depre-cate it as constitutively pernicious? Four complaints commonly lodged against gossip identify different characteristics as the root of its bad-ness: that it is malicious, that it is pointless, that its subject matter is trivial, that it addresses important subject matter in an inappropriate way. These complaints are rooted in a masculinist paradigm of "good" discourse.

Some would say my characterization of gossip has omitted its central feature: that all gossip is malicious. If this is intended as a stipulative truth, I will give the critic the term "gossip" and retain "quossip" as labeling a kind of discourse that is just like gossip, but not all of it is malicious. Actually, I will keep the term "gossip" for myself. If the critic's claim is intended to be empirical I challenge him to explain how the practice endures. In my view, only some gossip is malicious, and malicious gossip is parasitic on ordinary gossip, as lying is parasitic on sincere discourse.[3]

If all gossip aims at denigrating its subject, whom will it persuade? My malicious intent will usually only succeed where those whom I seek to persuade do not see my aim. If all those who gossip admit to the aim of denigration, their co-gossips have no reason to interpret their claim about S, the subject, as telling them anything about S, except that the malicious gossip does not like her. Conversely, if gossips do not recognize their aim as being to denigrate, it will be hard to hold them fully morally culpable, as the critics of gossip do. Part of the motive for holding that all gossip is malicious is a skepticism about our interest in other people—we are only really interested in others to the extent that they fit in with some project of ours—here, to damn them. My view is that we are gossips simply because we are interested in other people; and if we do not equate the empirical self with the egocentric self, then we do not need to posit a noumenal self to explain the possibility of unselfish practical and theoretical activity.

Is gossip wrong because it is not an end-directed discourse or because it is not backed by a controlling theory? The worry here is that gossip must collapse into nonsense or pointlessness, lacking criteria of relevance, sufficient justification, and so on. To such critics I prescribe a course in poetry appreciation, followed by a theater improvisation workshop. Like child's play, spending time with friends, and so on, the fact that an activity has no predetermined end does not mean it is pointless; indeed, its very openness may allow the formulation and achievement of other ends. The critics' paradigm of reputable discourse is the logically valid argument, with premises whose soundness is guaranteed by a well-confirmed theory—a masculinist and incomplete model.

Is gossip trivial because its subject matter, the personal, particular, and domestic, is trivial? Traditionally, these aspects of life have been regarded as both "feminine" and unimportant to what we are, qua moral beings. This assumption is now widely attacked in moral philosophy, especially in feminist works. One typical strategy is to claim that such views involve an excessively thin account of moral personhood. We are not Cartesian egos, Kantian noumena, detached existentialist wills. One problem such models encounter is persuading us that what such "thin selves" would do bears any relation to what we situated, psychologically complex and quirky folk should do. Further, if we do not give the living of our everyday "trivial" lives a constitutive role in the Good Life, we will end up with a moral philosophy that is unacceptably elitist (Plato, Aristotle), dull (Kant's uniformly dutiful selves Respecting, but not liking, each other), or episodic (Sartrian ungrounded choices), or one that fails to take needs seriously. Against this background, then, I deny that our everyday lives are trivial, and I assert therefore its subject matter does not ipso facto make gossip trivial.

Ironically, some critics deprecate gossip precisely because its subject matter is so important. Gossip is too trivial a medium to discuss the private. Here, deprecators divide into two groups according to the sense they give "private"—political or metaphysical. The first group appeals to the philosophical anthropology of liberalism; we each need and have a right to preserve a private part of our lives, free from intrusion.[4] It is essential to the good society that each of us have a "private life" in which we are free to be eccentric and wrongheaded, in contrast to our "public" life, and uninvited incursions into our private life may be resented. This is just what is wrong with gossip—it intrudes upon our "right to privacy."

It may be a brute fact that humans need privacy. It still would not follow from that fact that such a need must be met by institutionalizing a fixed "private sphere," nor that we have any correlative right to privacy, where my right entails a prima facie obligation on everyone else to respect my right.[5] The individual has no blanket right to control which aspects of her life may be scrutinized and assessed by other private individuals nor to control transmission of information about her "private life." There are norms of "tact" or "discretion," but these may be transgressed by anyone, not just gossips. Moreover, this may not be regrettable; for when the individual herself determines by which aspects of her life she is to be judged, hypocrisy and self-deception flourish. Precisely because gossip may refuse to take the individual on her own terms, to respect her definition of the split between public and private, it is particularly good at uncovering these vices. To be sure, there is a concomitant risk of gossip failing to respect her need for privacy. To assume against this background that gossip is a disreputable discourse is to contrast it with discourses that do respect the split between public and private. Thus, for instance, we are to deal with our colleagues and co-workers on a professional level only, thereby treating them as abstract entities rather than as human beings in all their fullness. This is quite characteristic of the ideology of male-dominated worlds of work; not only is this in bad faith, it also makes for bad management.

What of the worry that gossip is an inappropriate vehicle to carry the importance of one's metaphysically private life? Here, we are not talking of the Englishman's home as his castle, but the inner deliverances of the continental conscience. The worry here is that deep inner truths cannot be articulated in any language, or any public language, or at least not the leveling language of gossip or "chatter."

For obvious reasons I will not say anything about putatively ineffable aspects of individual moral experience. Why might one claim that one's understanding of moral concepts has a private aspect, which cannot, in principle, be shared with others, even through the medium of public language? One might argue that the individual's life history— the sequence of her experiences—contributes nuances to her understanding of moral concepts and hence her present moral experience.

This is plausible—my encounter with a gallant, house-bound old lady when I was sixteen changed my conception of courage. To argue from this to the claim that no one else could share this enriched conception is to assume that no one else could share my enriching experience. If this is claimed "as a matter of logic," it begs the question. If this is claimed as a matter of fact, then "only I can have my experiences" denies that there is another brain now causally connected to the sensory organs of this body. Thus the claim that "only I can have had my experiences (my life history)," rules out any branching in the causal chain stretching from the past enriching experiences to the brain of the present speaker. However, once we talk of experiences in terms of causal relations that hold between events, it is possible that someone else, then, may well have had a relevantly similar enriching experience and have come to share my present understanding of "courage."[6] The causal generalization under which my past experience falls would specify what "relevantly similar" means. Unless we assume that the experience, though shared, is ineffable, I could indeed talk about this "private" aspect of my conception, where someone else had shared the relevantly similar experience.

This interpretation does not make the standard masculinist assumption that, at the level of description relevant to moral agency "we are really all the same" and hence that moral concepts belong in universal discourse. It allows that differences among people may matter to their moral understanding. However, it concludes from this that the proper locus of moral development is in introspection, in radical isolation from public discourse. In the "feminine" model of self-understanding I will posit, this "private" discourse is replaced by semipublic discourse; discourse between people with relevantly similar, but not universally shared, experience. Gossip is an instance of such discourse.

The further claim against gossip, that it is a "leveling" discourse—it trivializes the differences between individuals by describing them all in the same terms—then also misfires. Not all gossip circles appeal to the same conceptions of moral concepts, for there is no universal language of gossip. Further, gossips are pluralists in explanation.

Now I want to argue that those very features of gossip that were deprecated above can be reevaluated positively. In order to do so, we require a different concept of moral agency. According to this alternative conception, the process of moral development is not a purely isolated, internal affair but occurs in relation to and interaction with others. The distinctive qualities and points of view play a role in these processes, and gossip can then appear as a suitable context for

1. learning about other people in general, formulating those loose generalizations about human motivation which inform "feminine intuition";
2. learning about other people in particular, which grounds our understanding of their difference and taken with (1) helps us develop empathy;
3. changing our moral views; and,
4. changing our self-understanding, with (1) and (2) above, or by reducing self-deception.

Gossip helps us to understand other people in general; by paying attention to details of their lives, we assess evidence for inductive generalizations. I am assuming that gossip is not all a tissue of lies or distortions, for as I argued above, it is not all distorted by malice, for such an intention would defeat itself. Expressions like "Don't exaggerate," and "That doesn't sound like her, are you sure?" also witness to gossip's concern for truth. The generalizations appealed to or generated in gossip do not form a unified theory, nor do they appeal to only one kind of explanatory factor or mode, for example, "It's her mother's influence," "It must have been something he ate," "She just likes that sort of thing." People in the grip of a monocausal theory are dull to gossip with—it is dreary to hear one man's thoughtful deed subsumed under "All men are pigs."

What we get from gossip will count as "understanding people" only if we do not presuppose that all people are "really" the same and that the way to reach understanding is to strip them of all their special empirical attributes until we reach a level which relates only to their sameness. Gossip gives us generalizations, not universal laws, and gossip teaches us about other people in particular, which together with general understanding helps us develop empathy, a morally crucial ability. Once we deny that at the morally relevant level of description, everyone is the same—contra Kant, for example—taking other people into consideration in moral decision making is going to require the attempt to imagine things from at least one point of view different from our own. Since we think that taking other people into consideration is partly constitutive of being moral, so too is empathy. How does gossip help develop empathy? Simply assessing information about the ways in which people are not like us does not yet teach us that their different outlooks may be legitimate. Information about the detail of their lives may fill out the backdrop to my project of imagining myself in their circumstances; it does not yet convert into the project of imagining myself to be someone else, with different desires, beliefs, or values, in those circumstances. How then does gossip help turn the trick?

The crucial feature of gossip here is that we share our general evaluations with our co-gossips. When we are discussing a particular case, we may find ourselves disagreeing with the judgment of our co-gossips. We find it harder to dismiss this disagreement precisely because of our shared background; we cannot assume they are simply mistaken. So we discuss our disagreement. Each of us invites the other to attend to various features of the case in virtue of which it can be seen as bearing a resemblance to some other case where we agreed in our judgments. But we relate it to different cases—hence the present disagreement. What this process may yield, if not consensus, is an example to me of what it is like to see the world from a different viewpoint, that of my co-gossip. Given the way she relates this case to others, I might see if I held slightly different beliefs and desires, the world could legitimately look slightly different. Thus gossip is a foothold for developing empathy because it discusses particular cases in detail. Gossip also enhances our capacity to project ourselves into increasingly alien circumstances and perspectives; and by evoking uncontrolled and serendipitous details, it enables the imagination to construct unexpected views of its subject.

How does gossip help us change or revise our moral views? I have just given part of the story: through gossip we may come to see that we might legitimately evaluate some cases differently from our initial inclination, that is, to interpret cases as our co-gossips do. Moreover, the ability to empathize allows us to check our moral intuitions. The golden rule, "Do unto others only what you'd have them do unto you," is only of any use in conjunction with empathy. For it is quite logically consistent for the racist to say that, were she black, she would not resent being done unto as the racist does. It is only when the racist is compelled to imagine her victim's own beliefs and values from within, rather than projecting her racist beliefs and values onto the victim, that the principle has any force. Of course, once this is done, the principle is otiose, which shows the priority of imagination over logic in moral thinking.

My account of the change in values allowed by gossip is a gradualist one, and the process is neither wholly rational (if this means motivated by a logically rigorous argument) nor ungrounded (some kind of reasoning goes on). Since we are creatures bound by context, we already have a set of moral beliefs that we share to some extent with others around us. The task of moral philosophy is not to generate principles a priori but to help us "fine-tune" those we have.

How does gossip help change our self-understanding? I suggested above that the Cartesian account of what it is to understand oneself will not do. Self-discovery is not introspecting a private, yet universally instantiated self. Given the relation between thought, language, and other speakers, to be a thinker is to be a language-user and thus a social being. In my account, self-discovery involves talking and interacting with others whose experiences and values overlap ours by greater or lesser degrees. Gossip is one kind of such talk.

People are notorious self-deceivers: that gossip does not usually take the co-gossips themselves as its subject is instructive here. For we often are more adept at seeing flaws in others than in ourselves. Having criticized our subject, we may then realize that we resemble her and warrant criticism ourselves; such a realization would perhaps be too painful to admit in direct discussion of ourselves. Further, if we manage through gossip to project ourselves onto another's perspective, we may be able to see aspects of ourself that we had denied from that external point.

Having seen some of the virtues of gossip against the background of a "feminine" philosophical anthropology, we reclaim the term "gossip" and give it a positive evaluation. The association of gossip with the feminine and a negative evaluation have a long history. Etymologically, the use of "gossip" as a derogatory term for trivial talk emerges at around the same time as its reference to specifically female friends. I have not argued that all and only women gossip. But from the work of Gilligan on female gendered moral and psychological development, it looks as though the characteristic self-understanding that emerges in gossip—the self as known in relation to other particular individuals and to an evaluative community—and the characteristic kind of moral reasoning which is involved in gossip—emphasizing concrete details and differences—converge with what is typically female. I suggest that we return to an early point in the word's etymological development when "gossip" referred to those people whom you would want to have attending you during your labor. These would have been women, but not necessarily close friends. Let "gossip" refer to talk about the particular, "personal," and concrete by well-disposed acquaintances, whereby we act as midwives to each other's moral development. Let it carry its association with the feminine and a positive evaluation.

Part 3 | Empirical Studies of Gossip

11 | Gossip, Reputation, and Social Adaptation
Nicholas Emler

"No man speaks concerning another, even supposes it be in his praise, if he thinks he does not hear him exactly as he would if he thought he was within hearing."
Samuel Johnson
"At ev'ry word a reputation dies."
Alexander Pope

GOSSIP HAS ENJOYED a miserable reputation. Hardly anyone has a good word to say about it. Almost every recorded comment on gossip, almost every fragment of folk wisdom, is negative. Thus it would seem that the scholar who wishes to claim something of value for this activity must overturn the considerable accumulated weight of common sense. Such is the aim of this collection of essays. I am pleased to contribute to this effort, for I believe there is much of value to be identified. My own thesis is that the activity we sometimes describe as gossip—and I must return to the qualifier "sometimes" here—is fundamental to the functioning of all human collectives. The functions I shall emphasize concern the successful adaptation of humans to the requirements of group living and the control mechanisms that operate to conserve effectively functioning human groups. Central to these functions are what may be called reputational processes. But first let us look at the reputation (cf. Spacks, 1985) of gossip and at some of the means by which scholars have sought to rescue and rehabilitate this activity.

The Public Reputation of Gossip

The common opinion of gossip is inclined to place it rather low on any scale of laudable, profound, or significant human behaviors. It has a reputation for triviality, for preoccupation with the thoroughly superficial and ephemeral in human affairs. It is regarded as the province of idle minds; only people who have nothing better to do stand around gossiping. It is unreliable and inaccurate, an entirely fallible source of information about other people. Its motivations are disreputable; tellers are motivated by mischief, rancor, or spite, listeners by a prurient and improper interest in matters that are none of their business. Gossips are often guilty of despicable violations of trust. The effects of gossip are frequently damaging—and sometimes catastrophically destructive—to the lives and livelihoods of those who are gossiped about. Finally, gossip is a quintessential female activity. Women chatter, tattle, gab, rabbit, prattle, nag, whine, and bitch. Men devote themselves to more consequential tasks; they build ships, discover continents, fight wars. They do not hang about nattering. The following provide a small but reasonably representative sample of common opinions of women and gossip across cultures and epochs: "The North Sea will sooner be found wanting in water than a woman at a loss for a word" (Jutland). "A woman does little, gossips much; you, youth, believe in wagging tongues?" (*The Magic Flute* [Mozart] libretto by Emanuel Schikaneder). But more ominously, "The tongue is the sword of a woman, and she never lets it become rusty" (China). Occasionally, of course, men do open their mouths, but then it is to accomplish something of consequence—to discourse, debate, philosophize, exchange ideas, conduct business, or engage in politics.

The reader may have spotted some contradictions in these common sense "truths" about gossip. For example, if gossiping really is so unimportant, trivial, vacuous, and idle, whence comes its dangerous qualities? Why is gossip so threatening and why should it be so violently condemned?

Before we go any further, let us be clear about the form and character of the reactions gossip has attracted. Contemporary views do tend toward mild disapproval, though not invariably. I recently heard about a hospital whose administrators placed a ban on gossip among the staff, and at least one contemporary religious order would like to see it stamped out altogether. In the past, reactions have been somewhat stronger. For George Eliot, gossip was "a sort of smoke that comes from the dirty tobacco pipes of those who diffuse it, proving nothing but the bad taste of the smoker." In Valloire, a small community in the French Alps, the women must take care when they go shopping not to stop and talk to anyone, less they be branded as gossips (Bailey, 1971). On Desirade, a small Carribean island, married women are so strongly condemned for associating with one another—and it is assumed that association means only one thing, that they are gossip-ing—that they must send the children to do the shopping.

In Britain there was a time when gossiping was proscribed by law (Oakley, 1972). From the fourteenth to the eighteenth century, it was the practice not merely to disapprove of gossip but to mete out more or less painful punishment to the offenders. At the milder end of the spectrum was public shaming, which might take the form of forcing the offender to wear a scold's bridle. Ducking stools and stocks were also used to chastise gossips. The city of Dundee contains among the instruments of medieval torture in its municipal museum some examples of the "branks," a kind of iron mask with a spike or pointed wheel that pro-jected into the mouth. The wearers were invariably women. The inten-tion, both symbolically and physically, was to stop their tongues. African slaves in America were treated in similar fashion, which per-haps reveals something of the status of women in British society over this period. At the extreme was death by burning. From the fourteenth to the seventeenth century, around half a million people in Europe were burned as witches (Harris, 1975). The overwhelming majority, more than 90 percent, were women. If we allow that there was no reality to the supernatural powers they were accused of exercising, then presumably they attracted this treatment for some more substantial reason. Quite plausibly, they were in effect burned for gossiping. In other, especially preliterate, tribal societies, there is frequently a strong association be-tween witchcraft accusations and accusations of gossiping.

Historically, men have feared the talk of women ("the tongue is the sword of a woman") and have sought all manner of ways to control it or better still to stop it completely. It is perhaps no accident that the pornography popular with a male audience so often depicts women not merely bound but gagged. But why should the inconsequential activity of gossip have produced such horror and dismay in decent folk that they had to humiliate or burn the offenders? It is possible the culprits were in breach of the Protestant work ethic—gossip is after all "idle" ("a woman does little gossips much"), and people hard at work do not do it. But you do not burn people to death simply because they are not working hard enough.

The answer seemed to be, or rather the answer given, was that gossip is not merely a sin of omission—one should have been using one's time more productively—but also a sin of commission. It is delib-erate mischief making. Gossips disseminate slanders, they stir up trouble, they create discord and dissension, they spread lies about their neighbors. They are a disruptive, destructive influence in the community. If a community found it hard to believe that anything as insubstantial as talk—and women's talk at that—could have such devastating effects, then they may have preferred to believe that these effects resulted from witchcraft, magic, the casting of spells, the deployment of evil powers procured from a pact with the devil.

Techniques of Rehabilitation

Gossip has not received a great deal of scholarly attention, but such treatment as it has been given has typically involved an attack on one of the negative elements in its reputation while retaining other details of the conventional image. Particularly interesting are a number of treatments that are highly critical of the ways in which it is disparaged but continue to emphasize that it is a female activity. Indeed, the objective in these treatments is often to defend the authenticity and value of women's talk rather than to examine gossip as such.

I would like to attack all the themes I have identified in gossip's public reputation: its triviality, its disreputable motives, its unreliability, its destructiveness, and its female character. The reader may feel that were I to succeed in these aims nothing would remain of what he or she understands by gossip. But my point is that the term "gossip" is often used in common parlance not as a neutral description of a phenomenon that has objective features but as a moral judgment. If one refers to a person as gossiping, one is not describing their behavior in the same way as if one had said they were breathing or running, but rather as if one had said they were lying or philandering. That is, the term "gossip" is used evaluatively, to criticize and censure, though not quite in the same manner as an accusation of "lying," for whether lying is an appropriate accusation can be decided with reasonable precision.

I believe there is a less evaluative and more objectively definable class of actions to which the term "gossip" can usefully be applied, and I hope the reader will bear with me as I work toward this definition. Its value lies in its capacity both to illuminate a significant phenomenon and to make sense of the historical association between women and gossip. My starting point is with some rather general questions about human nature. The first of these concerns the human use of time.

How Naked Apes Spend Their Time

On the basis of ethological studies we now know a great deal about the time-energy budgets of a number of mammalian species. We know something about the proportion of time spent sleeping or resting, feeding, foraging, and procreating. The interesting comparisons here are between humans and other social species, namely species in which evolved patterns of adaptation to the environment entail some degree of social structure, in which adaptation occurs at the level of social groups rather than single individuals. The debate about the defining characteristics of a "social" species is interesting and complex but somewhat beyond the scope of this chapter (see Wilson, 1974). It contains, however, a few points from which the present discussion can benefit.

First, there exists a fundamental division between social insects and social vertebrates (cf. Campbell, 1975; Wilson, 1974). Among the latter but not the former, social organization is based upon individual-level recognition. The individual members of a functional group of social vertebrates recognize and distinguish between one another as individuals. Second, the most sophisticated nonhuman societies, those of the primates, differ from others not particularly in terms of size—in absolute terms they are typically quite small—but in terms of such qualities as the fraction of time devoted to social behavior and the patterning of communication in social groups (Wilson, 1974). Thus a baboon troop will have a more complex internal patterning of communication than will a school of minnows or a flock of geese. Likewise, stump-tailed macaques will spend much more of their waking time in social acts (grooming, presenting, social observation), than ring-tailed lemurs.

For obvious reasons, similar information about humans is much more difficult to acquire. Sir Edward Coke (1552–1634) recommended the following time-energy budget for the good human:

> Six hours in sleep,
> in law's grave study six,
> four hours in prayer,
> the rest on nature fix.

We now have more reliable sources of information than Coke's prescriptive intuitions. A massive cross-national study on the use of time by Szalai and others (1972) reveals something of the characteristic daily pattern for a number of cultures and for different categories of people within these cultures. To take one example, on weekdays adult male Belgians spent an average of 8 hours in sleep, 6.3 hours working, 1.5 hours watching television, 1 hour traveling, 2.9 hours alone, and 1 hour reading. (Note that these are not all mutually exclusive categories).

Belgians, it turns out, are not unusual. They are much like the French, Germans, Yugoslavs, Hungarians, Russians, and Peruvians in their use of time. They are also somewhat like macaques in spending on average 80 percent of their waking time in the company of others. Only the inhabitants of Jackson, Mississippi, seemed to be different; adult males in Jackson spent 6.1 hours alone, 2 hours in front of the television, and 40 minutes reading. The amount of time spent in the company of others varied from 10 hours (in the American sample, which is ironic given the American reputation for friendly sociability) to 13-plus in Yugoslavia, over 80 percent. I shall consider below what people might be doing when in one another's physical presence.

Of course, the societies in Szalai's survey do not correspond to any natural pattern. All are products of historical and not merely biological evolution, all express the march of progress, a progress that we often are told has liberated people from the sheer physical toil required of our less "civilized" ancestors. Unfortunately for this popular and reassuring myth, a couple of studies of contemporary hunter-gatherers indicate considerably less than the ten to sixteen hours a day that one might expect to be spent in physical labor to secure the means of survival. The average may have been nearer to five hours (Sahlins, 1972), a good deal less time than contemporary Belgians work.

Language Use

Among the features that set humans apart from all other species, one stands out: the capacity for language. All social species have evolved specialized means for communication, whether these depend on visual, auditory, tactile, or chemical channels. But language is quite unique in its power and flexibility as a system of communication (Hockett, 1958). It is reasonable to ask how humans use this unique facility, how much of their time they spend using it, and with what consequences. It is also reasonable to expect that those scientific disciplines whose subject matter is humans and their social activities would by now have shed some light on these questions. It therefore comes as something of a surprise to discover just how scattered, fragmented, and limited the evidence remains. Thus, for example, my own discipline of social psychology purports to be the scientific study of human social behavior. Yet until very recently most textbooks in social psychology had almost nothing directly to say about language use.

Let us set up some basic questions and see what answers may be found. What do humans do with language? In so far as the uses include speech, how much time do they spend participating in spoken communication? In so far as they are speakers as well as listeners, to whom do they talk? Finally, what do they talk about?

To take the first question, spoken communication is an obvious use of language; but there are others, including thinking, reading, writing, and of course prayer. Academics may take comfort from the myth that the pinnacle of human evolution is represented by the scholar in his or her prototypical scholarly and language-using activities of reading and writing. But no one else is likely to believe this, nor should they. Reading and writing are very recent innovations in the natural history of the species, they are specialized and occasional activities, and they are generally very antisocial activities. Moreover, the Szalai survey confirms what many others have asserted: the average representative of a highly literate society spends little time reading and even less writing.

Language undoubtedly plays an important part in human thinking, and the psychological study of language has placed far more emphasis upon its role as a tool of thought than upon its manifestation as a form of social interaction. But it is not clear how much time the average human spends in silent reflections or mental calculations based on language. Some cognitive psychologists have begun to voice the suspicion that thought is an overrated activity, and we might now wonder whether we have not been the victims of another intellectual conceit here. Finally, *pace* Edward Coke, there is little evidence that the average member of any community now or ever has spent much time in prayer.

Speech Interaction

If we allow that spoken interaction may be a significant form of human social behavior, just how much of it is there? First, we need to recognize that people are more likely to participate in spoken interaction as listeners than as speakers. Studies of group interactions have established a strong size-inequality effect (Stephan and Mishler, 1952): as the group becomes larger, participation becomes progressively more unequally distributed and the differences between the most frequent contributor and the next most frequent increases. Hence, to the extent that human social existence involves face-to-face group interactions, we might expect that much of the time individuals spend in such interactions will be in the more passive role of listeners. The development of mass media technologies over the last one hundred years has vastly exaggerated this potential inequality. Cinema, radio, and television enable tiny elites of professional communicators to speak to passive audiences of millions (Lerner, 1958).

Similar trends were anticipated as features of the growth of large-scale social organization. Max Weber (1948), perhaps more than any other scholar, drew attention to the fundamental changes in social organization associated with the industrial revolution. Weber believed that economic and political organizations were becoming bureaucracies. One of the defining features of bureaucratic organization is that everything decided, ordered, and done is recorded in writing; hence the "bureau" as the hub of the organization. This social innovation not only allowed more rational and objective organization, it also supposedly multiplied the effective scale of organizations. Highly integrated and highly coordinated industrial and commercial enterprises with thousands of employees were now possible. The governments of nation states could effectively regulate the affairs of millions of citizens.

But this innovation had depended first upon improved technologies for mass producing messages and then upon a literate population able to decode them and to respond in kind (Lerner, 1958). The implication is that literacy fundamentally transformed the character of social life. Whereas oral cultures required face-to-face verbal exchanges to coordinate their affairs and were limited in scale by the constraints of such communication, in literate cultures the role of oral communication would be substituted by written or printed communications with their greater efficiencies and economies of scale.

In a certain sense, these expectations have not been supported by the evidence. Research from several sources indicates that the anticipated displacement of informal face-to-face communication by more formal and impersonal communication—written messages—has not occurred, even in the economic organizations that exemplify Weber's concept of bureaucracy (e.g., Davies, 1953; Mintzberg, 1973; Rogers, 1962). Likewise, Szalai's survey on the use of time reveals that diffusion of mass communication technologies has not resulted in the complete replacement of face-to-face interaction with mass consumption of mass-produced messages. The inhabitants of industrialized societies are spending 80 percent or more of their waking hours in the physical presence of others and much less than this watching television, listening to radios, or reading newspapers.

Some evidence on the question of how much time people devote to conversation is beginning to emerge from methods of research that allow recording of samples of natural human behavior. Observational methods tend to be reactive, intrusive, and costly. But self-recording, using a structured diary, is a reasonably cost-effective and reliable means for providing valid estimates of various parameters of human behavior (Reiss & Wheeler, 1991). Reiss, Wheeler, and their colleagues have developed and used such a procedure in a series of studies of social interaction. Wheeler and Nezlek (1977) asked a group of university students to keep a structured record of their own interactions over two separate two-week periods. Seventy percent of the recorded interaction was classified as conversation, and at least two of the other four categories of interaction were likely to involve primarily conversational exchanges. Their data also indicated that from five to six-and-a-half hours per day were spent in social interaction of some form.

For various reasons, this number is liable to be a significant underestimate. First, participants were asked to record only interactions of ten minutes duration or more. Mintzberg (1973), in a study of company presidents, found that between 50 percent and 90 percent of their activities, which included conversations and meetings, lasted less than nine minutes each. One might object that the activity patterns of students and managers may be very different. However, some evidence we have collected (Emler, 1990; Emler and Grady, 1989), also using diaries, indicates that students engage in many conversations shorter than ten minutes. Our structured diary provides a record only of conversational interactions; it is intended to cover all but the briefest of verbal exchanges, such as passing greetings or utterances employed to complete transactions such as paying for goods at a supermarket checkout. Wheeler and Nezlek's (1978) daily average for all interactions was 7.4; ours for conversational interactions only is in excess of 20 for all groups so far studied, including students. Second, any recording errors with such a technique are likely to be omissions.

This points to the conclusion that people spend a great deal of time in conversational interaction. The average is likely to lie somewhere between six and twelve hours per day. That is a large margin of error, but it begins to indicate the scale of investment that humans are making in conversational interaction. There remains at this point the possible objection that university students are an unusually talkative group, that they perhaps have more time on their hands and opportunities for conversational interactions than most other categories of person. We shall need to consider this objection below, but here we might note that students in higher education can hardly be characterized as foolish people with superficial minds. Should we reflect upon the other things that humans might be doing with their waking hours, we can begin to see that very few of the possibilities exclude talk.

If conversation is idle, then it might be supposed that labor will be silent. But quite the reverse: Burns (1954) found in a study of managers that more of their working day was spent in conversation than in all other activities combined. Mintzberg's study of company presidents revealed that the bosses of small enterprises spend 65 percent of their working days in conversations. For those heading large companies the respective figure was 78 percent. When we turn from those white-collar workers who can represent their talk as work, we find that others also talk while they work and that worker satisfaction is directly related to the opportunities a job provides to talk. Parenthetically, we may note that, this being one of the great rewards of employment outside the home, home-working is unlikely to prove as popular as some enthusiasts for information technology are now anticipating.

Eating and drinking also are routinely exploited as further occasions for talk—dinner parties are not for the food alone, still less coffee mornings for the coffee or bars solely for the consumption of alcohol. Note also that seating in places serving food and drink is arranged "sociopetally," to encourage interaction, rather than "sociogudally," to inhibit it (cf. Osmond, 1957).

The next question of significance concerns the proportion of conversational interactions that involve groups—and therefore inequality of participation—rather than dyads. The Wheeler and Nezlek (1977) data indicate that the majority of interactions are dyadic; our own data confirm this. Again, there is nothing peculiar about students in this regard. Managers, for example, also show a distinct preference for one-to-one conversations over larger meetings (Kaplan, 1984).

Who Talks to Whom

Whom, then, are we talking to? Much hangs on this question—nothing less than an entire model of society. Social theory in the nineteenth century and the early part of this century was preoccupied with the social consequences of industrialization and mass urbanization. According to a succession of theorists, these changes created new kinds of social relations that would progressively displace more archaic forms (e.g., Tonnies, 1887/1957). Whereas preindustrial society had consisted of small-scale, face-to-face, rural communities based on primary groups, the contemporary industrialized world would be characterised by large-scale, impersonal aggregations based on secondary groups. Beyond the rather limited world of the nuclear family, relations would be formal or bureaucratized. People would interact not as personal acquaintances but as the impersonal and generally anonymous occupants of formally defined roles. In the words of Louis Wirth (1938), life in the city would be "impersonal, transitory and segmental."

The implication of this "community lost" (Wellman, 1978) argument is that the conversations we have with others, unless these others are members of our immediate family, are likely to occur outside of any relationship of personal acquaintance. We are likely to be talking to people who are strangers to us or who might as well be. Our transactions with them will be predicated on our contextualized roles or functions—shopkeeper-customer, teacher-student, doctor-patient, worker-foreman—not on our respective personal identities or on any historical relationship between us as unique individuals. The further implication is that the substance of our talk is likely to be related to the immediate task of making a purchase, evaluating an essay, describing symptoms, or explaining job requirements.

In more recent years, scholars have begun to question the "community lost" model of social life (Boissevain, 1974; Fischer, 1981; Litwak and Szelenyi, 1969; Wellman, 1979). Influential among these critics has been J. Clyde Mitchell (1969), who offers a useful analysis of social organization. He suggests that three forms of social order can be distinguished analytically: the structural, the categorical, and the personal.

The structural is the formal order of a bureacratized society, as emphasized in classical social theory in the "community lost" model. The structural order articulates relationships in terms of more or less formal offices or roles and relationships between roles and in terms of the formally defined responsibilities, duties, powers, and spheres of jurisdiction linking these roles. The categorical order articulates social relationships on the basis of broad categories, such as gender, race, class, nationality, or religion, and on the basis of their associated stereotypes. It is founded on social identities and relations between social categories and the customs and traditions defining the proper conduct of category members.

The personal order has been the least emphasized or studied in the social sciences. It is the order created by relationships—of acquaintance, friendship, kinship, marriage—between specific individuals and by networks of such relationships and the qualities of the personal ties and loyalties that characterize them. It is the kind of social order that was supposed to have been lost with rural communities. Mitchell and others claim that even in cities this kind of order not only exists but predominates. People continue to dwell and interact within worlds consisting primarily of personal acquaintances. The evidence on which this claim has rested, however, is not especially robust. In several surveys of urban communities and personal networks, people have simply been asked how many friends they have or how often they meet friends or relatives. This places a rather high reliance on the accuracy of memory. Reiss and Wheeler (1991) found that correlations between interactions recorded by a diary method and interactions estimated from memory were extremely low and in some cases negative. Nor does the survey evidence tell us about the relative frequency of contact with friends or family as compared to contact with other kinds of people.

Our own procedure extends the diary record approach. Participants in our studies are asked to identify their relationship with the people with whom they converse. The major categories we have used in our research are (a) purely formal relations, that is, encounters occurring in a business or service context; (b) strangers outside the context of any business or service transaction; (c) partners in intimate relationships (husbands, wives, boy- or girlfriends); (d) immediate family members (mothers, fathers, siblings, offspring); (e) other relatives (grandparents, uncles, aunts, cousins, etc.); (f) close friends; (g) other friends; (h) acquaintances.

The data generated in this way can be examined in terms of the percentage of all encounters with people in different categories or in terms of the total number of people encountered within each category over the recording period. Our participants are asked to keep the diary records for a period of seven days. Among student samples, about 6 percent of all people encountered are classified as strangers and about the same percentage as purely business or service relationships. About 3 percent of all recorded encounters involve strangers, and approximately 4 percent are classified as business/service encounters. In samples of nonuniversity young people of the same age, young people living on their own in their hometowns, the percentages for business/service are very similar but those for strangers much lower. Contacts with immediate family members are more frequent among the latter group, but among both groups contacts with other relatives are very infrequent. For both groups, the largest categories, both in terms of numbers of different people encountered and frequencies of encounters, are close friends, other friends, and acquaintances. Young adults interact mainly with people they know personally.

At first glance, data we have collected from a sample of managers suggest that they may inhabit a very different kind of social world. For this group, the largest category, both in terms of number of people and frequency of encounters, was the business/service category. However, other data revealed that the people involved were by no means anonymous, interchangeable role-occupants. On average they were personally known to our managers for two years.

The Content of Conversational Interaction

If it is true that we not only spend a great deal of our time in face-to-face, one-to-one conversations but the people we talk with are known personally to us and probably known very well, what are we talking about? Malinowski (1932) suggested that speech can be divided into two basic forms, the task-oriented and the phatic (Bales [1950] was later to make a superficially similar distinction). The former refers to those utterances essential to securing the coordination of activities in some collective task. One might suppose this is the kind of talk our managers were engaged in when interacting in those "business/service" exchanges. In phatic communication, on the other hand, the meaning of the words spoken is almost completely irrelevant. Its purpose is to reconfirm social bonds, as in "how are you? I'm fine," "Nice weather," and other uninformative verbal rituals. Eric Berne (1966) made a similar point about the "stroking" function of informal talk.

But if this is all we do with language it hardly seems worthwhile for evolution to have bothered with something so complicated to do it with. After all, packs of hunting dogs have little trouble coordinating activities; and if talk is used for stroking or cementing social bonds, monkeys do this adequately by picking nits off each other. (Though interestingly Dunbar [in press] has recently argued that primates' grooming methods are very expensive in terms of time investment and that, in this respect, language potentially has some significant advantages—you can do it while doing other things and you can do it with more than one other person at a time.)

One might argue that at least with respect to cooperative problem solving, language gives humans significant advantages over dogs and apes. And the technical achievements of humans could be taken as evidence not just of the advantages of an opposable thumb and a large brain but of the capacity language provides to exchange complex technical information. Moreover, in the coordination of activities, language allows for advanced planning to a degree far beyond the capacity of any other gestural, vocal, or chemical communication system. One cannot imagine even chimpanzees making appointments with each other. So perhaps these functions are served by the conversational activities of managers: they are solving technical problems, coordinating tasks, planning and organizing productive activity.

This, however, still leaves all other talk in the category to which Malinkowski consigned it: content-free. Interestingly, research in sociolinguistics, in the psychology of social interaction, and in conversational analysis has all tended to reinforce the lack of serious scholarly interest in the substance of talk. Sociolinguists have shown more interest in speech style than speech content. Social psychologists have quite explicitly argued that the nonverbal accompaniments of speech can be more informative than the content. And conversational analysis has been more preoccupied with the mechanics of conversation—turn taking and topic switching, for instance—than with content or purpose.

Undoubtedly, more searching questions about the content of conversations have been neglected in part because of the technical difficulties surrounding their examination. One of the best-known procedures for examining conversational content is Bales's (1950) Interaction Process Analysis. This is a system for the classification of discrete actions and reactions, both verbal and nonverbal, occurring between two or more people in a face-to-face interaction. The method requires that interactions can be observed or recorded, and for these reasons it is only really practicable for interactions that occur under controlled, near-laboratory conditions. Eavesdropping (Webb et al., 1966; Levin and Arluke, 1985) or other covert recording of naturally occurring conversations is one possibility; but even if the ethical problems in this strategy can be overcome, what is available for observation in this way may not be representative of all conversations. Our own solution has been to adapt diary records in various ways. Whatever the method, it must include the classification of content, and it is very difficult to avoid imposing preconceptions at the point at which categories are defined. Bales's (1950) system used twelve basic categories, though the intention was to embrace more than the purely verbal. His categories imply two broad groups of action, those that are essentially social-emotional— joking, laughing, agreeing, expressing tension or irritation—and those which are task related. In effect, they echo Malinowski's dichotomy.

Bales (1958) reported data indicating 44 percent of actions falling into the first group and 56 percent into the second. It should be noted, though, that these data came from men working in small ad hoc groups under laboratory conditions on hypothetical tasks. Under these conditions, task-related acts—giving opinions, giving information—might be expected to predominate. But for other reasons Bales's categories cannot tell us all we want to know about the content of conversational interaction. We do not know if the findings generalize, whether to women, to natural settings and real tasks, or to interactions that do not have a problem-solving focus. Also, if in fact much of what happens in conversations more generally does involve statements of opinion or provision of information, about what matters precisely do people express opinions or exchange information?

Our own data shed further light on these questions. First, we found that impersonal topics form a minor proportion of conversations as a whole. People are far less likely to talk about art, literature, cuisine, religion, ideas, politics, or events in the national news than they are about specific names and known individuals. The latter appears to form 80 to 90 percent of the content of natural conversations. The focus of conversation is, in Rogers's (1983) terms, more often "localite"—the immediate social world inhabited by us and the people we know—than "cosmopolite."

Second, a significant proportion of this person-specific content, on the average two-thirds, is what Jourard and Lasakow (1958) have called self-disclosure. The speakers reveal personal details about themselves to each other. This content does not, however, correspond entirely with the kinds of disclosures in which researchers like Jourard have been interested, which seem to reflect the particular interests of the clinical psychologist—states of mind and body, fears, anxieties, and so on. Together these form a significant category but by no means the most important. In our work, states of mind and body have accounted for 11 to 12 percent of the personal information our participants recorded as exchanging. Larger categories were preferences (tastes/interests/attitudes) and plans/intentions (both about 25 percent), but the largest was doings. That is, people spoke most about what they or other people were doing or had been doing.

Finally, about one-third of the person-specific content of conversations referred to third parties known personally to one or other if not both or all those involved in the exchange. And a high proportion of this content concerned the doings of these third parties. Other data we have collected indicate that about two-thirds of all conversations include some reference to third party doings. Talk about the doings of acquaintances corresponds to a reasonably neutral or nonevaluative definition of gossip.

To sum up, people spend a great deal of time exchanging information and observations about themselves and other people they know. Moreover, the exchange of information that has a particularistic and personal reference—it concerns specific, named individuals—tends to have the following additional features: it occurs in conversations that are normally unscheduled, face-to-face, one-to-one, informal, and between people who are themselves mutually acquainted. How can such a pattern be explained? Given the current state of scientific knowledge, any answer is necessarily speculation but, I hope, informed speculation.

Social Adaptation

It is helpful to think first about the kinds of problems that the members of other social species, particularly those close to us in evolutionary terms, need to solve and the manner in which these are solved. As we have already noted, the societies of other primates are characterized by complex social systems based on individual-level recognition. Fundamental to the successful functioning of individuals within these societies is knowledge of social structure, where this means a knowledge of the other members of the group, including their individual idiosyncrasies, patterns of affiliation, and position in the status order.

Other primates, however, for all their sophistication as social actors, share one limitation with members of the most elementary insect societies. In one way or another, both groups share information about the material environment, but neither is able to share information about the social environment. Everything individual chimpanzees know about their society they must learn through direct personal observation of its members in action. Humans therefore stand apart from all other social species by their capacity to share information about the social and not just the material environment, a capacity provided by the power of language. Gossip, at the most basic level, can be regarded as the human equivalent of primates' "social observation"; it is the dissemination of knowledge about social structure. This very capacity, however, both transforms social structure itself and creates new problems. Humans do not need to spend time observing all the fellow members of their social worlds in order to know them well, nor do they need to sustain relations with all of them. Patterns of contact and acquaintance are consequently quite unlike those of primate societies; humans are not confined to constructing small-scale and entirely face-to-face societies. Social action is highly compartmentalized (see Wilson, 1974). Individuals continually group and regroup in different combinations and numbers for different purposes. Social structures are characterized by networks (cf. Boissevain, 1974) or affiliations of varying strengths and sustained for diverse purposes. Knowledge of the social landscape, exchanged as gossip, is thus crucial knowledge about the links in social networks.

Language also contains a greater potential for prevarication than other, nonverbal forms of communication (Hockett, 1958), and, in particular, it creates an enhanced capacity for deliberately false communication. It is not that the members of other animal societies make no attempts to deceive one another (see Byrne and Whiten, 1988). Rather, both the power of language to mislead and the human dependence on verbally transmitted information about social structure make the reliability of communication a special problem for humans (see Ekman, 1985). Gossip both poses problems about its own reliability and provides solutions to these problems, insofar as any individual human observer is not dependent on a single source for social information. I believe a fundamental purpose of gossip as social observation is to make reputational inquiries. The continual activity of gossip allows individuals and communities to accumulate behavioral evidence about others and to form and refine judgments about their vices and virtues.

To see why reputational inquiry should be so fundamental and why indeed we devote so much time to it, let us again start from a parallel with primates. Among humans as among primates, social observation supports social action. For monkeys and apes such action has both defensive and assertive features. It is defensive in that each individual seeks to avoid being harassed, victimized, exploited, or manipulated by others. Each individual will draw upon accumulated knowledge of others based either on its own past exchanges or encounters with those others or its observations of their other interactions. Social action is assertive in so far as individuals seek power within the group by forming alliances with some while manipulating, exploiting, harrassing, or victimizing others. Primates, as de Waal (1982) has demonstrated, play politics. And their political action draws upon their accumulated knowledge of individuals and social structure.

We humans are really no different in our endless curiosity about the other people around us and particularly about those whose actions might affect us. Our curiosities are especially sharpened with respect to consequential differences between people, differences that come under the broad headings respectively of powers and character. By powers I mean to include such attributes as physical strength and stamina, manual skills, specialist knowledge, and intellectual talents. Power also involves control of valued resources. Character judgments are likewise multidimensional and might include estimates of trustworthiness, responsibility, courage, cool-headedness, friendliness, tact, sensitivity, generosity, and tolerance, among other qualities.

Is gossip directed more towards judgments about other people's powers or to judgments about their moral attributes? Given, on the one hand, evidence that character traits are quite stable over time (Hogan, 1983) and, on the other, the fact that powers or capacities are liable to change, one might expect that gossip would be more concerned with monitoring the latter set of attributes. However, there are counter-indications. There is some evidence that the substance of gossip is often more negative than positive (but see Levin and Arluke, 1985). Better established by research (e.g., Skowronski and Carlston, 1987) is the finding that negative information is more diagnostic of moral traits than positive information, whereas the reverse is true for abilities (and indeed for powers; both a rich and a poor man might afford to ride a bicycle every day but only a rich man could afford to drive a Rolls Royce as regularly). It may be that reliable character judgments are more difficult to make or more vital to get right. But in the current state of our knowledge about the substance of gossip, it is too early to draw firm conclusions here.

Our adaptation to the informal economy of life is more successful the more detailed our reputational knowledge is—to whom can we safely lend our garden tools and who is in a position to lend us theirs; whom can we trust to support our political ambitions; to whom should we turn for the best advice about buying a new car or about investment opportunities; with whom should we form partnerships, whether business or marriage; whom should we particularly avoid offending; and so on. This list of examples reminds us that people do make mistakes, forming ill-advised alliances, making bad marriages, misplacing their confidence and trust, heeding poorly informed advice, picking fights they cannot win. But I would contend that a person who gossips extensively, and thereby keeps informed, is less, not more, likely to experience such misfortunes.

The wide dissemination of reputational information has advantages for the collective as well as for its individual members. Identifying fools and scoundrels is advantageous to individuals whose circumstances might otherwise be adversely affected. In these terms it may be that the communal or collective advantage only describes the sum of individual benefits obtained by limiting the damage and mischief done by the incompetent or the immoral. But communities as social organizations depend for their survival and prosperity on allocating responsibilities and powers to particular individuals. Accurate appraisal of character and talent in the form of reputational judgments allows the selection of individuals likely to do the most good and least harm to the collective. Gluckman (1963) makes precisely this point about the role of gossip in selection for leadership positions. He also points out that gossip can function as a form of social control, discouraging individuals from straying too far from collective standards through fear of public criticism and its consequences. Likewise Sabini and Silver (1982) observe that gossip, by dealing with concrete instances of moral transgression, gives routine operational definition to otherwise rather abstract principles of morality.

Gossip as information and opinion exchange is a two-way process: we give as well as receive. And as should by now be obvious, gossip does not merely disseminate reputational information but is the very process whereby reputations are decided. Reputations do not exist except in the conversations that people have about one another. Certainly my neighbor's reputation depends upon what he does—whether he beats his wife or makes beautiful furniture—but this is only the starting point for his reputation. Unless others both observe and then discuss his actions, there is no reputation, whether for cruelty or craftsmanship. I may overhear my neighbor routinely beating his wife or spy his handmade furniture through the window and conclude that he is a cruel man or talented woodworker, but unless my conclusion is shared by others, then he still has no reputation for cruelty or woodwork. This then lends a further dimension to gossip: its social nature provides the potential for political action. In this it is a two-edged weapon. Gossip offers scope to manipulate the reputations of others, but with risks to the self when such manipulation is too transparently self-serving or clumsy.

Finally, it might be expected that we would be keenly interested in our own reputations insofar as these describe the kinds of moral credit and credibility we have within the community. Our own reputations play an important role in determining our capacity to secure help and cooperation, to persuade or intimidate, and to avoid exploitation. Gossip affords us possibilities of monitoring our reputations but also of managing them. It allows us to discover what others may be saying about us that they would not say to us (though here again is a well-known political tactic—the false confidant, using the intermediate position to poison relationships), and it allows us some influence over what they will say about us by priming their future conversations with our versions of events (see Emler, 1991).

The Characteristics of Gossip

We are now in a position to appreciate why the exchange of personal information should so often occur in unscheduled, informal, one-to-one, face-to-face conversations between acquaintances. Such conversations provide a number of advantages over any alternatives. Let us take these features in turn and mention briefly some of the advantages they might provide.

Unscheduled. There are probably a number of reasons why so many of our daily conversations are neither deliberately sought nor arranged in advance. One concerns costs. There is good evidence that human patterns of association are powerfully shaped by the principle of least effort (e.g., Catton and Smircich, 1964). Allowing conversations to arise out of routines minimizes effort. The benefits people derive from routine encounters may well, of course, depend on their skill in initiating conversations and taking them in productive directions. Commentators on gossip have more than once noted its incidental character. It is possible that the benefits derived from gossip are unpredictable; we accumulate information about other people almost at random without knowing in advance which bits will prove to be useful or when. If we cannot know in advance which conversations will turn out to be informative, there is little benefit in arranging or contriving in advance to talk to particular people on particular occasions. But this remains for the present a hypothesis to be verified or rejected, and it is not difficult to think of counter-arguments. There may prove to be an optimal mix of strategies, and perhaps people differ in their skills at approximating this optimum.

Informal. Such encounters have no fixed agenda. The conversation can therefore take any direction. Formality also works against intimate disclosure or the taking of risks.

Face-to-face. First, the audience wishes to evaluate the credibility of what they are being told (Is this all true? Does this person know what he or she is talking about? Is he/she attempting to manipulate or mislead me?). The range of vocal and visual cues available in face-to-face interaction allows an audience a more reliable basis for making these kinds of judgments. Second, the speaker can more effectively monitor audience reaction as revealed through their own nonverbal feedback. From this feedback the speaker is better able to answer such questions as: Are they interested in this? Do they believe me? Am I revealing too much or being too critical of a mutual friend? Third, the value of gossip in determining reputations depends on its candor, although this can conflict with other informal rules of relationships— not to speak ill of friends behind their backs, not to betray confidences (cf. Argyle and Henderson, 1984). Thus every occasion for gossip is potentially a conspiracy to bend or break these rules, a conspiracy against other friends and acquaintances. And potential co-conspirators must negotiate their mutual willingness to enter into such a pact and establish the limits to which they are prepared to go. The various nonverbal channels play an important part in such delicate negotiations.

One-to-one. The information and observations a speaker provides can be fine-tuned for a very specific audience. The information can be that of most relevance to the co-gossip and the opinions of a kind that he or she is likely to sympathize with. Explanations and accounts can be matched to ensure comprehension with minimum redundancy, and what is said can be continually modified and adjusted on the basis of feedback about reception of the message. These tasks can be managed far less easily with any audience greater than one. Furthermore, there will seldom be any two people with whom a third would wish to share precisely the same confidences. Accordingly, Taylor, De Soto, and Lieb (1979) have found that the level of disclosure is dramatically lower in triadic as compared to dyadic conversations. Criticisms of a friend voiced to one mutual acquaintance would not necessarily be voiced in the same way, if at all, to another.

Between Acquaintances. There is an efficiency to such conversations, given that the participants are more likely to know how much the other already knows about any particular matter and to know what might actually be news and of interest to the other. A bore is among other things someone who fails to make such discriminations. Acquaintances will be more familiar with one another's nonverbal style and thus better able to read the cues that each provides. Knowledge of the other also allows a more accurate appraisal of the value of his or her own observations and disclosures. Finally, the moral relationship between friends and acquaintances provides some protection against being duped, manipulated, or misled and a better chance that one's own disclosures will not be grossly abused.

The foregoing claims are for the most part working hypotheses that await more systematic tests against evidence. But if gossip has been sadly neglected by researchers in the social sciences, this neglect is more likely to be remedied if one can first show that the phenomenon is amenable to systematic analysis and that testable hypotheses can be framed.

The Reputation of Gossip Reconsidered

We now have arrived at the point at which at least a preliminary reconsideration of gossip's reputation can be made. Certainly, we can see that there are prime facia grounds for challenging most of the elements of its traditional reputation. I do not propose to offer a detailed reexamination of that reputation here. The other chapters in this book already make a substantial contribution in this direction. I will instead confine myself to two brief points.

First, far from being a trivial and superficial activity that appeals only to shallow and idle minds, gossip is intelligent action. It is a complex and sophisticated instrument of adaptation. Humphrey (1976) observes that primates are much more intelligent than the demands of the material environment would appear to require. He argues that there must nonetheless be something in the primate's environment sufficiently challenging and imperative to require such a high level of intelligence, and concludes that the environment inhabited by a chimp or a baboon is made intellectually demanding by the other chimps or baboons it contains; high-level intelligence is required primarily to solve the problems of living in a social group. It has since been shown (Dunbar, in press) that the size of the neocortex among primate species is directly related to the typical group size occurring in each species. The human neocortex is considerably larger than that of the chimpanzee, and human social structures are likewise substantially larger. As an exchange of information and observations about the inhabitants of one's environment, gossip contributes centrally to successful functioning in that environment. Successful gossip requires delicate judgments about what precisely to say to whom, how to say it, and what to hold back. It also involves skill in extracting disclosures from others. If we recognize its many functions and its often high level of sophistication, we then may begin to appreciate the sheer scale of the intellectual achievement competent gossip represents.

My second and final point concerns the association between gossip and women. Gossip is a powerful process in the politics of everyday life. This inevitably makes it the target of attempts at control. The traditional image of gossiping and the gossip can be seen in this light. The various elements that make up this image have, in combination, the effect, first of all, of discouraging women from participating in the political process at all and, second, if they are incautious enough to do so, of discounting their involvement and legitimizing a punitive response (Emler, in press). The moral, perhaps, is that the truth about gossip will continue to be distorted while gender inequalities in political and economic life persist.

12 | Used and Abused: Gossip in Medieval Society

Sylvia Schein

THIS STUDY DEALS with various aspects of gossip that found expression in medieval society: attitudes to gossip, the carriers of gossip, motives for gossiping, subject matter of gossip, gossip as a part of the stereotype of feminine behavior, and, finally, the power of gossip.

The scarcity of medieval sources prevent us from conducting an empirical-statistical study on the order of Levin and Arluke's "An Exploratory Analysis of Sex Differences in Gossip" (Levin and Arluke, 1985, pp. 281–86). The scarce, sporadic data provided by contemporary sources enables us to formulate therefore only the most general hypotheses. Medieval society was a "close" society, and most information passed from person to person through oral communication. These conditions fostered gossip, created a propensity to believe it (as there were no counter checks to information received through oral communication), and contributed to its power. Indeed, as in other "close" societies, gossip played a most powerful role.

Gossip was defined as a repetition of a rumor, of something heard from someone else. A woman called a "gossip" was someone "who likes to go about repeating what she hears" (Harrison, 1974, pp. 356–57).[1] Sometimes a woman's girlfriends are called "her gossips" (Pitts, 1985, pp. 12, 22). Gossip is often described as being geographically limited to a certain place, a village, a town, or a neighborhood. In Jean de Meun's continuation of the *Romance of the Rose* (ca. 1277), a jealous husband accuses his wife of being so impudent as to provoke gossip that runs throughout the town (Robbins, 1962, p. 171). The Wife of Bath in Chaucer's *Canterbury Tales* (1387–1400) likes to wander "from house to house for a chat and village malice" (Coghill, 1973, p. 291). Boccaccio refers to both "a district's gossip" and "a city's gossip." In one of the tales of the *Decameron* a man says to a lady: "You deceive yourself if that is what you believe [that only she and her maid know about her secret love] for the people where he [the lover] lives, as well as of your own [people] talk about nothing else" (McWilliam, 1972, p. 637). In another story a certain lady tells her neighbor that she slept with Angel Gabriel; the neighbor recounts the news while attending a party with a number of ladies. The ladies pass the tale on to their husbands and to various female acquaintances and "thus within forty-eight hours the news was all over Venice" (McWilliam, 1972, pp. 349–50). Sometimes a piece of gossip was so sensational that it spread beyond the boundaries of a diocese (Power, 1964, p. 458).

Gossip was censured as a negative activity in medieval society, due partly to the influence of Scripture. According to Leviticus: "You shall not go up and down as a slanderer among your people" (Lev. 19:16), and Proverbs: "He who goes about as a talebearer reveals secrets" (Prov. 11:13), as well as: "Like a gold ring in a swine's snout is a beautiful woman without discretion" (Prov. 11:22), and: "He who goes about gossiping reveals secrets; therefore do not associate with one who speaks foolishly" (Prov. 20:19). In the New Testament, gossip appears among such serious transgressions as malice, envy, murder, and deceit. (Rom. 1:29; 2 Cor. 12:19). It also appears as a feminine activity. St. Paul dwells upon young widows "who learn to be idlers gadding about from house to house and are not only idlers but gossips and busy bodies saying what they should not" (1 Tim. 5:13). His remedy for such a sinful occupation is to marry and bear children (1 Tim. 5:14). In ca. 1370 William Langland counts "sloth" among one of the seven deadly sins (Goodridge, 1959, p. 73).

Gossip was considered most "uncourtly" by the code of courtly love. Andreas Capellanus in his famous *Art of Courtly Love*, a sort of summary of the rules or the doctrine of courtly love (composed between 1174 and 1186), warns the lover that "love decrees that if the lady finds that her lover is foolish and indiscreet . . . or if she says that he has no regard for her modesty, she will not forgive his bashfulness" (Locke, 1957, p. 28). The perfect lover, according to the doctrine, should be discreet and should not gossip about his lover to his friends. Moreover, according to John Gower's *Confessio Amantis* (ca. 1390) the chief care of the lover should be "all speech and to gossip to forbear / that may concern my lady's name" (Tiller, 1963, v. 525–27, p. 107). Similarly, a lady should avoid gossiping, provoking gossip, and even listening to gossip (Bornstein, 1983, p. 34). Gossip appears in the courtly love literature as the enemy of love. Guillaume de Lorris in his *Romance of the Rose* (ca. 1237), an allegoric epic about ideal love, includes among the allegoric figures (all personified by women) a figure he calls "Evil Tongue" "who thinks or fancies wrong / in all affairs and retells all she knows or weans," "who will no woman spare," and "who is accustomed to recount false tales of squires and demoiselles." "Evil Tongue," an enemy of the lovers, arouses "jealousy" against the "lover" and thus comes between him and his love (Robbins, 1962, pp. 76–77, 85). Jean de Meun, in his continuation of the *Romance of the Rose* (ca. 1277), instructs the "lover": "if a man or a woman come to you with tales / About your lady saying what they've seen / Never believe a word of it, assert / That they are foolish to report such news" (Robbins, 1962, p. 196). Moreover,

> Let him [the lover] give her [his love] no cause
>   to fear his boast
> vile shame it is that many a one defames
> With false and feigned stories the good name
> Of many a lady he has never possessed.
> Such are not courteous or worthwhile men,
> But ones whose failing hearts impede success.
> A villain vice is vaunting; he who brags
> Is worse than fool; the wise man who succeeds
> Conceals the fact. Love's treasures are best hid
> From all but faithful friends who'll quiet keep;
> To him the sweetheart's boons may be revealed.
> (Robbins, 1962, pp. 198–99)

Describing the death of "Evil Tongue," Jean de Meun refers to her having now no "power to see or hear whatever may occur / There is no one now who can carry tales to her / So she is able to surprise no more." Therefore: "Jealousy no longer is to be feared; / To lead the good life one no longer dreads" (Robbins, 1962, p. 453). Besides being condemned by the Scriptures, then, gossip was considered "uncourtly," an initiator of jealousy and therefore a foe of love and of lovers, and even one of the deadly sins.

Who Gossiped?

Though condemned as an immoral occupation, gossip appears to have been a daily occupation of all the strata of society, of both women and men and even children. It was, however, the burgesses, the dwellers of the towns, who had the bad reputation of being gossips. Chaucer, for example, presents his Wife of Bath, a satirical figure of a bourgeois woman, as one who likes "in company to laugh and chat" and who admits freely that "As I so often did, I rose and went / To see her [Dame Alice] ever wanting to be gay / and go a-strolling, March, April and May / From house to house for chat and village malice." Her husband is presented as trying in vain to prevent her spending time in this occupation. According to the *Wife of Bath* the unfortunate husband swore when she "went off gadding . . . from house to house," and he even "would take the Bible up and search for proverbs in Ecclesiasticus / Particularly one that has it thus: 'Suffer no wicked woman to gad about.'" When the wife used to see her "gossip or a friend" the husband used to "scold" her "like a devil" (Coghill, 1973, pp. 32, 283, 291, 294). And indeed the bourgeois husbands often tried to prevent their wives from gossiping. In a book of directions written in the late fifteenth century by a sixty-year-old bourgeois from Paris for his fifteen-year-old wife, the husband advises his wife "not to speak too much, not to say anything in jest or mockery that she might regret, not to laugh too much and to speak humbly and courteously to everyone . . . She should not gossip with other women, and not reveal the secrets of her husband" (Bornstein, 1983, p. 57).

In the *Fifteen Joys of Marriage*, a satire composed about 1400 by an educated bourgeois probably in one of the busy commercial towns of western France, gossip plays an important role, especially in marriage. Though women gossip more, men are not silent. Women gossip mainly with other women, men mainly with other men; but sometimes men and women gossip together (Pitts, 1985, pp. 12, 40, 46, 62, 75, 123). Within marriage wives often use gossip to get what they wish from the husbands. Wishing to get for herself a new gown a wife refers while in bed to whispering of others that she heard from her "gossip" about her being shabbily dressed (Pitts, 1985, p. 12). Another wife declares, again in order to get herself a gown from her husband, that: "as far as I am concerned I'd be glad to go round dressed in homespun but then what would people say?" The poor husband, who is stingy or perhaps thinks his wife has enough gowns already, tries vainly to dismiss the importance of gossip, replying: "Don't worry, sweetheart, just let them talk. Why should we follow the pack?" (Pitts, 1985, pp. 46–47).

More often, however, the husband dismisses gossip not on purpose but out of naivety. A "good fellow, who is a sincere and a goodnatured type," upon hearing rumors about his wife's fling, "had several good folk swear that these were only malicious lies and groundless fabrications, just as many ladies are woefully slandered heavens know, by the gay blades prowling the streets; such carousers only set their tongues awagging about decent respectable women when they can get nothing else from them" (Pitts, 1985, p. 40). Such a naive husband often becomes a subject of gossip. After vowing that he'll never believe "stories nor listen to babble" about his wife's flings, "he becomes a laughing stock: she calls him Old Johnny Cuckold, another points at him in the street, another says it's a great misfortune for such a fine fellow as he.

Still another remarks that it makes no difference, that such are the rules of the game, and that the husband is a dull sort anyway. Finer folk will turn him out and steer clear of him" (Pitts, 1985, pp. 74–75). Similarly, Boccaccio presents men as ignoring gossip. When a wife refers to "mischievous things" said about her and a man, her husband replies: "Away with you . . . Do you suppose I pay any attention to gossip-mongers" (McWilliam, 1972, pp. 292–93). Sometimes, however, the betrayed husband believes the gossip. In a meeting of "gossips" a wife tells the following story: "When that rumour of you know what was circulating about so-and-so and me, my husband confronted me with it, but I defended myself well, thank God. Why, he went more than three months without food or sleep, and he tossed and churned so in bed, sighing all the while" (Pitts, 1985, p. 123).

Though on the whole women are presented as spending more time gossiping than men, men obviously gossiped among themselves too. A group of male guests after leaving their host's house listen to what their servants, who were talking to the host's servants, have to say about the host's marriage and the behavior of his wife and "they have a good laugh as they trot along" (Pitts, 1985, p. 62). That gossip was common among men is also clear from *The Butcher of Abbeville*, a popular fabliaux by Eustache of Amiens (ca. 1400). The butcher is described as "well liked by his neighbours for he is not one of these malicious gossips, but an honest, trustworthy and well bred" man (Hellman and O'Gorman, 1965, p. 31).

Children gossiped, too. In the *Decameron*, Boccaccio describes a rector who, after having been discovered in bed with a most ugly servant girl named Ciutazza, was for a long time afterwards unable to walk down the street without being pointed at by small boys, who would taunt him with the words "There goes the man who went to bed with Ciutazza" (McWilliam, 1972, p. 610).

That gossip abounded among the members of the lower classes of society, particularly among domestic servants, is reflected in the references to the subject in the didactic literature of the Middle Ages. Jacques of Vitry, in his most popular and influential collection of exempla (fables intended as examples of good or bad behavior), regards male servants as no less garrulous and apt to gossip about their lords' secrets than their female counterparts (Crance, 1890, p. 85). Servants gossiped among themselves, with other people's servants, and with their employers. Courtesy books for women exhort servant women and chambermaids not to gossip about their employers, which seems to indicate that this was the main subject matter of servants' gossip. Christine de Pisan, in *Treasure of the City of Ladies* (1405), warns ladies not to show their servants any little sign of some vice so as to prevent them "talking about her behind her back," and she warns servant women not to defame their employer "either among themselves or elsewhere," "for words can never be said privately enough that they may not be reported. If they hear evil spoken of their employer they must try to tone down the gossip and explain it away." Answering a servant's argument that "I see something I have reason to talk and gossip about and there is nothing else very interesting about my work," Christine de Pisan argues as follows:

> Go away if you do not like it but if you need to be employed as a servant . . . just keep quiet . . . and pretend that you do not see the least thing and that you notice nothing, since it is not within your ability to remedy it nor is it any of your business . . . If you see evil and if you hear someone talk about her [the mistress] play down the gossip if you can, or if not, keep your mouth shut about it, and for this you will be esteemed the more. God knows that many women who talk about their mistresses do it more out of spite because they are not in on the secret, and out of envy that other women know more about it, than for any other motive. (Lawson, 1985, pp. 110–15, 124–26)[2]

Motives for Gossiping

What indeed were the motives for gossiping? Since oral communication was the main method of passing information from person to person, there was no way to distinguish precisely between "gossip," "information," or "news." They were often and sometimes even maliciously and intentionally confused. Christine de Pisan, referring to the court gossip of ladies in waiting and servants, mentions motives of spite, envy, and boredom (Lawson, 1985, p. 127). Sometimes repeating a piece of gossip had the concrete aim of achieving a wish. In other cases, gossip evolved from the frustration of being denied one's wish. Men, for example, spread malicious gossip about women they failed to seduce (Pitts, 1985, p. 40).

Often, however, gossip was idle and purposeless, simply an enjoyable manner of spending time. During the time of the Black Death (1348), Boccaccio's ladies of Florence complain that "all we ever hear is so-and-so is dead and so-and-so is dying" (McWilliam, 1972, p. 60), bemoaning lack of juicy gossip. As an enjoyable pastime gossip is sometimes linked to a good laugh (Coghill, 1973, p. 32) and joking, and thus something that encourages jokes and merryment. In William Langland's *Piers the Ploughman* (ca. 1370), for example, "sloth," one of the seven deadly sins, admits that she "enjoys a bawdy joke, a riotous day at the village wake, or a juicy bit of scandal about some neighbour more than all that Matthew, Mark, Luke and John ever penned" (Goodridge, 1959, p. 73). It would appear therefore that gossip was not only sometimes malicious, motivated by feelings like spite, envy, revenge, or frustration, but that it was often motivated by a keen and healthy interest in one's neighbors or friends, in the affairs of one's prince or king, or by one's wish for a good time.

Subject Matters of Gossip

> Of wars, and peace and marriages, of rest and work
>   and voyages,
> Of suffering, of health and life,
> Of love and hate, accord and strife,
> Of praise, of loss and then of gain,
> Health, sickness, then of cure again,
> Of tempests and of zephyrs mild,
> Plague deaths of men and creatures wild,
> Of various sudden transmutations
> Of circumstances and locations,
> Of trust and doubt and jealousy,
> Of wit and folly, victory,
> Of plenty and of great starvation,
> Of trade, of death, of mination,
> Of good rule and bad governments,
> Of fire and various accidents.

Thus describes Chaucer the topics of the various chitter-chatter jangles (Stone, 1983, p. 116) in the Hall of Rumour of the *House of Fame* where truth and lies fought together to escape.

> Was whispering in another's ear
> Some novel tidings secretly,
> Or else was talking openly
> As thus. . . . "What's happened? Have you heard?
> And do you know the latest word?"
> "No" said the other "tell me what"
> The other told him this and that,

And swore that all of it was true.
"He say so" and "He's going to do,"
"He's at it now."
"I heard some chat,"
"You'll find it's true!" "I'll bet on that."
(Stone, 1983, p. 118)

It follows then that the subject matters of gossip were most various and diverse.

The most popular subject of gossip, it seems, was love, especially extramarital love affairs. A wife's flings were very often a subject of village or town gossip (Pitts, 1985, p. 123). No less favorite subject was the betrayed husband, the "Cuckold" (Pitts, 1985, pp. 74–75). At court the main subject of gossip was the behavior of the lord and lady but other members of the court received attention, as well (Lawson, 1985, pp. 110–15, 124–46). One usually gossiped within one's social group. Courtiers gossip about other courtiers, and townfolk about fellow townfolk, and village dwellers about their neighbors (McWilliam, 1972, p. 610; Pitts, 1985, pp. 46–47). In several tales of the *Decameron* a wife complains that she "has no single neighbor who does not gape and laugh at her for slaving away as she does" (McWilliam, 1972, p. 529). In one of the poems of the *Carmina Burana*, the *"Pity me,"* a girl complains that after her lover left her pregnant: "I am all they [folks] ever talk about—pride of their gossiping" (Parlett, 1986, p. 128). John of Joinville in his *Life of Saint Louis* (ca. 1307) reports that the people of Champagne gossiped about him, for they were jealous of the love the king showed him (Shaw, 1963, p. 330).

Within their communities, people gossiped about the most usual and trivial events, as well as about the most extraordinary ones. The Venetian humanist Gregorio Correr writing in 1443 to Celila Conzaga, a Patrician of Mantua, ordered her to refuse to hear about such matters as "who marry, who swells in pregnancy, to whom infants hail from the cradle . . . Let your conversation to be serious and modest" (King and Rabil, 1983, p. 101). If trivialities and trivial events and behavior were subjects of gossip, even more so were unconventional and eccentric ones. Margery Kempe, the eccentric wife of a burgess of Lynn, complains in her autobiography (ca. 1433) that whatever she did became town gossip. She knew that people "made many adverse comments about her, because she wore gold pipes on her head [i.e., fashionable hair dress of goldwire and mesh] and her hoods with tippets were fashionably slashed . . ." When she failed as a horse-mill owner "it was raised about the town . . . that neither man or beast would serve [her] and some said she was accursed; some said God openly took vengeance upon her; some said one thing and some said another." Following Margery's spirited conversion "she was slandered and reproved by many people because she led so strict a life" (Windeatt, 1985, pp. 43, 45, 47).

Sometimes, however, people in other communities were the subject of gossip. People of a certain town sometimes gossiped about a nearby court or monastery or nunnery. For example, in 1432 the bishop of Lincoln wrote to a canon of Lincoln about

> an abundant rumour and loud whisperings [that] have brought to our hearing that in the priories of the Holy Trinity of the Word by Markgate and of St. Giles by Flamstead . . . certain things forbidden, hateful, guilty and contrary to holy religion and regular discipline are daily done and brought to pass in damnable vice by the said prioresses, nuns and other, serving men and agents of the said places; by reason whereof the good report of the same places is set in jeopardy, the brightness and comeliness of religion in the same persons are grievously spotted, inasmuch as the whole neighbourhood is in commotion herefrom.

As the result of inquiry into the scandal it was discovered that the prioress of Markgate consorted for more than five years, up to the time of his death, with the steward of the priory, so that "public talk and rumour during the said time were busy touching the premises in the town of Markgate and other places, neighbouring and distant, in the diocese of Lincoln and elsewhere" (Power, 1964, pp. 457–59). In this case, the gossip was so scandalous that it spread beyond the boundaries of the diocese of Lincoln. One of the most comical tales of the *Decameron* offers another example of gossip about a convent: an abbess bribes a gardener who slept with her as well (as with all the other nuns in the convent) in order to prevent him from going away and "spread[ing] tales concerning the convent." As a result the gardener stays on at the convent as its steward, and "although he fathered quite a number of nunnlets and monklets, it was all arranged so discreetly that nothing leaked out until after the death of the abbess" (McWilliam, 1972, pp. 234–41).

Nuns were not only a subject of gossip but they often gossiped among themselves. In the tale of the "Abbess and the Breeches," included in the *Decameron* but older than Boccaccio, nuns gossip about a nun who receives a lover in her cell and even report her to the abbess (McWilliam, 1972, pp. 688–91; Power, 1964, pp. 522–23 and n.3).

In *Piers the Plowman*, the sin of anger boasts that when she was a cook in a convent she

> brewed them [the nuns] broths of every conceivable slander—that mother Joanne was an illegitimate child, that Sister Clarice might be a knight's daughter, but her mother was no better than she should be, and that Sister Peacock had an affair with a priest— "She'll never be a prioress," they said, "She had a baby last year in cherry time, it's the talk of the convent!" And I fed them with such a hash of spiteful gossip that two of them would sometimes burst out "liar" together, and slap each other the face. Christ! If they'd both had knives they would have slaughtered each other! (Goodridge, 1959, pp. 65–66)

In nunneries, by the way, the person most prone to spreading gossip about the nuns was the portress, or doorkeeper, whose duty it was to receive guests and all comers. Abelard, in his instructions to Heloise as abbess, argues therefore that the portress should not carry any rumors heard from people outside into the convent, "but if she hears what ought to be known she should report it privately to the abbess" (Radice, 1981, pp. 218–19).

Gossip as a Part of the Stereotype of Feminine Behavior

It was commonly believed that women were more apt to spend their time gossiping than men. Early in the Middle Ages, St. Jerome, echoing St. Paul (in 1 Tim. 5:13), argues in a letter to Eustochium that one should cast out "like the plague those idle and inquisitive virgins and widows who go about to married women's houses, who outdo the parasites in plays by their unblushing impudence as 'evil communications corrupt good manners'" (1 Cor. 15:33) (Mierrow, 1962, p. 164).[3]

The architect of courtly love, Andreas Capellanus, shows that gossiping became a topos of medieval misogyny:

> No woman can make you such a firm promise that she will not change her mind about the matter in a few minutes . . . woman is by nature a slanderer, because only slander can spring from envy and hate. It is not easy to find a woman whose tongue can ever spare anybody or who can keep from words of detraction. Every woman thinks that by running down others she adds to her own

praise and increases her own reputation . . . never rely upon a woman's promise or upon her oath, because there is no honesty in her; always be careful to keep your intentions hidden from her and never tell her your secrets . . . every woman is a liar . . . a drunkard . . . loud mouthed. (Locke, 1957, pp. 44–54; Bloch, 1989, pp. 1–24)

Writing in the late Middle Ages, Boccaccio held the opinion that women gossip more than men and presents gossip as being "passed throughout the town from one woman to the next" (McWilliam, 1972, p. 350). In his highly didactic and misogynist treatise *Concerning Famous Women* (ca. 1355–1359), he complains, while praising Proba the wife of Adelphus, about "those women who yield to pleasure and idleness, think it wonderful to stay in their rooms wasting irrevocable time in vain stories, and often spend their time from morning to night and stay awake through the night in harmful or useless gossip" (Guarino, 1964, p. 22).

Most medieval men agreed with the argument of Andreas Capellanus that because they are apt to gossip women are unable to keep a secret. One of the most popular and widely read collections of exempla, that of Jacques of Vitry (ca. 1240) includes the story of a wife who asked her husband to tell her what went on in the meetings of the city council of which he was a member. The husband made her believe that the council decided to allow each of the city's citizens to take several wives and to keep it a secret. The wife, unable to keep the secret, protested before the council, which understood the husband's precaution and praised him highly for not confiding secrets to his wife because of the "frivolity" (*levitas*) of some women (Crance, 1890, p. 98). Another popular collection of exempla, the so-called *Gesta Romanorum* (compiled in ca. 1473), includes stories whose main moral is that "there was never a woman who could keep a secret" (Swan and Hooper, 1959, pp. 226–28). William Langland used this moral to explain why prioresses could not hear confessions of their nuns and praised Pope Gregory IX for forbidding it in the strongest terms, arguing that "otherwise they [the nuns] would all have been disgraced on the very first day for women can never keep anything secret" (Goodridge, 1959, p. 66).

Because gossip became a topos of the misogynist stereotype of women, they were constantly instructed by courtesy books for women not to gossip, not to listen to gossip and not to provoke gossip and thus become a subject of gossip. The French troubadour Garin lo Brun (twelfth century) argued in his courtesy book for women that a lady should never be in an intimate situation with a man unless he is a relative, or she has known him for a long time. Otherwise people will gossip about her. A friar from Bèziers, Matfre Ernengaud in his *Breviari d'amor* (1288) argued that a woman should be affable and friendly but must not do anything dishonorable; she must have the tact to know when to stop a flirtation so that people will not gossip about her. According to *The Good Wife Taught Her Daughter* (an address from a mother to her daughter ca. 1350), a girl should not gossip or reveal secrets while visiting other women; neither should she gossip with friends or family members in church, but attend church with serious intentions. Similarly, Suzanne of Bourboun, Anne of France, the wife of Louis XII of France, advised her daughter in a letter ca. 1504–1505 not to engage in gossip or mockery and to be gracious and humble to everyone (Bornstein, 1983, pp. 34, 63–64, 72). Christine de Pisan, in *The Treasure of the City of Ladies*, advised young princesses to pursue the virtue of sobriety that will prevent her, among other matters, "from ever speaking badly of any other person." They should not talk behind the back of their enemies about them and moreover they should keep their women of the court "in order just as the good and prudent abbess does in her convent, so that bad reports about it may not circulate in the town, in distant regions or anywhere else" (Lawson, 1985, pp. 58, 69, 76). To protect themselves from gossip, the princesses should avoid foolish love affairs. They should not easily believe hearsay nor fall into the habit of whispering privately in secluded places, even to any of her own people or her women (Lawson, 1985, pp. 96, 100).

Concerned with the ill fame of ladies of the court as gossips, Christine de Pisan argued that

> it is a very great shame that down in the town or elsewhere they may say: "The ladies and the women of the court certainly know how to slander each other! I have heard about such-and-such lady or maiden such-and-such a thing and something else about such another. In this respect the court of a princess ought to be like a well-regulated abbey where the monks have an oath that they will say nothing to outsiders about their secrets or anything may happen among them. (Lawson, 1985, p. 126)

Did medieval women indeed gossip more than men? Is the insertion of gossip into the misogynist stereotype of women really justified? The answers to both these questions is yes. Faced with limited opportunities to exercise real power over their own or others' lives, barred from holding office and from direct lines of political influence, relegated to the domestic arena, medieval women, especially from the ranks of nobility, tried to procure a share of the power by using such tools as kinship, gifts, and patronage and such weapons as intrigue, deceit, and gossip. It was their very powerlessness that forced medieval women to ridicule, gossip, and use other intrigues to gain their ends (Hanawalt, 1988, pp. 188, 207). Spreading gossip was a means to gain power, albeit a potentially dangerous one if allowed to get out of control.

The Power of Gossip

"Good Lord, how many kingdoms, how many countries and how many good people have been destroyed by mischievous gossip." With these words Christine de Pisan describes the power of gossip (Lawson, 1985, p. 127). To understand this power in medieval society we must remember that in the Middle Ages the chief source of vital information was oral narrative, a means of communication characterized more than any other by uncritical acceptance of what is said (Gurevich, 1990, pp. 1–8). Not only was communication predominantly oral, but the medieval legal system was mainly oral, in the sense that verdicts were often delivered upon sworn oaths of the plaintiff or the defendant. In legal proceedings witnesses were often used as well as juries. The twelve-member juries were mostly people (often neighbors of the litigants) who, before coming to the court, knew the truth of the matters at issue and were therefore more witnesses to than judges of the fact (Maitland, 1908, *passim*).

The power of gossip in medieval society also arose from its social structure, which was highly hierarchic, with strict and well defined codes of behavior for every social class. Social immobility was accompanied by what may be defined as "topographical stagnation." People traveled little and very seldom changed their place of habitation; if they did, they generally moved only a short distance. People lived in remote, relatively small, and therefore closed communities (in villages, cities, castles, or monasteries), each ruled by its specific laws and codes of behavior.

Together, these factors—the credibility of oral information, the strict codes of behavior, as well as immobility and closeness of the relatively small communities—gave gossip great potency. Gossip was often accepted as truth, and, given the strict codes of behavior, gossip could destroy people's reputation and their position in society. Gossip spread to all members of the small, close communities of the Middle Ages, and often a consensual "group opinion" developed.

Gossip was therefore very much feared. The specter of acquiring a bad reputation at a lord's court, or of being the butt of malicious gossip haunted many noble families, some of which pursued with vengeance those who were said to have spoken ill of them. Often, then, gossip was too dangerous a weapon to use (Hanawalt, 1988, p. 208). Indeed courtly literature emphasizes the consequences of the power of gossip. One of the most popular medieval courtly romances, the *Chatelaine of Vergy* (ca. 1288), makes it a point to demonstrate to its readers (or listeners) that there exists a class of people who make so good a pretense of loyalty and discretion that one cannot but trust them; yet when it happens that someone opens his heart to them, acquainting them with his love and private affairs, they spread the knowledge abroad and make it a matter for raillery and mirth. Moreover, the romance attempts to show that an act of spreading gossip can cause such tragedies as death and suicide (Maratasso, 1972, pp. 138–51). A *lais* of Mary of France (from the second half of the twelfth century) attempts to teach its readers a similar lesson. In *Le Fresne* two neighboring knights took wives, and one of the ladies gave birth to boy twins. The other lady, upon hearing the news, said in front of her household that it had never occurred to her that a woman gave birth to two sons at once, nor ever will, unless two men are the cause of it. Those in the house took note of these words, which were repeated and became widely known throughout all Brittany. In the same year the slanderer herself conceived twins and gave birth to two daughters, which grieved and distressed her greatly. She lamented to herself: "The worst has befallen me! / He who calumniates and lies about another / Is completely unaware of what has before him / One may gossip about someone / Who is better fit for praise than oneself" (Freeman, 1988, p. 251; Burgess and Busby, 1986, pp. 60–62). To ward off shame she decides to murder one of the children, thinking that she would rather make amends to God than shame and dishonor herself (Burgess and Busby, 1986, p. 62). In this *lais* slander and fear of gossip, not simply gossip alone as in the *Chatelaine of Vergy*, produce tragedy. Due to the intervention of a maid, none of the babies is murdered; instead one is removed from the house and abandoned near an abbey where she is brought up. When after many years the daughter is found, the mother confesses her deed before her husband and says: "Once, in my great wickedness, I slandered my neighbor. I spoke ill of her two children, but in fact I did myself harm" (Burgess and Busby, p. 61). In the Middle Ages "gossip" or "public rumor" could ruin an individual, or at least his or her reputation, which later often could not be rebuilt.

In a "close" and predominantly oral society like the medieval one, where gossip could destroy one's honor, reputation, or even one's life, it was greatly feared. Nevertheless, and in spite of repeated warnings and admonitions against gossip in the various genres of medieval literature, people from all the classes gossiped. Women had the reputation of gossips, and indeed, as a result of their status in society, did gossip more than men; but men and children gossiped as well. Gossip served as a means to achieve their ends as well as a powerful weapon against their enemies. Moreover, it served as an informal control over relationships between the sexes. Furthermore, the gossip of men and women contained similarities as well as differences. In the whole, men's gossip was more "idle," whereas women's gossip had often well-defined motives and objects; the object was more often than not political, social, or domestic power. In the Middle Ages, as in other chapters in human history—gossip was both used and abused.

13 | Gossip, Gossipers, Gossipees

Marianne E. Jaeger, Anne A. Skleder, Bruce Rind, and Ralph L. Rosnow

GOSSIP IS A SLIPPERY subject. Everyone seems to know what everyone else means by gossip, except the researchers who have wrestled with it as a technical term. Although it is described as a pleasurable activity, its consequences may be anything but pleasurable for its targets. It is often defined as idle talk about trivial matters, yet it serves important functions, both intra- and interpersonally. It is a universal activity, yet some of us seem to gossip more frequently than others.

Our knowledge about gossip and gossiping is rudimentary. Some researchers acknowledge that gossip gets little serious attention, but add that it is a waste of time for investigators to study such a trivial activity. What little we do know about gossip—that it has derogatory connotations—comes from such diverse sources as literary, religious, and philosophical writings, as well as anthropological studies that document sanctions against the telling of unfounded stories about others. Some investigators have attempted, however, to repair the good name of gossip. Levin and Arluke (1985), for example, offer instances of positive gossip in an empirical study of its contents drawn from interpersonal contexts, from conversations overheard among college students, and from comments appearing in gossip columns in the mass media. Aaron Ben-Ze'ev (Chapter 1), in turn, provides a philosophical analysis of the premise that gossip is an intrinsically valuable activity.

Indeed, a number of writers agree that, despite its apparently trivial or superfluous nature, gossip serves a number of useful psychological functions. According to Levin and Arluke (1987), we gossip to enhance our self-esteem or status in a group, to obtain information that serves our need to evaluate ourselves through comparison with others in a reasonable and nonpainful way, to establish or maintain social cohesiveness within a group, to define ambiguous or anxiety-laden situations, or more simply to entertain or relax. Ben-Ze'ev highlights the role of gossip in satisfying certain basic human needs, namely, the need to know the personal and intimate details of others' lives in order better to understand and control our own lives, and a so-called tribal need, the need to be accepted by an exclusive group characterized by intimate and affective ties. Rosnow and Georgoudi (1985) outline three general, though not mutually exclusive, functions of gossip that operate at the individual and interpersonal level: to inform, to influence, and to entertain.

Attempts to describe the typical gossiper result in seemingly disparate portraits. For example, we recognize the social isolate, the least popular member of a group, who suffers feelings of worthlessness, social anxiety, and need for esteem from others and who gossips to gain attention and status or esteem from others (cf. Levin and Arluke, 1987; Ben-Ze'ev, Chapter 1). On the other hand, gossipers are "often quite sensitive, curious, social-minded and involved" (Ben-Ze'ev, Chapter 1), and it is the nongossiper who is uninterested in the affairs of others and who has no friends to gossip with or about (Levin and Arluke, 1987). Although these disparate claims seem intuitively correct, there is, unfortunately, no direct evidence to support them.

At best, there is only sparse indirect evidence, garnered through the study of rumor, concerning the nature of the gossiper. Rosnow and his associates, in an exploratory study of the spread of the "Paul is dead" rumor,[1] found that people who spread this rumor had fewer dates and got together less frequently with friends than those who had heard the story but had not passed it on (Rosnow and Fine, 1976a). Rosnow (in press) metaanalyzed seven studies that showed that anxious people are more likely to transmit a rumor, and he found the average effect ($r = .48$ or $d = 1.10$) was comparable in magnitude with the linear effects of several well-known and important situational factors that affect behavior (cf. Funder and Ozer, 1983). However, it is problematic whether results pertaining to rumormongering also apply to gossiping.

And who are the targets of gossip? The subject of gossip columns, talk shows, or "people in the news" features on television and in print concerns either the ordinary, everyday aspects of the lives of famous people, or extraordinary events in the lives of ordinary people (cf. Levin and Arluke, 1987). Ben-Ze'ev suggests further that the targets of gossip may be the subject of envy (Chapter 1). It is almost a given that the target of gossip is someone familiar to its participants, but little else is known about the person others are discussing behind his or her back. If we know little of the characteristics of the gossiper, however, we know even less about the targets of the garden variety gossip that occurs in face-to-face interactions.

The purpose of the present investigation is to learn something about the gossiper and the gossipee, as well as about commonsense views of the nature of gossip. By examining the characteristics of the gossiper empirically, we may confirm or modify the seemingly disparate portraits of the gossipmonger outlined above.

One obstacle to studying gossip empirically is its secretive nature. According to Sabini and Silver (1982), we all gossip, but feel that we should not. Therefore, we gossip discreetly. Rosnow and Georgoudi (1985) point out that feelings of privacy and protection are necessary preconditions of gossip. The empirical investigator faces the difficult task, then, of finding individuals who are willing to talk about their gossip or the gossip of others. Another precondition of gossip is sociability (Rosnow and Georgoudi, 1985). Gossip rarely occurs among strangers or among acquaintances whose relationship is characterized by aloofness. As a result, the situation in which one attempts to search for gossip should be characterized by a level of amiable familiarity among potential gossipers and gossipees. A third precondition of gossip is a common frame of reference (Rosnow and Georgoudi, 1985). This frame of reference may include shared values and attitudes and access to background knowledge within which a particular piece of gossip may be understood. In the words of Levin and Arluke (1987), "in order to gossip together, people must share the same set of values and must know a third person in common whose behavior either upholds or violates those values" (p. 24).

We chose to examine gossiping within a college sorority, because many of the characteristics of sororities provide the preconditions for gossip to occur. They are exclusive groups of young women, situated within the wider university population, which are characterized by a sense of community and communality. A shared frame of reference is virtually insured in such a group. Young women no doubt choose a particular sorority because the values and goals of the group are similar to their own. Furthermore, all potential sorority sisters go through a stage of pledging in the sorority, which further socializes them in its prevailing values and goals. Sororities are usually small enough that everyone knows everyone else, and their relative exclusivity provides a sense of privacy and protection from the hurly-burly of life in a large university.

Method

Overview

We initially made contact with a sorority to obtain approval to conduct a study about gossip within the group. Once permission was obtained, the present study was introduced to the sisters as a study of "communication networks," and information about their sisters and themselves was obtained by means of confidential or anonymous questionnaires in two phases.

Participants

The participants were thirty-six women who belonged to a service sorority at a large public university in the northeastern United States. The sisters ranged in age from eighteen to twenty-two (traditional college age). Many of the sisters lived on campus, either in the sorority house or in campus dormitories, while others lived off campus.

Questionnaires

Questionnaire 1. In the first questionnaire, which was filled out anonymously, the sisters were asked a number of questions about their fellow sisters. The purpose of the first questionnaire was (a) to identify who gossiped about whom and from that information to determine how frequently someone gossiped or was the target of gossip; (b) to determine the friendship groupings or cliques within the sorority and the relative popularity of each sister within the sorority; and (c) to determine the extent to which each sister was viewed as likable or not. The fifteen sisters who returned the first questionnaire were considered anonymous informants to help us determine the extent of gossiping in the sorority.

Respondents were first provided with a list of 143 adjectives and a list of all the sisters in the sorority and asked to indicate, next to the name of each sister, those adjectives that best described each sister. No minimum or maximum number of adjectives was suggested. Second, they were asked to list, for each sister, others in the sorority that the particular sister tended to gossip about. The respondents were instructed to write "no one" if they felt a particular sister did not engage in gossip about others. The sisters were asked to make a best guess if they were uncertain, but to indicate with an X next to a sister's name if the respondent did not know the person well enough even to make a guess. As a check on the extent to which each sister gossiped, the respondents were also asked to indicate, for each sister, how much that person gossiped in general by rating her on a scale from 0 (indicating that the sister never, or hardly ever, gossiped) to 100 (indicating that the sister gossiped all the time). Respondents were also asked to list, for each sister, that person's close friends in the sorority. Again, they were instructed to make a best guess in case of uncertainty or to indicate whether they did not know the sister well enough even to make a guess.

In the final portion of the questionnaire, respondents were asked to define gossip, in their own words. They were instructed to be as brief or thorough as they wished.

Questionnaire 2. The second questionnaire consisted of measures of various personality traits that have been thought to characterize gossipers.

Need for approval by others was measured by the Marlowe-Crowne Social-Desirability Scale. The higher the score, the more strongly motivated the respondent is to seek the approval of important others, and it follows that the person's behaviors should be bent to serve this aim (Crowne and Marlowe, 1964, p. 39). If gossiping is normatively acceptable, we should expect those people with a high need for approval and the expectation that approval can be attained by behaving in culturally acceptable ways to be more likely to gossip. On the other hand, if gossiping is normatively unacceptable, we should expect that gossipers will be lower in the need for approval than nongossipers.

Self-esteem was measured by Rosenberg's Self-Esteem Scale (Rosenberg, 1965). The picture of the individual with low self-esteem that emerged from Rosenberg's validation research corresponds to the nature of the gossiper as hypothesized by others. Individuals with low self-esteem were characterized by self-rejection, self-dissatisfaction, and self-contempt, and they were more likely to be on the periphery of a social group.

The Taylor Manifest Anxiety Scale (MAS) was used to measure trait or chronic anxiety (Taylor, 1953). This scale had been used in previous research on rumor by Rosnow and his colleagues, which demonstrated a consistent relationship between anxiety and awareness of a rumor (Anthony, 1973) or propensity to transmit a rumor (Jaeger, Anthony, and Rosnow, 1980).

Respondents were asked to indicate their names on the second questionnaire so that their responses could be related to information obtained in the first questionnaire. They were, however, assured of the confidentiality of their responses. Previous research implied that more honest responses can be expected when confidentiality is guaranteed (Esposito, Agard, and Rosnow, 1984).

Thirty-one sisters returned the second questionnaire, for an 86 percent return rate.

Procedure

At a monthly meeting of the sorority, one of the authors introduced the present study as an investigation of "communication networks" and obtained the necessary informed consent from each sister. The first questionnaire was distributed to each sister at this meeting. The sisters were instructed to complete the questionnaire in the privacy of their own rooms, to seal the completed questionnaire in the envelope provided with the questionnaire, and to place the sealed envelope in an enclosed box placed in the sorority house within two weeks. They were told not to discuss their answers with the other sisters.

When the sisters dropped off the first questionnaire, they collected the second questionnaire, which was to be mailed to the investigator in the stamped, addressed envelope provided. Reminders were sent to the sisters two weeks later, and the investigator later attended the next monthly meeting in order to ask all the sisters to complete the second questionnaire even if they had not completed the first one.

Derived Measures

In order to reduce the data to a manageable form, various measures were derived from the initial questionnaire, most of which involved obtaining scores for each sister by taking the mean ratings provided by the fifteen informants.

Likability. The 143 adjectives used by the respondents in the first questionnaire to describe each sister were personality-trait words that had been given likableness ratings in a previous study (Rosnow, Wainer, and Arms, 1969). These ratings ranged from -42 (the least likable trait) to $+37$ (the most likable trait), and had a test-retest reliability of $r = .97$. Likability scores for each sister in the sorority were determined by obtaining the mean of those previously derived ratings; these means ranged from -6.88 (most unlikable) to 25.95 (most likable).

Gossipers. From the informants' reports about who gossiped about whom, a general gossiping propensity score was derived. This indicated the mean number of people, averaged across the informants, each sister was reported to have gossiped about.[2] Each sister was then classified into a high, moderate, or low gossiper group using cut-off points that roughly divided the distribution of gossiping propensity scores into thirds. These cut-off points were adjusted slightly in order to ensure that sisters within a group were more similar to other group members than to sisters in the neighboring group. As a result, fourteen were identified as low gossipers, thirteen were identified as moderate gossipers, and nine were identified as high gossipers.

Gossipees. From the same information given above, a score was derived that reflected the propensity for each sister to be the target of gossip. This score indicated the mean number of people, averaged across informants, who were reported to gossip about a given individual.[3] Each sister was again classified into a high, moderate, or low gossipee group, using cut-off points that roughly divided the distribution of propensity to be a target of gossip into thirds. Again, these cut-off points were adjusted slightly to ensure that sisters within a group were more similar to each other than to sisters in the neighboring group. As a result, twelve sisters were identified as low gossipees, eleven as moderate gossipees, and thirteen as high gossipees.

Popularity. A sociometric matrix was constructed to reflect the modal perceptions, based on data from the informants, of who chose whom as her close friends in the sorority. From this matrix, it was possible to determine how many individuals a given sister was reported having as close friends. It was also possible to determine the number of times a given sister was mentioned as a close friend of another sister.

Results

We first examine the characteristics of the gossiper and of the gossipee. Then we present a more fine-grained analysis of who gossips about whom. In the discussion section, we touch on the commonsense understandings of gossip among sisters in this sorority.

Gossipers

High, moderate, and low gossipers were compared on three personality measures: their need for social approval, their self-esteem, and their anxiety; they were also compared on their likableness; and on three indicators of popularity. For each independent variable, the following set of contrasts was examined (cf. Rosenthal and Rosnow, 1985, p. 1): 1) comparison of high and low gossipers, 2) comparison of high gossipers with the average of the moderate and low gossiper groups, 3) comparison of low gossipers with the average of the moderate and high gossiper groups, and 4) comparison of the moderate gossipers with the average of the high and low gossiper groups. We report both significance levels and the effect size r of these contrasts. By way of comparison, Cohen (1969) defines effect sizes of $r = .1$, .3, and .5 as small, medium, and large effects, respectively, although even small effects can have great practical significance. For example, aspirin's effect in preventing heart attacks was $r = .03$ in one major biomedical study (see Rosnow and Rosenthal, 1989). The effects obtained here were substan-

Table 13.1. Means and standard deviations of those with high, moderate, or low propensity to gossip on need for social approval, self-esteem, anxiety, likableness, and popularity

Dependent Variables	Gossipers		
	High (n = 7)	Moderate (n = 11)	Low (n = 12)
Need for social approval	14.29 (5.79)	14.91 (5.11)	19.67 (5.96)
Self-esteem	31.00 (5.16)	31.64 (3.85)	30.75 (3.84)
Anxiety	17.14 (4.85)	12.09 (4.72)	12.33 (5.38)
	High (n = 9)	Moderate (n = 13)	Low (n = 12)
Likableness	10.25 (8.87)	12.75 (9.40)	18.76 (5.92)
Number of close friends	2.11 (1.27)	3.08 (1.32)	1.64 (1.01)
Number of times chosen as close friend	2.67 (1.22)	2.92 (1.89)	1.50 (0.86)

tially larger than that effect. Means and standard deviations of the high, moderate, and low gossiper groups are presented in Table 13.1.

Low gossipers scored significantly higher in need for social approval than moderate and high gossipers combined ($F(1,29) = 5.74$, $p = .02$, r 0 .41). The related contrast comparing high and low gossipers was also significant ($F(1,27) = 4.05$, $p = .05$, r 0 .36). None of the comparisons on self-esteem was significant (all F s < .25). Indeed all groups were equally high on self-esteem. High gossipers were significantly more anxious than moderate and low gossipers combined ($F(1,27) = 5.16$, $p = .03$, r 0 .40). The related contrast comparing high and low gossipers was also significant ($F(1,27) = 4.05$, $p = .05$, r 0 .36).

Low gossipers were found to be significantly more likable than the moderate and high gossipers combined ($F(1,33) = 6.85$, $p = .01$, r 0 .41). The related contrast comparing high and low gossipers also indicated that high gossipers were perceived to be significantly less likable than low gossipers ($F(1,33) = 6.11$, $p = .02$, r 0 .40). Moderate gossipers were reported as having more close friends in the sorority than high and low gossipers combined ($F(1,33) = 8.24$, $p = .007$, r 0 .45). In addition, low gossipers had significantly fewer friends than the moderate or high gossipers combined ($F(1,33)$ = 5.36, p = .03, r 0 .37). A similar pattern emerges when the number of times a sister is named as a close friend of someone else is examined. Low gossipers were less frequently identified as someone else's close friend ($F(1,33)$ = 7.25, p = .01, r 0 .42). The related contrast comparing high and low gossipers approached the conventional 5 percent significance level ($F(1,33)$ = 3.82, p = .06, r 0 .32). In addition, there was a nonsignificant trend for moderate gossipers to be named more frequently as someone else's close friend ($F(1,33)$ = 2.95, p = .09, r 0 .29).

Gossipees

There was a high correlation between the tendency to gossip and the frequency with which sisters were named as a target of gossip (r = .76). Because of this high correlation it was expected that comparisons among high, moderate, and low gossipee groups would be similar to those found for the gossiper contrasts. Hence, the four contrasts outlined in the previous section were repeated for the high, moderate, and low gossipee groups. The means and standard deviations of the high, moderate, and low gossipee groups on the personality and popularity measures are presented in Table 13.2.

Sisters least frequently named as targets of gossip were significantly higher in need for social approval than those most frequently named ($F(1,27)$ = 4.94, p = .03, r 0 .39). In addition, low gossipees scored higher in need for social approval than moderate and high gossipers combined ($F(1,27)$ = 4.85, p = .04, r 0 .38). None of the contrasts on self-esteem even approached significance (F s < .36). Contrary to the findings when gossipers were contrasted, none of the contrasts on anxiety approached significance (F s < .09).

Those sisters most frequently named as targets of gossip were perceived as less likable than those who were least frequently the target of gossip ($F(1,33)$ = 11.96 p = .002, r 0 .52). The related contrast comparing high gossipees with moderate and low gossipees was also significant and impressively large ($F(1,33)$ = 10.80 p = .002, r 0 .50). Those least frequently named as targets of gossip had significantly fewer close friends than others ($F(1,33)$ = 11.63 p = .002, r 0 .51). Those most frequently named as targets of gossip also had more close friends than the low gossipees ($F(1,33)$ = 10.50 p = .003, r 0 .49) or the low and moderate gossipees combined ($F(1,33)$ = 4.52 p = .04, r 0 .35). A similar

Table 13.2. Means and standard deviations of those with high, moderate, or low propensity to be named as targets of gossip on need for social approval, self-esteem, anxiety, likableness, and popularity

Dependent Variables	Gossipers		
	High (n = 11)	Moderate (n = 8)	Low (n = 11)
Need for social approval	14.36 (5.78)	15.63 (5.34)	19.73 (5.75)
Self-esteem	31.18 (3.99)	30.38 (3.16)	31.64 (4.88)
Anxiety	13.09 (5.91)	13.88 (5.59)	13.27 (4.92)
	High (n = 13)	Moderate (n = 11)	Low (n = 12)
Likableness	8.90 (9.56)	15.68 (7.87)	19.37 (4.47)
Number of close friends	2.85 (1.35)	2.64 (1.36)	1.33 (0.65)
Number of times chosen as close friend	3.08 (1.75)	2.19 (1.47)	1.58 (0.79)

pattern emerged when the frequency with which the sisters were named as someone else's close friend was examined. High gossipees had significantly more close friends than low gossipees alone ($F(1,33) = 7.02$ $p = .01$, r 0 .42) or the low and moderate groups combined ($F(1,33) = 5.97$ $p = .02$, r 0 .39). The contrast comparing low gossipees with moderate and high gossipees was also significant ($F(1,33) = 4.40$ $p = .04$, r 0 .34).

Gossiping and Friendship

Even though a sorority shares common values and goals, smaller groupings or cliques are likely to appear. A sociogram constructed from the friendship choice sociometric matrix revealed a number of more or less interconnected clusters of friends or cliques (groups where three or more individuals mutually choose each other as friends [cf. Festinger, Shachter, and Back, 1950]) and a variety of friendship pairs (see Figure 13.1). Two clusters stand out in contrast when gossiping tendencies

Figure 13.1. Sociogram indicating friendship choices within the sorority

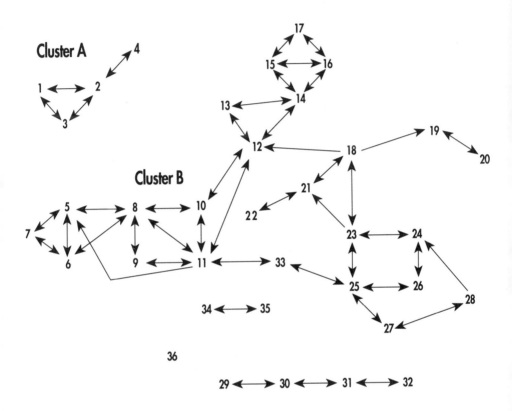

are examined within the sorority. Cluster A has no connections with other cliques in the sorority, and the members of this group rarely gossip or are the targets of gossip. Cluster B, on the other hand, is connected to at least two other identifiable cliques in the sorority, and the members of this group are among the most gossiping and gossiped about sisters in the sorority.

We wished to determine whether sisters gossiped about their close friends, nonfriends, or both. To examine who gossiped about whom, specific targets of gossip for each sister were identified through the modal ratings of the informants. Gossipers and their targets who could be reliably identified (i.e., where at least one-third of the informants had agreed on whom had been gossiped about) are indicated in Figure 13.2, which superimposes who gossips about whom in the friendship

Figure 13.2. Gossipers and their targets of gossip in relation to friendship choices

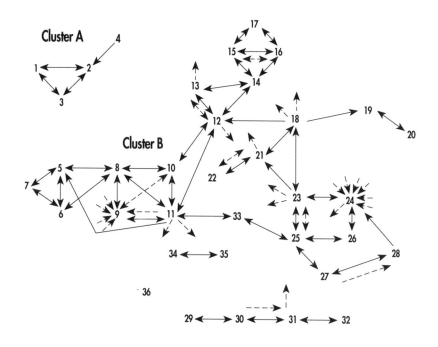

Note: Dashed lines indicate gossip targeted at close friends, short outward arrows indicate gossip targeted at nonfriends, short inward arrows indicate sisters targeted by nonfriends.

sociogram. Sisters were as likely to gossip about their close friends as about other women in the sorority. There were also seven instances of mutual gossiping where a sister was also the target of her target's gossip. Mutual gossiping was more likely to occur between sisters who were mutual friends than between members of different friendship clusters.

Discussion

This study was our initial investigation of the characteristics of the gossiper and the gossipee. Although gossiping can be found everywhere, we limited our search for gossiping to a single group of individuals within which the preconditions of gossip would be met, namely a college sorority, and thus we limit also the generality of our findings. We may, nonetheless, shed some light on the seemingly disparate portraits of the gossiper that exist in the literature.

Within the group that we studied, the individuals with a tendency to gossip were perceived to be less likable than those who gossiped less or not at all. Because we asked the informants to describe each sister before we asked anything about their gossiping tendencies, it is unlikely that the lower likableness of the gossiper is a measurement artifact resulting from being labeled a gossip. Although gossipers were generally less favorably perceived by others, it did not in fact emerge that they had lower self-esteem than others. Nor did they have a greater need for social approval; in fact, the opposite appears to be the case. Individuals who rarely gossip have a greater need for approval from others. Sisters with a greater tendency to gossip about people in the sorority were, however, more anxious than others; this finding is reminiscent of research results indicating that anxious individuals are more likely to pass on rumors about unknown others (Jaeger et al., 1980).

Contrary to other characterizations of gossipers, the most frequent gossipers in this study do not appear to be social isolates. People are necessary to gossip with and to gossip about. The sociogram identified a clique of some of the most popular sisters in the sorority (see cluster B in Figure 13.1). According to the member of our research team who had direct contact with the sorority, this clique appeared to contain the "movers and shakers," that is, the more active and influential sisters in the sorority. The members of this clique were also among the most active gossipers and the ones most frequently gossiped about. In general, however, moderate gossipers tended to have more close friends within the sorority than high gossipers, whereas those who rarely gossiped had the fewest. Within the sorority, gossipers were also more likely to be the targets of gossip. In general, therefore, the characteristics of the gossipees were similar to those of the gossiper, with a couple of exceptions. Like gossipers, the gossipees were less likable than others, yet they had esteem for themselves and a lower need for social approval. Although gossipers were generally more anxious than others, gossipees were no more or less anxious than those less frequently the targets of gossip. Gossipees also had the greatest number of close friends within the sorority, and were most frequently seen to be the close friends of other sisters.

We have acknowledged some of the seemingly contradictory views on gossip. Now we ask, what does gossip mean to those who provided us with information within the sorority? Although we received comments about gossip from only nine of the sisters, their responses reflect the complex and sometimes contradictory nature of gossip. About half of the remarks emphasized the negative nature of gossip, either explicitly or implicitly. For example, gossip is "catty remarks" or "when someone talks about another person in a negative way." Or, gossip is implicitly negative because it involves talk about people "behind their backs." The remainder felt that gossip was basically a harmless activity that could sometimes "get out of hand"; for example, "some people definitely come close to crossing the line between innocent gossip and malicious intent to destroy a reputation." Three of the comments indicated that gossip is a source of information about others: "what's going on, and who is doing what to whom." Gossip was also seen as entertaining, "hanging out and talking" or "a fun diversion." The sociability inherent in gossip can be seen in the following excerpt: "What else do you call it when a group of friends get together and talk about what happened that day or a funny story?" That gossip could be used to influence the thoughts or feelings of others appears implicit in the views that gossip involves talking about another "in a negative way," or when it involves "malicious intent to destroy a reputation." Clearly, the way our informants construe gossip reflects the theorized nature and functions of gossip.

The present investigation confirms certain accepted truths about gossip even as it calls others into question. Gossip, according to our informants, serves to inform, entertain, and/or influence perceptions of others. Gossip may be harmless, but it may also involve negative intent. Our results contradict the image of a gossiper as a social isolate with low self-esteem who gossips to gain social approval. Whether our results in fact serve to revise the accepted truth about gossipers is a question we have begun to investigate further. As Rosnow and Georgoudi (1985) point out, what constitutes gossip is context dependent. A piece of information may be gossip in one context, information or news in another, depending on the nature of the social exchange and the intention behind the act. Characteristics of the gossiper and the functions of gossip may also vary according to the nature of the social group to which the gossiper belongs. We studied a college sorority, membership within which already may have met subjects' need for affiliation, self-esteem, and social approval. We plan next to undertake an investigation of a college fraternity. Fraternities, like sororities, provide the necessary preconditions for gossip, and like sororities, they are exclusive social groups characterized by mutual choice between the group and its members. Here, too, we might expect that gossip may serve needs other than those for affiliation, esteem, and social approval. However, gossip is stereotypically a female activity, so it is possible that the nature of gossip and of the gossiper and gossipee would differ in this exclusively male domain.

Gossip is a slippery subject, but not so slippery that it cannot be studied. The study of gossip, gossipers, and gossipees in different contexts may encourage the theoretical attention gossip deserves by confirming or revising certain accepted truths or by raising new questions as yet unasked.

14 | Medical Gossip and Rumor: Their Role in the Lay Referral System

Jerry M. Suls and Franklin Goodkin

MEDICAL GOSSIP AND RUMOR can arise from a range of sources: from the alarm or assurance expressed by a relative or friend, from information provided by the mass media, or from organized groups offering alternatives to conventional medical treatment. In each case, information about health and illness is transmitted by individuals with no medical training whose proposed treatments or claims undergo no expert systematic review. The implications are important because medical gossip and rumor can significantly influence an individual's decision to seek medical attention.

There has been little systematic study of medical gossip and rumor and their effects on health and health care. Practically, this area of study has much to offer to the understanding of how people use or fail to use health care facilities, and theoretical value lies in the fact that medical gossip and rumor are continuously available and serve as models to determine the validity of hypotheses regarding gossip and rumor in general. Medical gossip and rumor may adversely affect health care by leading patients to reject medical attention when care is needed or, conversely, to overuse a physician's time.

Medical psychologists and sociologists have long recognized the importance of friends and relatives for health behaviors, what people do to prevent future health problems, as well as illness behaviors, what people do to assess their health or find remedies. Suchman (1974) found that three-quarters of the symptoms described to a physician had first been discussed with a layperson, typically a relative. Lay consultation is believed to be one factor that explains why most symptoms of illness are either ignored or receive nonmedical attention. Only about one-third of those with physical symptoms refer themselves for professional medical consultation. For example, in a prospective diary study with women, there was one medical consultation for every eighteen symptom episodes (Scambler, Scambler, and Craig, 1981). If the symptoms untreated by physicians are mild and do not indicate diseases that require medical intervention, of course, then people ignore them wisely. But, in fact, symptoms in need of expert attention are frequently not being referred for professional consultation (Ingham and Miller, 1979). For example, a study using a mobile health clinic and an extensive battery of medical tests on citizens of a borough in the United Kingdom found 57 percent of the 3,160 subjects presented symptoms of sufficient severity to require additional referral (Epsom, 1978). These studies establish the important point that most symptoms do not lead to medical consultation; this phenomenon has been called the "illness iceberg" (Scambler and Scambler, 1985). Stated simply, many people underuse professional medical services.

To complicate the picture, however, a large proportion of the people who do seek professional medical attention to report symptoms have no demonstrable disease. Studies estimate that 25 to 40 percent of all patients seeking primary care have no major medical disease, and 30 to 60 percent of all visits to primary care physicians involve symptoms for which no serious underlying medical cause can be detected (Barsky, 1981; Backett, Heady, and Evans, 1954). Of course, in some portion of the patient population there may be underlying disease that goes undetected, but for others medical visits may be prompted by hypochondriacal tendencies. Finally, laypeople may label as severe some symptoms that are benign, such as those caused by stress. It must be recognized, of course, that contemporary biomedical science and practice are not error-free.

Lay interpretation of symptoms has been discussed by Leventhal, Meyer, and Nerenz (1980) in terms of common-sense representations. A common-sense representation refers to the symptoms that lay people associate with disease. When a man diagnosed with essential hypertension reports that he knows his blood pressure is elevated when he has headaches, this represents an inaccurate lay interpretation of his condition. Although elevated blood pressure does not cause headaches, the belief that the two are related can influence the patient's decision to take medication (Meyer, Leventhal, and Gutmann, 1985). It follows that such beliefs may also influence the layperson's choice to inappropriately seek medical attention or inappropriately terminate treatment based on his or her misinterpretation of the symptoms. Thus, the man in our example may notice he has had no recent headaches and decide to stop taking antihypertensive medication. The larger point is that both failure to seek needed medical care and consultation for unnecessary care are common events that reflect the result of marked disjunctions between lay interpretations of illness and medical perspectives on disease (Scambler and Scambler, 1985). To anticipate our argument, some portion of the disjunction may result from medical gossip and rumor.

The disjunction between professional medical conceptions of illness and illness behavior and those of lay people may result from several factors, some of which, such as access to medical care, economic and geographic factors, psychological stress, and hypochondriacal tendencies, are acknowledged by the medical community. In addition, social psychological factors have been identified. Freidson (1970) observes that "what the layman recognizes as a symptom of illness is in part a function of deviation from the culturally and historically variable standard of normality established by everyday experience" (p. 285). What the layperson understands to be a sign of illness is defined partly by the lay referral structure to which he or she belongs, that is, the network of personal influences—friends, relatives, neighbors—who organize "the process of becoming ill by pressing the sufferer into or away from the professional consulting room" (Freidson, 1970, p. 292). This network not only provides lay consultants to whom the individual can turn for advice but also influences the extent to which the lay culture directs individual's actions (Scambler and Scambler, 1985, p. 39).

In some instances, particularly when the lay culture's perspective is more or less congruent with that of the medical establishment, the lay referral system facilitates the use of professional health care services. Sometimes, however, the lay system may inhibit health service utilization. The latter probably results from several different factors that are currently not well understood. It is plausible, however, that friends and relatives may fail to understand the significance of symptoms or that they may reject mainstream medical care and instead recommend the exploration of alternative forms of care, such as self-care or treatment by folk practitioners.

Personal communication in the lay referral network is typically described as one-on-one conversations about the significance of physical symptoms, their likely duration, and avenues of care. The information transmitted probably originates from other sectors of the network or from the transmitter's personal experience. As noted above, this information may or may not accord with conventional medicine, but one thing is sure: it is filtered through a nonprofessional. We know from empirical studies (see Skipper and Leonard, 1965; Samora, Saunders, and Larson, 1961) that physicians' tendency to spend litte time explaining disease and treatment and to use "Medspeak," or medical jargon, with their patients contributes to misconceptions about disease.

Our analysis proposes that the lay referral system draws heavily on medical gossip and rumor as well as on personal experiences. Some cases of medical rumor and gossip originate from other members of the network, but some emerge from such impersonal sources as the mass media, which have no connection to the medical establishment and for which there may be little, if any, "gatekeeping," or critical review of information. (In fact, in these nonscientific, unreviewed sources, the more fantastic or exaggerated the claims, the better.) These nonofficial sources of medical information may be assimilated into the personal communications of the members of the lay referral network. Although many of these "nonmedical" media sources have no credibility with biomedical practitioners or scientists, we propose that their influence on the lay public may, in fact, be substantial.

The frequency with which medical gossip and rumor is transmitted between close or casual acquaintances is unknown and remains an important question for future research. The tabloids suggest, however, that medical gossip and rumor are common. The following lists show the medically-related gossip and rumor topics in just two issues of the *Sun* and the *Star*. At least one-third of the articles in these publications were devoted to unauthenticated information about health or illness.

Gossip

"Doogie's Acne Agony"
"Raymond Burr, 73, has tumor removed in a 4-hour surgery"
"Nichollette Sheridan fights paralyzing disease with diet"
Secret behind Michael Jackson's nose jobs
Judy Garland kept her tv show going on wine and pills
Sadam Hussein has terminal cancer

Rumor

New drug to treat hypertension invented by teenager
Poison from tainted food can be a miracle drug for eye and neu-
  rological disorders
Vegetarian diet for dogs
Strange allergy forces women to stay naked at all times
Paralysis from spinal cord injury can be cured using aborted fetuses
Gorilla diet makes you strong and powerful
Boy, 2, addicted to cigars
Armless patient gets a new limb from leg of corpse
Healing touch can cure any illness says psychic healer
Spices can add zest to your love life

Gossip + Rumor

Dixie Carter: Indian potion makes me twenty years younger
Fergie's Diet and exercise plan
How celebrities beat chronic fatigue syndrome

To suggest that medical gossip and rumor are integral to the lay referral system is not a radical proposal. Once their roles are acknowledged, however, the unique features and effects of gossip and rumor can be discerned.

Why Medical Gossip and Rumor?

First, some definitions. Rumor is unauthenticated information about an event or issue that is nonnormative (i.e., suspect). Gossip is (usually negative) hearsay about the personal affairs of others (Rosnow and Fine, 1976b). It is the convention to distinguish rumor from legend or folklore; rumors tend to be topical, folklore is long-term. Legends may, of course, reappear occasionally embodied as rumors, particularly in the case of medical rumors. Garlic has been proposed as a preventative for heart problems and cancer on and off for centuries. Folklore and legends are not profit making, however, whereas medical rumor may often be transmitted with the intention of making a profit. The recommendation to take chicken soup for a cold is folklore. In contrast, numerous "wonder" diets appear to be promoted exclusively for profit.

Although rumor and gossip are both forms of suspect, nonnormative hearsay, they are thought to serve different functions, which the topic of social comparison helps to elucidate (Festinger, 1954; Suls, 1977; Suls and Miller, 1977; Wills, 1981). Comparisons with other people have two primary functions: self-assessment and self-enhancement. Self-assessment refers to the process of gaining information about the accuracy or appropriateness of one's opinions, abilities, or behavior and is usually instigated when people are uncertain of their standing or what a situation means. Anxiety or fear may be accompanying emotions. Self-enhancement refers to the restoration or protection of self-esteem by comparing oneself with others worse off—so-called downward comparison (Wills, 1981). When a person is uncertain or anxious about one's performance standing, whether to vote for a particular candidate, or the significance of a new dark-colored blemish, social comparisons may provide direct evaluative information. In some cases, however, direct comparisons are unavailable or potentially embarrassing. Rumor provides an indirect source of comparison information that can clarify situations that engender anxiety and uncertainty (Schachter and Burdick, 1955). Indeed, Allport and Postman's (1947) classic experimental studies showed that rumors are more likely to be transmitted and believed by people experiencing uncertainty or anxiety. Rumor, then, may have special significance to health care because the perception of novel or debilitating physical or psychological symptoms creates uncertainty and anxiety. Lacking objective information, people should be responsive to and eager for rumors about "bugs" going around, physical signs to look for, information about the expected course of the illness, and, of course, remedies.

Rumors primarily serve a self-evaluative function, but gossip would appear to be more useful for self-enhancement. The negative information about specific people usually conveyed by gossip places the object of the gossip in a worse position in comparison to the self and constitutes a downward comparison, which should bolster the self-esteem of the recipient of the gossip (Wills, 1981). For example, learning that a celebrity has gained an enormous amount of weight may boost one's self-esteem, at least temporarily, via downward comparison obtained from gossip. Downward social comparison theory (Wills, 1981) also predicts that people who are chronically low in self-esteem or have received an acute threat to self-esteem (such as loss of a job, or a divorce) may be keen to learn of other people's misery, which increases one's own feelings of subjective well-being in the short-run. In the present context, interest in medical gossip may be motivated by general threats to self-esteem or by more specific medical/health threats to oneself.

Like rumor, gossip is an indirect source of comparison information because one does not interact with the person who is less fortunate. Taylor and Lobel's (1989) analysis of social comparison activity under threat is relevant here although they have not written about gossip per se. According to their analysis, persons under threat, such as cancer patients, frequently cope by thinking about other patients who are even sicker (Wood, Taylor, and Lichtman, 1985). Cancer patients do not prefer to interact or affiliate with these others, however, because actually seeing someone in a worse condition can produce revulsion and fear. When breast cancer patients do not have targets for downward comparison directly available, they may invent them; for example, "those other women" who seem to have so much difficulty adjusting (Taylor, Wood, and Lichtman, 1983, p. 34). In addition to cognitive fabrication of worse-off targets, gossip about people who are worse off provides an opportunity to make one's own situation seem better while avoiding actual interaction or direct exposure to more unfortunate individuals.

A conspicuous exception to the pattern is gossip that communicates positive news. For example, the tabloids frequently circulate stories about movie stars with weight problems who are reported to have conquered obesity with a miracle diet. In these cases, the gossip affords an upward comparison that serves as a source of motivation or inspiration. Given our previous discussion, one might assume that such an upward comparison would generate negative affect in the recipient of this news, particularly if the recipient had a weight problem. Positive affect can be generated by upward gossip, however, if it communicates a method that is available to the recipient to reduce weight. In other words, upward gossip should generate positive affect only if it holds out the possibility of self-improvement for the recipient; otherwise, upward gossip should be uncommon and, when it does occur, generate negative affect instead (Major, Testa, and Bylsma, 1991).

Although rumor has been conceptualized as serving an evaluative function and gossip as serving an enhancement function, the reality is more complicated. The list above shows that some tabloid stories mix rumor and gossip (e.g., a TV star uses an Indian potion to gain a more youthful appearance). In these cases, hearsay serves an evaluative and an enhancement function. Another complication concerns whether the transmitter of the gossip reaps any benefits from being the source of the gossip or rumor. We might speculate that transmitting rumors allows the sender the opportunity to build consensus and gain validation to the extent that the audience agrees; at the very least, the transmitter gains status for having special knowledge. In sum, gossip and rumor serve functions that are consistent with self-enhancement and self-evaluative motives. These functions should apply to hearsay about medicine, health, and other domains, and the implications for the health domain are especially rich.

Medical rumor and gossip can either strengthen or weaken the appeal of conventional medicine. Consider the following scenario: after a stressful day at work, you come home with a stomachache, tired, and headachy. Although you attribute the symptoms to the kind of day you had, your son mentions that your symptoms sound like those he heard precede a terrible flu going around his school. That rumor may send you to the physician's office, or at least prompt you to monitor future symptoms more carefully. Persons who are chronically negatively affective (NA), a personality trait that characterizes about 25 percent of community samples (Costa and McCrae, 1987; Watson and Clark, 1984), tend to be somatically overconcerned. This means they tend to interpret benign and minor physical sensations as possible signs of physical disease (Watson and Pennebaker, 1989). It is plausible that persons high in NA are more susceptible to medical rumors, particularly about infectious diseases, and may comprise a large proportion of those persons who overuse medical care in the absence of underlying physical disorder.

The role of medical gossip and rumor can also be seen in cases of mass psychogenic illness (i.e., epidemic transient situational disturbances). In such instances, a group of people in the same occupational setting or attending the same school exhibit physical symptoms for which no physical explanation can be found. The symptoms tend to appear during periods of extreme psychologic stress and are characterized by rapid onset. In general, the "illness" spreads among people with whom one works closely, or knows personally.

A classic example of mass psychogenic illness is the "June Bug" episode studied extensively by Kerckhoff and Back (1968). During an especially busy time of the year, an industrial plant was closed down because of a mysterious illness afflicting about one quarter of the plant's two hundred employees. The symptoms included nausea and feverishness that sent several workers to their physicians and a few to the hospital, although no objective evidence of illness was found. Upon being interviewed, many of the stricken workers reported seeing or being bitten by an insect at the plant sometime prior to symptom onset. Careful examination failed, however, to find evidence of insect bites or strange insects. After a few days, all of those affected recovered fully and there were no subsequent reports of illness. After conducting a complete examination of the plant and the victims, researchers from the Communicable Disease Center concluded that the afflicted were "victims of nothing more than extreme anxiety" (Kerckhoff and Back, 1968, p. 7). Apparently, those who became "ill" showed a classic pattern of hysterical contagion in which symptoms of stress were misinterpreted as physical illness. Most important for our discussion is that the pattern of symptoms and the supposed cause (i.e., insects) was spread via rumor and gossip among work associates.

Hearsay can also discourage people from seeking conventional care or expert opinion. A rumor has been circulating in France for some years that twenty well-known brands of food products are toxic and produce cancer (Kapferer, 1985). This rumor is interesting because it is transmitted hand-to-hand on a leaflet. Despite official denials from the food industry and governmental regulators, the rumor continues. Another medical rumor is very popular in Egypt. Despite the need for birth control in that country, a belief circulates that oral contraceptives cause weakness (DeClerque, Tsui, Abul-Ata, and Barcelona, 1986). A national survey of currently married men and women indicated that this rumor decreased the probability of current and future use by previous users and by those who never used the Pill.

Perhaps the most striking example of how medical rumor can prompt people to seek alternative care is laetrile, a sham treatment for cancer with no documented therapeutic value. False claims about the success of laetrile, which has failed all scientific tests, have prompted many cancer patients to seek laetrile therapy in clinics that make considerable profit. What makes laetrile claims especially serious is that laetrile is a highly toxic substance containing high levels of cyanide and therefore can be fatal.

An important question for further study is whether we can define more specifically the conditions in which gossip or rumor will bring people to seek conventional or alternative care, or indeed to seek no care at all. In the absence of prior systematic study, our hypotheses will necessarily be speculative, but amenable to empirical scrutiny. First, we hypothesize that people will rely more on gossip and rumor as the medical domain becomes increasingly complex. Although rumor and gossip may make outlandish claims, both forms of hearsay tend to be framed in plain and simple language. Also, because of the tendency for hearsay to become leveled and sharpened (Allport and Postman, 1947; Rosnow and Fine, 1976b), gossip and rumor will probably convey more direct messages than conventional medicine, which understands the uncertain state of medical knowledge about many diseases and makes more balanced and complex claims.

Second, to the extent that conventional medical care has had adverse consequences and little success in improving the patient's situation, people should be more responsive to gossip and rumor. The result of this tendency would be to increase the appeal of quacks or alternative forms of care. Laetrile is, again, a good example. A study of patients who self-referred for a trial of laetrile indicates that they tend to have more negative feelings about conventional care (Cooper, 1983). Laetrile and vitamin treatments are heavily used unconventional treatments that may gain currency, in part due to gossip and rumor, because conventional medicine has only limited success in treating cancer.

A third hypothesis is related to a classic phenomenon of attitude research. Independent of an individual's history of success with conventional care or the complexity of the particular health domain, there are sociopsychological factors that may contribute to people believing and acting on unsound claims. A message conveyed by an incredible communicator may have a minimal impact initially, but gain impact over time (the so-called "sleeper effect," Hovland and Weiss, 1951). This effect happens only under certain conditions: when recipients do not learn who the source is until after receiving the original message, but then some time later forget the source. The basis of the sleeper effect is that people will reject a message from an unreliable source if they know the source before hearing it. If the source is not known until afterward, however, the audience will consider the message with an open mind only to reject it afterward. After some weeks, the information has had a chance to "sink in," but the source may be forgotten, leading to more persuasion over time (Gruder et al., 1978).

We think medical gossip and rumor may frequently gain its persuasiveness in just this way. A finding reported by Barbour et al. (1985) suggests that the sleeper effect may have been operating when researchers found that five of twelve patients receiving laetrile therapy volunteered that the "nontoxic" nature of laetrile was important in their decision to choose that treatment. Clearly, claims that laetrile is "nontoxic" can only have arisen from a nonexpert source. If a persuasive message about the merits of laetrile were presented without first mentioning the source, the audience might have been receptive to the information until learning the source. With the passage of time, the noncredible source may be forgotten, and the nontoxic benefits of laetrile recalled.

In view of the prevalence of medical rumor and gossip in the tabloid media, sleeper effects regarding the health domain are highly likely. Systematic study of the extent to which fantastic stories of cures by psychics, exotic plants, and bizarre procedures promoted by tabloids or described in fiction are believed deserves empirical attention. Our reasoning suggests the following hypothesis: belief in medical gossip and rumor will be greater when the source of the hearsay is not revealed until weeks or months after the message is received. Another hypothesis is based on the notion that chronic illnesses tend to be associated with more diverse symptoms than acute illnesses. Consequently, the former may create greater uncertainty and anxiety, independent of illness severity. If our earlier reasoning about the role of uncertainty and anxiety is correct, then hearsay about chronic illness should be more common than about acute illness.

In order to study the generic features of gossip and rumor, past researchers have tended either to wait for a relevant piece of hearsay or to plant elaborate stories in the hope they would be transmitted (Schachter and Burdick, 1955). Our observation is that medical gossip and rumor is everpresent and available from a wide variety of sources, making medical and health domains excellent vantage points from which to study general patterns of rumor and gossip transmission and factors that increase or decrease transmission reception. We hope that this chapter will provide impetus for the systematic study of medical hearsay and its consequences for health care.

15 | The Tendency to Gossip as a Psychological Disposition: Constructing a Measure and Validating It

Ofra Nevo, Baruch Nevo, and
Anat Derech-Zehavi

THE IDEA FOR THIS STUDY originated during long hours of case conferences, when it sometimes appeared that in discussing their clients psychologists were involved in an activity that strikingly resembled gossip. We were impressed by the similarity between the activity of analyzing patients' personal problems and what takes place in social groups when gossip occurs. The comparison was not to our liking. We would like to make sure that in spite of the similarity we are aware of the significant differences between the two activities. Psychological discourse concerning a patient is undertaken for the professional purpose of understanding the patient in order to help him. Discussion of a patient occurs within a theoretical framework for professional reasons, whereas gossip does not appear to have a conscious or explicit purpose. At staff meetings, for example, the participants seem to know the difference between gossiping and discussing cases, and whenever a discussion strays from professional seriousness, someone is bound to say something like, "Well, let's not gossip." Nevertheless, the activity at case conferences and at therapy and supervision sessions resembles gossip insofar as it concerns intimate facts about other people. In both instances people talk and exchange information about other people. Thus we were led to the present study.

As social scientists, we employed the methodology of our field. Accordingly we proceeded by reviewing the existing literature for definitions of gossip and for accounts of its nature, reasons, and functions. We then arrived at an operational definition of gossip and constructed a reliable and valid measure of the personal disposition to gossip. This furnished us with the basis for testing the relationship between vocational interests and the disposition to gossip.

Rosnow and Fine (1976b, p. 87) describe gossip as referring to "news about the affairs of another, to one's own memoirs or confessions, or to any hearsay of personal nature be it positive or negative, spoken or in print." Hannerz (1967) has rightly pointed out that the "same information may be gossip or nongossip, depending on who gives it to whom." Therefore the context and intentions of gossip must be considered, not only the nature of the information itself. Rysman (1977) traces the development of the use of the word from a positive term used to describe both sexes to a derogatory term applied principally to women. By the twentieth century the use of gossip in regard to males has become rare. If two people, one a man, the other a woman, engage in the same behavior of talking too much, the woman is likely to be called a gossip, whereas the man will not. By extension perhaps, a man who gossips is often called "an old woman."

Three approaches to gossip exist in the social science literature: the sociological-anthropological approach, the social psychological approach, and the individual approach. The sociological-anthropological approach to gossip is based on observations of various ethnic and social groups and emphasizes the social functions of gossip. Gossip transmits information in order to teach and enforce group norms. Gossip thus contributes to group cohesion, serves as means to create stronger group identification, and helps to clarify group boundaries (Colson, 1953; Gluckman, 1963; Hannerz, 1967). Gossip has been condemned in Jewish tradition, and later in the traditions of other religions (e.g., Leviticus 19:16). Schein (Chapter 12) traces the negative connotations of gossip to the influence of teachings of the Bible and to moral and religious sanctions in the Middle Ages. As one can learn from modern etiquette manuals (Levin and Arluke, 1987, pp. 218–19), those sanctions persist to our day. Yet gossip has prevailed notwithstanding. Apparently, people obtain a great deal from the activity of gossiping. A person does not gossip alone, but needs a partner and a human object to talk about. Moreover, gossip occurs in a social setting and must therefore operate within group norms and rules of behavior that determine its content and form. The individual brings to gossip his own interests and needs, which interact with the norms of the group.

Social psychology, for its part, focuses more on the individual within groups than on the group itself. Apart from the contribution of gossip to group norms and cohesion, it is important to remember that it is the individual who gossips. We must therefore consider what that individual gains from such behavior. Social comparison, raised status, enhanced power, and entertainment are some of the results of gossip that have been highlighted by social psychologists. Suls (1977) has suggested that gossip operates through the process of social comparison, as proposed by Festinger (1954). The individual is interested in information in order to compare him- or herself to others. These comparisons enable an evaluation of one's own achievements and abilities and the development of a sense of self and self-esteem. Suls points out that one can increase one's status by spreading gossip about others, either by attaching oneself to high status figures or by criticizing them. Rosnow (1977) elaborates on the functions of exchanging gossip, by describing it as an instrumental transaction whereby A and B exchange trivial stories about C with the aim of receiving more gossip in exchange, obtaining status and power, or even just being entertained. Indeed, some gossip is engaged in solely for the sake of enjoyment and fun, usually in an intimate and unstressful atmosphere (Rosnow and Fine, 1976a).

The individual and, especially, the dynamic psychological approach regard gossip as part of the fantasy life of the individual person. Gossip resembles illusions, dreams, jokes, and stories in that it offers an ambiguous, unstructured stimulus that allows hidden fantasies to surface. Whether they are those who offer the information or only passive listeners, people project their own wishes, anxieties, and unconscious needs onto the objects of gossip. Gossip activates unconscious motivations. Through it the individual can legitimately express aggressive and sexual fantasies or work out themes that arouse personal anxieties. Thus gossip serves as an adaptive defense mechanism.

Medini and Rosenberg (1976) argue that the very existence of gossip throughout the centuries must be taken as evidence of its fulfilling a deep human need. They observe that gossip contains "the issues of the human condition, the human community, issues of secrecy, self-esteem, pride, voyeurism, intimacy and search for security." They point, as well, to the similarity between gossip and psychotherapy, and note that "of the many things that psychotherapists do, one of the most effective might be called the reassurance of humanity. Placing a patient's impulses, thoughts, or behavior into understandable human context can have a very powerful therapeutic result." This effect of psychotherapy is called by them the "same boat" phenomenon. Through psychotherapy, the patient and the therapist both learn that even the most secret and frightening of thoughts, feelings, beliefs, and deeds are human. Much the same effect can be achieved by gossip. Rosnow and Fine (1976b) have found that individuals who score high on the Taylor Manifest Anxiety Test tend to spread more rumors and gossip. This suggests that gossip may have some therapeutic effect.

Although gossip is differentiated from other forms of social discourse by the qualification that it is engaged in without any special goal, it does serve a number of functions: the transmitting of information, the enforcement of group norms and values, and the creation of group cohesion and group identification. Gossip provides the opportunity to test one's conceptions about oneself and one's abilities, as well as one's social perceptions and values. It can help build self-esteem through the agency of comparison. One can achieve status, power, and control by participating in the process of gossip. From the psychodynamic point of view, gossip is a mechanism that facilitates the expression of hidden fantasies and repressed drives in a socially legitimate way. It may provide reassurance and encouragement.

When we consider the important place that gossip has in the life of the individual and of social groups, it is surprising that no test or measure has been devised of the tendency to gossip. The principal method used in studying gossip in the empirical studies reviewed so far has been that of natural observation. Other methods include the analysis of newspaper gossip columns and interviews (Levin and Arluke, 1987). Rosnow and Fine (1976b, p. 81) have proposed that "it is possible that a persistent tendency to gossip is in part a character trait or psychological disposition, although there is no psychological evidence in support of this hypothesis." We have elected to follow their suggestion and to furnish evidence in kind: first, to develop a reliable and valid measure of the disposition to gossip that would quantify the tendency, and second, to examine the relationship between this tendency and vocational interests in people-oriented vocations.

Our working definition for gossip is a verbal or written communication having no clear purpose, between two or more persons about another person or persons, the content of which consists in personal matters. Accordingly, gossip is a social activity that centers on people and is engaged in by people. Although it does not have a conscious purpose, it nevertheless may serve social and personal needs. We exclude from the category of gossip discussions about one's own affairs, since it seems to us that gossip implies a third person as its object (see for example, Ben-Ze'ev, Chapter 1).

Any attempt to design a self-report questionnaire must address the issue of social desirability; that is, the tendency of people to report behavior that accords with social norms and conventions. Because gossip is generally regarded as being socially undesirable, people do not accurately report their own conduct. For example, Levin and Arluke (1985) have found that when conversations at a university cafeteria were monitored by trained observers, they recorded that 68 percent of all talk consisted in gossip. On the other hand, Shapersteen (1987) reports that when he asked students to report directly about how much they gossiped in an ordinary conversation, men reported that they did so 21 percent of the time and women that they did so 27 percent of the time. The difference between the two studies probably derives from the methods of research they employed, and it may be that under-reporting in the latter case is due at least partially to respondents' awareness that gossip is an undesirable mode of behavior.

In addition to examining the reliability and validity of our Gossip Tendency Questionnaire (GTQ), we addressed four specific hypotheses that were derived from literature:

1. There are individual differences in the tendency to gossip; they are expected to distribute approximately normally in the population, that is, about two-thirds of subjects will score around the mean of GTQ, and the rest will get extreme scores (either low or high).
2. There is a negative relationship between social desirability and the tendency to report gossip.
3. There are gender differences in tendency to gossip, with women tending to gossip more than men.
4. Those with vocational interests in people-oriented professions tend to gossip more than those with vocational interest in other fields.

Following our definition, we worked out thirty items that sampled behaviors from several domains of gossip (e.g., achievements in work and study, relationship between sexes, physical appearance, newspaper stories about celebrities, voyeurism). We tried to sample as many different items of gossip as occur in everyday life. After experimenting with various item contents and formats, a Gossip Tendency Questionnaire, or GTQ, research form was prepared that consisted of a total of twenty items (see Appendix 15A). We should note that in our first draft of the GTQ we included items referring to voyeurism (e.g., "When I am in a bus or public place I tend to listen in on the private conversations of other people"). Analysis of the homogeneity of the questionnaire revealed that items of this kind did not pertain to the GTQ, since they were negatively correlated with the other items of the questionnaire. Apparently gossip involves communication or intended communication.

We took three measures to get round the problem of social desirability. First, in making up specific items of the questionnaire we avoided mentioning the word gossip, choosing rather to describe the particular behavior that takes place. Second, our instructions presented gossip as an accepted everyday mode of behavior (see Appendix 15A). Finally, all subjects filled out the Social Desirability Questionnaire (Marlowe and Crowne, 1960), and the score of each subject was calculated and used as a control for the statistical analysis of the GTQ.

Subjects were asked to rate each of the twenty items of the GTQ on a scale from 1 (Never) to 7 (Always), to characterize the extent to which the item typified their behavior. The item scores of each subject were summed over all items, and this represented their individual score as regards tendency to gossip. Two samples were used. Sample A was made up of thirty members of a kibbutz in northern Israel and comprised fifteen males and fifteen females, aged 20–30. Sample B consisted of 120 students at the Technion and the University of Haifa, of whom fifty-eight were males and sixty-two females, and whose ages ranged from 19 to 30. All subjects received the GTQ first, followed by the Marlowe and Crowne Social Desirability scale, and then the occupational interest inventory, Ramak (Meir and Barak, 1974). It consists of seventy-two names of occupations, nine from every vocational field as classified by Roe (1956). Several studies have shown that the tendency to prefer certain groups of occupations may serve as reliable and valid measure of vocational interests (e.g., Peiser and Meir, 1978). Subjects answered the questionnaires individually after receiving a general explanation about the nature of the study (see Appendix 15A).

The Psychometric Characteristics of the GTQ

Reliability. Homogeneity coefficients (Cronbach alpha) for the two samples were found to be .80 and .87 respectively. This means that the items of the questionnaire measure a homogenous entity and the questionnaire has internal consistency.

Validity. To check the validity of the GTQ, two members of the same kibbutz as the respondents in sample A were asked independently to rate each of the subjects on a scale from 1 to 9, regarding the extent of the subject's gossiping.

There was high interjudge agreement between the two judges: $r = .92$. The correlation between the total score of GTQ and the mean of the two ratings was .53 ($p < .01$). This correlation shows quite a strong relationship between the GTQ self-report and peer rating. It supports our claim that the GTQ measures gossip as observed by outside observers. Hence, the GTQ has empirical validity.

Hypothesis 1. Distributions of scores in GTQ: The possible range of scores in the GTQ was 20–140, the mean score was 73.17, and the median score 73, with a standard deviation of 16.66. None of the respondents received extreme scores. About 65 percent of the subjects received gossip scores of 60–80 (around the mean) and the rest consisted of 15 percent below and 15 percent above the mean, approximating the normal curve and indicating that the tendency to gossip distributes normally in the population, like many other personality and disposition traits.

Factor analysis. The matrix of intercorrelations among the twenty items of the GTQ was factor analyzed by the principal components method with rotation, Varimax (SAS, 1985). Factor analysis revealed the following four different scales within the GTQ:

1. Physical appearance scale: The items included are 2, 10, 14, 20 (e.g., "I like talking to friends about other people's clothes"). The first three items deal with physical appearance and are highly loaded on this factor (.73, .71, .56, respectively). The last item is a general question about tendency to gossip, and its association with this factor is somewhat surprising. It may reflect the centrality of talking about physical appearance.

2. Achievement scale: The items included are 15, 11, 5, 6, 13. These items are loaded with the second factor (.71, .58, .57, .56, .34, respectively). All of them deal with other people's achievements in their studies, work, or personal lives (e.g., "I like talking to friends about other people's grades and intellectual achievements"). Item 13 deals with other people's salaries and was added to this scale, although it was loaded equally with factors 3 and 4 below.

3. Social information: This category deals with talking about a variety of social subjects, such as the love affairs, relationships, and problems of other people, and generally reveals social involvement (e.g., "I tend to talk with friends about the love affairs of people we know"). This factor includes items 7, 16, 8, 17, 9. Their loading as regards this factor is .68, .59, .56, .53, .53, respectively.

4. Sublimated gossip: Included are items 1, 19, 18, 12. These concern activities not in themselves gossip, but rather the intellectual activity of gossip, such as reading biographies, analyzing other people's motivations, and so on (i.e., "I like reading biographies of famous people"). The loading as regards this factor was .62, .55, .51, .49, respectively.

The only item that did not belong to these factors was item 4:

"I prefer listening to conversations about other people rather than taking part in them." Item 4 thus reflects the passive side of the gossiper, and may be a factor that our questionnaire fails to represent.

As a result of the factor analysis, the questionnaire was divided to four subscales. Each respondent was able to receive five gossip scores: one total score and four scores on the different subscales representing the four factors set out above.

Hypothesis 2. Social desirability: The relationship with social desirability was examined through subjects' response to the social desirability scale of Marlowe and Crowne (1960). The correlation between the two questionnaires in the two samples was −.37 and −.33, respectively. Both correlations were significant. The implication of this finding is that, although we took measures to reduce it, the influence of social desirability nevertheless persisted and any substantial research in this field must control for social desirability.

Hypothesis 3. Gender differences: Since self-reports about gossiping are influenced by social desirability, we have computed the gender difference while statistically partialling out the effect of social desirability. Gender difference (net effect) was found to be significant ($f = 6.41$, $p \leqslant 0.02$), with higher scores for women (75.6 − 69.8). For gender differences in the content of gossip as defined by the four factors described above, the only significant difference found between sexes was that more women reported gossiping about physical appearance ($T = 3.94$; $p \leqslant 0.001$).

Hypothesis 4. Vocational interests: The relationship between tendency to gossip and vocational interests was measured by calculating for each subject his interests in people-oriented professions and non–people-oriented professions. A partial correlation (which partials out the effect of social desirability between the tendency to gossip and vocational interests in people-oriented profession) was = 0.47 ($p \leqslant 0.02$). This correlation could be attributed to gender differences, since women more than men tend toward people-oriented professions and tend to report more on their gossip. Covariance analysis revealed a significant difference in the tendency to gossip among subjects that prefer people-oriented professions as compared to subjects that prefer non–people-oriented professions ($F = 8.88$; $p = 0.0036$). This means that subjects that prefer people-oriented professions tend to gossip even when the effects of gender and social desirability are controlled.

The point of departure for this study was the perceived similarity between discussions of patients by psychologists and the social phenomenon of gossip, which led us to undertake the scientific adventure of constructing a measure of the individual tendency to gossip. Our preliminary results suggest that the tendency to gossip is a personal trait distributed normally among the population tested. The GTQ was validated by means of peer rating, and we can conclude that we succeeded in operationalizing the personal tendency to gossip. Construct validity was used, as well, to validate the questionnaire; that is, we checked and predicted theoretical relationships, such as those between gossip and gender and between gossip and social desirability. As predicted, a negative relationship was found between social desirability and the self-reporting of gossip. This finding accords with observations in the literature and reflects the burden of centuries of sanctions against gossip. The predicted gender difference was also found by using the questionnaire. Women were found to gossip more than men, as indicated by other studies as well. The above two results add to the validity of the GTQ.

Regarding the issue of gender difference, it would seem that when gossip is measured by the subscales and social desirability is controlled, a more accurate picture emerges in which men and women are found to gossip almost to the same extent. In fact, it would be safe to say that the two sexes engage in more or less the same amount of gossip. In other words, social pressure may lead men to underreport their gossip. The only difference found between genders regards gossip about physical appearance. In agreement with Ben-Ze'ev (Chapter 1) and Levin and Arluke (1985), we assume that, had we asked about gossip on the sports achievements of other people, we might have found that men gossiped more than women. Society expects women to be more interested in physical appearance, so it is not surprising to find that they also talk more about the physical appearance of others. It appears, therefore, that both sexes engage in gossip, but that content differs.

The most interesting finding for us was the relationship between vocational interest in working with people and the tendency to gossip. It would appear that people bring to gossip the same motivations they bring to vocations dealing with people. These motivations have to do with power, the need for comparison, and curiosity. One can hypothesize that the tendency to gossip derives from the same source as vocational interests. One difference between the two is that talking about people in the context of one's profession is highly approved by society, whereas gossip is not. Psychotherapy is in a way a sublimation of the needs reflected in gossip. This is by no means to say that we intend psychologists to take up gossiping instead of discussing cases.

Yet they ought to be aware of the similar motivations that underlie the two behaviors, as well as of the dangers. This conflation illustrates why the ethics of psychology is so important. It ensures that professionals will restrain their natural disposition to gossip, so that the inclination to gossip about patients should remain within the limits of professional concerns.

Having succeeded in constructing this questionnaire, we suggest that future research concentrate on the relationship between the tendency to gossip and other personality traits and needs. One might hypothesize that the tendency to gossip will correlate highly with other personality traits such as extroversion and the need for power, control, and affiliation. Of special interest is the relation between the specific content of gossip (e.g., achievement, social appearance, etc.) and particular traits and needs. If we are right in saying that gossip is a way of expressing needs and motivations, it should follow that people will choose different topics to gossip about according to their personal needs.

Appendix 15.A | GTQ Research Form (translated from Hebrew)

This research is being carried out by the Department of Psychology at the University of Haifa to measure certain social and personal attitudes. Please read the instructions and circle the answers you think are right.

Instructions:

This questionnaire concerns the tendency of people to talk about other people. It is a tendency which occurs almost every day, and most people engage in it. Read the statements below carefully, and try to estimate the extent to which they characterize your own behavior.

Example: I tend to talk about other people.

1 never   2 once   3 rarely   4 infrequently   5 frequently   6 usually   7 always

circle the number that fits your behavior for each item on the questionnaire.

1. I read gossip columns in newspapers

Never 1 2 3 4 5 6 7 Always

2. I like talking to friends about other people's clothes.

Never 1 2 3 4 5 6 7 Always

3. I tend to talk with my friends about relationships between men and women (example, couples or break-up between couples).

Never 1 2 3 4 5 6 7 Always

4. I prefer listening to conversations about other people rather than taking part in them.

Never 1 2 3 4 5 6 7 Always

5. I tend to gossip with a good friend about people who left the country.

Never 1 2 3 4 5 6 7 Always

6. I like talking to friends about other people's grades and intellectual achievements.

Never 1 2 3 4 5 6 7 Always

7. I think that I can contribute interesting information to almost any conversation about people.

Never 1 2 3 4 5 6 7 Always

8. I tend to talk to friends about the problems some of our friends have at work.

Never 1 2 3 4 5 6 7 Always

9. I like analyzing with a friend the compatibility of various couples.

Never 1 2 3 4 5 6 7 Always

10. I like talking with a friend about the personal appearance of other people.

Never 1 2 3 4 5 6 7 Always

11. I tend to talk with friends about the educational level of people in important positions we know.

Never 1 2 3 4 5 6 7 Always

12. I enjoy analyzing with my friends the motives and reasons for other people's behavior.

Never 1 2 3 4 5 6 7 Always

13. I like talking with a friend about the salaries of our mutual friends.

Never 1 2 3 4 5 6 7 Always

14. When I come back from a party or some other event, I tend to talk about my impressions about the personal appearance of the others who were there.

Never 1 2 3 4 5 6 7 Always

15. I tend to talk to friends about the success of certain people in their job.

Never 1 2 3 4 5 6 7 Always

16. Usually I feel I know what is going on, who is going with whom, etc.

Never 1 2 3 4 5 6 7 Always

17. I tend to talk with friends about the love affairs of people we know.

Never 1 2 3 4 5 6 7 Always

18. I like reading biographies of famous people.

Never 1 2 3 4 5 6 7 Always

19. I like to tell friends about interesting details concerning other people.

Never 1 2 3 4 5 6 7 Always

20. I tend to gossip.

Never 1 2 3 4 5 6 7 Always

Notes

Chapter 1. The Vindication of Gossip

I am grateful to Lisa Frank, Robert Goodman, William Lycan, Cynthia Miller, and Amelie Rorty for helpful comments. The work on this chapter began while I was on sabbatical leave at the Center for the Philosophy of Science at the University of Pittsburgh. The hospitality and support of the center are gratefully acknowledged.

1. Aristotle has a somewhat similar distinction between *poesis* (productive action) and *praxis* (activity). The following formulation of the distinction is that of Michael Strauss.

2. Gossips often envy the objects of their gossip. What underlies gossip and envy is a constant comparison with others. In envy this comparison is accompanied by a concern over the unequal, inferior position of the agent (Ben-Ze'ev, 1992a); in gossip this concern is less important. Despite the negative attitude toward the object that is often present in envy and gossip, both attitudes frequently involve some kind of admiration for certain aspects of the object.

3. The relation between the truth-value of the information conveyed in gossip and its moral evaluation is not simple. On one hand, true information does not distort the character of the object; but, on the other hand, intimate and personal information may hurt more when it is true, as one cannot refer to it as merely unsubstantiated rumor. Moreover, truthful information may be partial, e.g., when one takes things out of their context, and hence distorted after all.

Chapter 2. In Praise of Gossip

This paper grew out of remarks provoked by presentations by Louise Collins and Maryann Ayim at the Canadian Philosophical Association meetings in June 1990. It owes much to both those presentations, which are included in this volume.

1. For examples of these terminological meanders, see Copp and Wendell, 1983.

2. Louise Collins (Chapter 10) has in fact made a similar suggestion. For the Kantian principle at stake, see Kant, 1949.

3. In de Sousa, 1987, I have defended a notion of objective value, compatible with granting the relativity of value to human capacities and experiences, of which appropriate emotional response constitute the apprehension.

4. Ayim, who compares the cooperative search for truth in gossip and the search for truth in science, observes that "the test for truth in investigative

gossip [as in science] is inherently social" (see Chapter 8). But she clearly acknowledges the problem of size.

    5. See Peirce,1931–1958, 5:316; quoted by Ayim (Chapter 8).

Chapter 3. Gossip as Moral Talk

    1. A further example of this attitude may be found in Henry James's novel *The Sacred Fount*. The narrator provokes gossip-talk for the specific purpose of testing the hypothesis that one partner of a couple will draw on the gifts of the other and so deplete that person's vitality.

    2. See, for example, Gilbert Ryle's, 1954, discussions of pleasure.

    3. For reactions to watching soap opera see Ien Ang, 1985.

    4. Aaron Ben Ze'ev, Chapter 1, defends this view.

    5. For an account of the position opposed to that of the theoretical critic see, e.g., Thomas Nagel, 1970, pp. 1–10.

    6. Various aspects of this view are defended by Iris Murdoch, 1970; Mary Midgeley, 1983; John McDowell, 1978, 1979.

    7. This point explains why it is impossible to gossip about certain people, viz, those from whom we are unable to withhold moral concern, e.g., our children, and presumably ourselves.

    8. See, for example, Rowbotham, 1983. In her view, although gossip (in a wider sense than mine) can provide women with important ways of perceiving and describing the world, there are also drawbacks: "For the woman dependent on men it provides also a powerful form of social control over the behavior of other women. Gossip can determine who is within the protection of society and restrict other women from moving over into self-determination and giving the game away."

Chapter 4. The Logic of Gossip

    1. See the account of friendship in L. Thomas, *Living Morally: A Psychology of Moral Character* (Temple University Press, 1989), ch. 4.

Chapter 5. Gossip and Humor

    1. See Morreall, 1983b, ch. 7, for a discussion of humor and aesthetic experience.

    2. The fact that the appeal of gossip is largely to the imagination is often overlooked in attacks on gossip that charge it with sensationalism and epistemic irresponsibility.

    3. See Cohen, 1983.

    4. See Morreall, 1987, ch. 20 and 22.

Chapter 6. The Legal Regulation of Gossip

1. On the purpose of defamation law, see Robert Post, 1986, The social foundations of defamation law: Reputation and the constitution. *California Law Review* 691:707–21.

2. See *Florida Star v. B.J.F.*, 1989 (Scalia, J., concurring): In the present case, I would anticipate that the rape victim's discomfort at the dissemination of news of her misfortune among friends and acquaintances would be at least as great as her discomfort at its publication by the media to people to whom she is only a name. Yet the law in question does not prohibit the former in either oral or written form. Nor is it at all clear, as I think it must be to validate this statute, that Florida's general privacy law would prohibit such gossip. . . . This law has every appearance of a prohibition that society is prepared to impose upon the press but not upon itself.

3. See Robert Post, 1990, The constitutional concept of public discourse: Outrageous opinion, democratic deliberation, and *Hustler Magazine v. Falwell*, *Harvard Law Review* 103:601.

4. For an example of both attitudes compressed into a single case, see *Arrington v. The New York Times Co.*, 434 N.E.2d (N.Y. 1982), cert. denied, 459 U.S. 1146 (1983).

Chapter 7. Gossip and Privacy

1. For an illuminating discussion of the different senses to the public/private distinction, as well as of the importance of maintaining the private realm as private.

2. See Flaherty, 1972. Many colonial towns, as well as many ancient and modern cultures, required single people to belong to a household.

3. The Turkish movie *Yol* explores the conflict between family roles and personal or expressive relationships.

4. "Shame and the feeling of shame," in Max Scheler, *Posthumous papers*. I am very grateful to Eugene Schoeman for painstakingly translating this essay from the German for me.

5. Robert Post insisted on my personal recognition of this as a problem.

6. "Make your contribution as informative as is required (for the current purposes of the exchange)."

Chapter 8. Knowledge Through the Grapevine

1. Interestingly, Manber's 1989 treatment of logarithms labels as "the gossip problem," the determination of the smallest number of steps in which a complete interchange of information can occur within a group, under the condition that only two people can talk together at a time. The solution is $\log 2n$; for some indication of how efficiently Manber perceives gossip to be, $\log 2n$ is twenty where n is one million (p. 416).

2. Ben-Ze'ev argues in Chapter 1 that gossip is by definition an idle pursuit, pursued for its own sake, that is, for the pleasure inherent in the activity itself rather than for any extrinsic end to which it may lead. If this is

true, then the activity I am addressing in this paper is not pure gossip, or "paradigmatic gossip," as Ben-Ze'ev calls it, but either a peculiar brand of gossip or the use of gossip to achieve an extrinsic end, namely, the furthering of one's knowledge of information. The sort of gossip in which I am interested, investigative gossip, will be by definition purposive, for the gossiper engages in it precisely in order to enlarge her knowledge or information.

3. 1931–1958, paragraph 1.8; hereinafter references to Peirce's writing will indicate the volume number (1), followed by the paragraph number (8).

4. For very interesting discussions in the literature, however, see Spacks, 1985, pp. 83–105; Medini and Rosenberg, 1976, pp. 452–62; epistemological approaches to gossip are also found, although not explored to any length, in Arno, 1980, p. 347; Fine and Rosnow, 1978, p. 161; and Brenneis, 1984, p. 492.

5. For a current description of how the chilly climate operates at the University of Western Ontario, see Backhouse et al, 1989.

6. Jones, 1980, p. 195, discusses this perception of gossip. Oakley, 1972, p. 12, describes a proclamation issued in 1547 in response to the perceived excess of independence and other male features among Elizabethan women. This proclamation forbade women "to meet together to babble and talk" and ordered men "to keep their wives in their houses."

7. Gluckman's (1963) perception of the relationships between witchcraft and gossip is interesting; see also Oakley, 1974, p. 16.

Chapter 9. Gossip, or in Praise of Chaos

1. See Chapter 10, Louise Collins. "Gossip: A Feminist Defense."

2. I discuss the adequacy of social scientific practice to its subject matter, and the exemplary nature of knowing other people, in *What can she know? Feminist theory and the construction of knowledge.* Ithaca, NY: Cornell University Press, 1991.

Chapter 10. Gossip: A Feminist Defense

This paper was originally written for the Canadian Society of Women in Philosophy (C-SWIP) conference on Women and Language, Sept. 1989, at the prompting of Prof. M. Deslauriers. It was then read at the Canadian Philosophical Association conference, May 1990, with the encouragement of Prof. L. Code. I am grateful to both, and to Prof. R. de Sousa for referring me to the present project. I have received helpful suggestions from them and many others. Special thanks are also due A. Skorzewska, for helping me first articulate my view.

1. M. Deslauriers has suggested that there is a skill in gossiping, the skill of storytelling, and characteristically the skill of extrapolating a tale from apparently inconsequential details. There are particular people to whom we turn when we would gossip for the sake of entertainment—the gifted raconteuse, the wit, and so on. However, dull gossip is nonetheless gossip. And the notion of "entertainment" suggested as the constitutive end here would have to be broadened to vacuity. I therefore deny that the skill of storytelling is skill

in promoting the constitutive end of gossip, for there is no such end. It does not follow from this that no skills are exercised or developed while gossiping.

2. It is also tricky for an outsider to recognise what is "gossip-worthy" to the group and hence for her to bid her way in with information to which she has access. John Sabini, in *Moralities of everyday life*, Oxford University Press, 1982, points out that even to recognize an episode of gossip as such may depend on already sharing some background assumptions. I thank Prof. S. Mullett for drawing my attention to Sabini's work.

3. The malicious gossip, M, seeks to harm her subject, S, by, one, saying what she believes false of S, two, selecting from what she believes true of S, or, three, doing both, to perform a speech act intended to produce an unflattering belief about S in her co-gossips. She does this by pretending to be engaged in ordinary gossip, making statements that apparently aim at truth, that her co-gossips will take at face value. However, her statements actually aim at persuasion by any means and are therefore governed by expediency, not sincerity. Were her malice discovered, her co-gossips would accordingly cease reading her claims as prima facie evidence of truths about S. Hence, the possibility of some malicious gossip on this account rests on the innocence of most ordinary gossip.

4. Classically, the intruder to be repelled was the state, and private individuals could exercise their free speech about my domestic life, so long as this did me no "harm." Subsequently, liberals have been concerned with intrusion by other institutions, e.g., those which exchange my banking and health records, and their representatives, journalists of the gutter press, for example. I am not suggesting that liberal theorists would ever limit individual freedom to gossip about me; they are squeamish enough about legislating against, for example, racist organizations that actually defame people.

5. Cases where we appear to recognize information about S's "private life" as appropriately subject to her control, for example, letting S herself be the first to tell other friends of her pregnancy, need not be construed in terms of S's rights at all. I just do not want to preempt her pleasure in telling them.

6. Or, more accurately, to make a singular causal statement commits us to the view that there is some causal law under which the events fall, even if we do not know that law. So even if we do not know the relevant description of the events (the description under which the law subsumes these events), we know that there must be such a description. I thank Prof. R. de Sousa for referring me to Donald Davidson, "Causal Relations," *Journal of Philosophy* 64 (1967): 691–703.

Chapter 12. Used and Abused

1. In his "House of Fame" (ca. 1379) Geoffrey Chaucer distinguishes between "news," "rumours," and "tales"; tales originated in news and were turned into tales as they "went from mouth to mouth / Each time increasing more and more . . . growing greater on each tongue / that told it /." He defines a "tale" as "false and true confounded" (Stone, 1983, v. 2070–2150, pp. 119–21).

2. On the reputation of female servants as gossips see also Goodich, 1985, pp. 119–36.

3. According to Johan Le Fèbre, *Les Lamentations de Matheolus*: "Why are women more noisy, full of foolish words, and more garrulous than men? Because they are made of bones and our [male] persons are made of clay; bones rattle louder than earth" (Bloch, p. 18).

Chapter 13. Gossip, Gossipers, Gossipees

1. In 1969 there circulated a story that the Beatle, Paul McCartney, had been decapitated in an auto accident, and that he had been replaced by a double. Many clues to his death purportedly appeared in several Beatles albums, most notedly, *Abbey Road* (see Rosnow and Fine, 1976a for more details about the rumor).

2. A number of informants indicated that some girls gossiped about "everybody." To protect us from possibly misleading interpretations based on the large number (35) implied by this remark, we trimmed the highest and lowest numbers before calculating the overall propensity scores (cf. Rosenthal and Rosnow, 1991).

3. For reasons outlined in the previous footnote, these averaged gossipee propensity scores were also based on trimmed means.

References

Allport, G., and L. Postman. 1947. *The psychology of rumor.* New York: Holt, Rinehart, and Winston.

Ang, I. 1985. *Watching Dallas: Soap operas and the melodramatic imagination.* London: Methuen.

Anthony, S. 1973. Anxiety and rumor. *Journal of Social Psychology* 89:91–98.

Arendt, H. 1958. *The human condition.* Chicago: University of Chicago Press.

Argyle, M., and M. Henderson. 1984. The rules of friendship. *Journal of Social and Personal Relationships* 1:211–37.

Aristotle. 1941. Politics. In R. McKeon, ed., and B. Jowett, trans., *The basic works of Aristotle.* New York: Random House.

Arno, A. 1980. Fijan gossip as adjudication: A communicative model of informal social control. *Journal of Anthropological Research* 36:343–60.

Austen, J. 1946. *Emma.* Oxford: Clarendon Press.

Backett, E. M., J. A. Heady, and J. C. G. Evans. 1954. Studies of a general practice. II: The doctor's job in an urban area. *British Medical Journal* 1:109–23.

Backhouse, C., R. Harris, G. Michell, and A. Wylie. 1989. The chilly climate for faculty women at U.W.O.: Postscript to the Backhouse Report.

Bailey, R. 1971. *Gifts and poison: The politics of reputation.* Oxford: Blackwell.

Bales, R. F. 1950. *Interaction process analysis: A method for the study of small groups.* Cambridge, Mass.: Addison Wesley.

———. 1958. Task roles and social roles in problem-solving groups. In E. E. Maccoby, T. M. Newcomb, and E. L. Hartley, eds., *Readings in social psychology.* 3d ed. New York: Holt.

Barbour, J. S., et al. 1985. Psychosocial characteristics of cancer patients who choose Laetrile therapy. *Journal of Psychosocial Oncology* 2:93–108.

Barfoot, Joan. 1989. Toronto: Macmillan.

Barsky, A. J. 1981. Hidden reasons some patients visit doctor. *Annals of Internal Medicine* 94:492–97.

Benn, S. 1984. Privacy, freedom, and respect for persons. In Schoeman, ed., *Philosophical dimensions of privacy: An anthology.* Cambridge: Cambridge University Press.

Ben-Ze'ev, A. 1992a. Envy and inequality. *Journal of Philosophy* 89:551–81.

———. 1992b. Pleasure-in-others'-misfortune. *Iyyun* 41:41–61.

———. 1993a. Another look at pleasure-in-others'-misfortune. *Iyyun* 42:431–40.

———. 1993b. *The perceptual system: A philosophical and psychological perspective.* New York: Peter Lang.

Bergson, H. 1956. Laughter. In Wylie Sypher, ed., *Comedy.* Garden City, N.Y.: Doubleday Anchor.

Berne, E. 1966. *Games people play.* London: Deutsch.

Bloch, R. H. 1989. Medieval misogyny. In *Misogyny, misandry, and mis-*

anthropy, ed. R. H. Bloch and F. Ferguson. Berkeley: University of California Press.

Boddy, J. P. 1989. *Wombs and alien spirits: Women, men, and the Zar cult in northern Sudan.* Madison: University of Wisconsin Press.

Boissevain, J. 1973. An exploration of two first order zones. In J. Boissevain and J. C. Mitchell, eds., *Network analysis: Studies in human interaction.* The Hague: Mouton.

———. 1974. *Friends of friends: Networks, manipulators, and coalitions.* Oxford: Blackwell.

Bornstein, D. 1983. *The lady in the tower: Medieval courtesy literature for women.* Hamden, Conn.: Archian Books.

Brenneis, D. 1984. Grog and gossip in Bhatgaon: Style and substance in Fiji Indian conversation. *American Ethnologist* 11:487–516.

Burgess, G. S., and K. Busby, trans. 1986. *The lais of Marie de France.* Harmondsworth, Eng.: Penguin.

Burns, T. 1954. The directions of activity and communication in a departmental executive group. *Human Relations* 7:73–97.

Byrne, R., and A. Whiten, eds. 1988. *Machiavellian intelligence.* Oxford: Oxford University Press.

Campbell, D. T. 1975. On the conflicts between biological and social evolution and between psychology and moral tradition. *American Psychologist* 30:1103–26.

Catton, R. W., and R. J. Snircich. 1964. A comparison of mathematical models for the effect of residential propinquity on mate selection. *American Sociological Review* 29:522–29.

Christie, A. 1930. *The murder at the vicarage.* New York: Berkley Books.

Coghill, N., trans. 1973. Chaucer, Geoffrey. *The Canterbury tales.* Harmondsworth, Eng.: Penguin.

Cohen, J. 1969. *Statistical power analysis for the behavioral sciences.* San Diego, Calif.: Academic Press.

Cohen, T. 1983. Jokes. In Eva Schaper, ed. *Pleasure, preference, and value: Studies in philosophical aesthetics.* Cambridge: Cambridge University Press.

Colson, E. 1953. *The Makah Indians.* Manchester: Manchester University Press.

The Compact Edition of the Oxford English Dictionary. 1971. Oxford: Oxford University Press.

Cooper, S. E. 1983. Some social-demographic characteristics of patients self-referred for a clinical trial of laetrile. *Journal of Psychosocial Oncology* 1:83–91.

Copp, D., and S. Wendell, eds. 1983. Pornography and censorship. In *New concepts in human sexuality.* Buffalo: Prometheus Books.

Costa, P. T., Jr., and R. R. McCrae. 1987. Neuroticism, somatic complaints, and disease: Is the bark worse than the bite? *Journal of Personality* 55:299–316.

Crance, T. F., ed. 1890. Jacques de Vitry, *Exempla.* New York: Franklin.

Crowne, D. P., and D. Marlowe. 1964. *The approval motive: Studies in evaluative dependence.* New York: Wiley.

Davies, K. 1953. Management communication and the grapevine. *Harvard Business Review* 31:43–49.

DeClerque, J., A. O. Tsui, M. F. Abul-Ata, and D. Barcelona. 1986. Rumor, misinformation, and oral contraceptive use in Egypt. *Social Science and Medicine* 23:83–92.

Dennett, D. 1984. *Elbow room: The varieties of free will worth wanting.* Cambridge, Mass.: MIT Press.

de Sousa, R. 1987. *The rationality of emotions.* Cambridge, Mass.: MIT Press.

de Waal, F. 1982. *Chimpanzee politics.* London: Jonathan Cape.

Douglas, M. 1966. *Purity and danger: An analysis of concepts of pollution and taboo.* New York: Praeger.

Dunbar, R.I.M. In press. Co-evolution of neocortex size, group size, and language in humans. *Behavioral and Brain Sciences.*

Ekman, P. 1985. *Telling lies: Clues to deceit in the marketplace, politics, and marriage.* New York: Norton.

Emler, N. 1990. A social psychology of reputation. In W. Strobes and M. Hewstone, eds., *European Review of Social Psychology,* vol. 1. Chichester: Wiley.

———. In press. *Secrets and scandals, rumours and reputations: The social science of gossip.* Hemel Hempstead: Harvester.

Emler, N., and K. Grady. 1989. The university as a social environment. Paper presented at British Psychological Society, Social Psychology Section Annual Conference, Brighton.

Epsom, J. 1978. The mobile health clinic: A report on the first year's work. In D. Tuckett and J. Kaufert, eds., *Basic readings in medical sociology.* London: Tavistock Publications.

Erikson, K. 1966. *Wayward Puritans: A study in the sociology of deviance.* New York: Wiley.

Esposito, J. L., E. Agard, and R. L. Rosnow. 1984. Can confidentiality of data pay off? *Personality and Individual Differences* 5:477–80.

Festinger, L. 1954. A theory of social comparison processes. *Human Relations* 7:114–40.

Festinger, L., S. Schachter, and K. Back. 1950. *Social pressures in informal groups.* New York: Harper and Row.

Fine, G. A. 1977. Social components of children's gossip. *Journal of Communication* 27:181–85.

Fine, G. A., and R. L. Rosnow. 1978. Gossip, gossipers, gossiping. *Personality and Social Psychology Bulletin* 4:161–68.

Fischer, C. 1981. *To dwell among friends: Personal networks in town and city.* Chicago: University of Chicago Press.

Flaherty, D. 1972. *Privacy in colonial New England.* Charlottesville: University of Virginia Press.

The Florida Star v. B.J.F. 1989. 491 U.S. 524, 533.

Freeman, M. 1988. The power of sisterhood: Marie de France's "Le Fresne." *Women and power in the Middle Ages,* M. Erler and M. Kowaleski, eds. Athens: University of Georgia Press.

Freidson, E. 1970. *Profession of medicine: A study in the sociology of applied knowledge.* New York: Dodd Mead.

Freud, S. 1959. Humour. In *Collected papers,* vol. 5. New York: Basic Books.

Funder, D. C., and D. J. Ozer. 1983. Behavior as a function of the situation. *Journal of Personality and Social Psychology* 44:107–12.

Gavison, R. 1984. Privacy and the limits of the law. In F. Schoeman, ed.,

Philosophical dimensions of privacy, pp. 346–402. New York: Cambridge University Press.

———. 1991. The private-public distinction: Why the (feminist) invitation to abolish it should be declined. Manuscript.

Gleason, J. B., and E. B. Greif. 1983. Men's speech to young children. In B. Thorne, C. Kramarae, and N. Henley, eds., *Language, gender, and society,* pp. 140–50. Rowley, Mass.: Newbury.

Gluckman, M. 1963. Gossip and scandal. *Current Anthropology* 4:307–16.

Godkin, E. L. 1890. The rights of the citizen to his own reputation. *Scribner's.*

Goffman, E. 1959. *The presentation of self in everyday life.* Garden City, N.Y.: Doubleday.

Goodich, M. 1985. Ancilla Dei: The servant as saint in the late Middle Ages. *Women of the medieval world,* J. Kirshner and S. F. Wemple, eds. New York: Basil Blackwell.

Goodridge, J. F., trans. 1959. William Langland, *Piers the Ploughman.* Harmondsworth, Eng.: Penguin.

Gouldner, A. 1976. *The dialectic of ideology and technology.* London: Macmillan.

Greenhouse, C. 1986. *Praying for justice.* Ithaca, N.Y.: Cornell University Press.

Grice, P. 1989. Logic and conversation. In *Studies in the way of words.* Cambridge, Mass.: Harvard University Press.

Gruder, L., T. M. Cook, K. M. Hannigan, B. R. Flay, C. Alessis, and J. Halamaj. 1978. Empirical tests of the absolute sleeper effect predicted from the discounting cue hypothesis. *Journal of Personality and Social Psychology* 36:1061–74.

Guarino, G. A., trans. 1964. Giovanni Boccaccio, *Concerning famous women.* London: Allen and Unwin.

Gurevich, A. 1990. *Medieval popular culture: Problems of belief and perception.* Cambridge: Cambridge University Press.

Hanawalt, B. A. 1988. Lady Honor Lisle's networks of influence. *Women and power in the Middle Ages,* M. Erler and M. Kowaleski, eds. Athens: University of Georgia Press.

Hannerz, U. 1967. Gossip, networks, and culture in a black American ghetto. *Ethos* 32:35–60.

Harris, M. 1975. *Cows, pigs, wars, and witches: The riddles of culture.* London: Hutchison.

Harrison, R., trans. 1974. *Salic salt. Eighteen fabliaux translated from the Old French.* Berkeley: University of California Press.

Heidegger, M. 1962. *Being and time.* New York: Harper and Row.

Heilman, S. C. 1973. *Synagogue life.* Chicago: University of Chicago.

Hellman, R., and R. O'Gorman, trans. 1965. *Fabliaux: Ribald tales from the Old French.* New York: Cronell.

Hershkovits, M. 1937. *Life in Haitian valley.* New York: Knopf.

Hochschild, A. R. 1983. *The managed heart: Commercialization of human feeling.* Berkeley: University of California Press.

Hockett, C. 1958. *A course in modern linguistics.* New York: Macmillan.

Hogan, R. 1983. A socioanalytic theory of personality. In M. Page, ed., *Nebraska symposium on motivation.* Lincoln: University of Nebraska Press.

Hovland, C., and W. Weiss, 1951. The influence of source credibility on communication effectiveness. *Public Opinion Quarterly* 15:635–50.

Hull, D. L. 1988. *Science as a process: An evolutionary account of the social and conceptual development of science.* Chicago: University of Chicago Press.

Humphrey, N. 1976. The social function of the intellect. In P. P. G. Bateson and R. A. Hinde, eds., *Growing points in ethology.* Cambridge: Cambridge University Press.

Hupka, R. B. 1991. The motive for the arousal of romantic jealousy: Its cultural origin. In P. Salovey, ed., *The psychology of jealousy and envy.* New York: Guilford Press.

Hurka, T. 1990. "Principles." *Toronto Globe and Mail,* April 17.

Ingham, J., and P. Miller. 1979. Symptom prevalence and severity in a general practice. *Journal of Epidemiology and Community Health* 33:191–98.

Jaeger, M. E., S. Anthony, and R. L. Rosnow. 1980. Who hears what from whom and with what effect: A study of rumor. *Personality and Social Psychology Bulletin* 6:473–78.

Jones, D. (1980). Gossip: Notes on women's oral culture. *Women's Studies International Quarterly* 3:193–98.

Jourard, S. M., and P. Lasakow. 1958. Some factors in self-disclosure. *Journal of Abnormal and Social Psychology* 56:91–98.

Kant, I. 1949. *Fundamental principles of the metaphysics morals.* Indianapolis: Bobbs-Merrill. First published 1785.

———. 1950. *Grundlegung zur Metaphysik der Sitten.* Translated by H. J. Paron as *The moral law.* New York: Barnes and Noble.

———. 1963. Jealousy, envy, and grudge. In *Lectures on ethics.* New York: Harper and Row.

Kapferer, J. N. 1985. A mass poisoning rumor in Europe. *Public Opinion Quarterly* 53:467–81.

Kaplan, R. E. 1984. Trade routes: The manager's network of relationships. *Organizational Dynamics* 12:37–52.

Kerckhoff, A. C., and K. W. Back. 1968. *The June bug: A study of hysterical contagion.* New York: Appleton-Century-Crofts.

Key, M. R. 1975. *Male/female language, with a comprehensive bibliography.* Metuchen, N.J.: Scarecrow Press.

Kierkegaard, S. 1962. *The present age.* New York: Harper and Row.

King, M. L., and A. Rabil, eds. 1983. *Her immaculate hand: Selected works by and about women humanists of quattrocento Italy.* Medieval and Renaissance Texts and Studies 20. New York: Center for Medieval and Early Renaissance Studies.

Kinsey, A. C., W. B. Pomeroy, and C. E. Martin. 1948. *Sexual behavior in the human male.* Philadelphia: W. B. Saunders.

Kinsey, A. C., W. B. Pomeroy, C. E. Martin, and P. H. Gebhard. 1953. *Sexual behavior in the human female.* Philadelphia: W. B. Saunders.

Kuhn, T. 1970. *The structure of scientific revolutions.* 2d ed. Chicago: University of Chicago Press.

Lakoff, G. 1987. *Women, fire, and dangerous things.* Chicago: University of Chicago Press.

Lakoff, R. 1975. *Language and women's place.* New York: Harper.

Lawson, S., trans. 1985. Christine de Pisan, *The treasure of the city of ladies; or, The book of the three virtues.* Harmondsworth, Eng.: Penguin.

Lerner, D. 1958. *The passing of traditional society: Modernising the Middle East.* New York: Free Press.

Leventhal, H., D. Meyer, and D. Nerenz. 1975. The common sense representation of illness danger. In S. Rachman, ed., *Psychology and medicine,* pp. 7–30. London: Temple Smith.

Levin, J., and A. Arluke. 1985. An exploratory analysis of sex differences in gossip. *Sex Roles* 12:281–86.

———. 1987. *Gossip: The inside scoop.* New York: Plenum Press.

Levin, J., and A. J. Kimmel. 1977. Gossip columns: Media small talk. *Journal of Communication* 27:169–75.

Litwak, E., and I. Szelenyi. 1969. Primary group structures and their functions. *American Sociological Review* 35:465–81.

Locke, F. W., trans. 1957. Andreas Capellanus, *The art of courtly love.* New York: State University of New York Press.

McDowell, J. 1978. Are moral requirements categorical imperatives? *Proceedings of the Aristotelean Society,* supp. vol. 52:13–29.

———. 1979. Virtue and reason. *The Monist* 62:331–50.

McWilliam, G. H., trans. 1972. Giovanni Boccaccio, *The decameron.* Harmondsworth, Eng.: Penguin.

Maitland, F. W. 1908. *The constitutional history of England.* Cambridge: Cambridge University Press.

Major, B., M. Testa, and W. H. Bylsma. 1991. Responses to upward and downward social comparisons: The impact of esteem-relevance and perceived control. In J. Suls and T. A. Wills, eds., *Social comparison: Contemporary theory and research,* pp. 237–60. Hillsdale N.J.: Lawrence Erlbaum Associates.

Malinowski, B. 1932. The problem of meaning in primitive language. In C. K. Ogden and I. A. Richards, eds., *The meaning of meaning.* London: Routledge.

Manber, U. 1989. *Introduction to algorithms: A creative approach.* Don Mills, Ont.: Addison-Wesley.

Maratasso, P., trans. 1972. *Aucassin and Nicolette and other tales.* Harmondsworth, Eng.: Penguin.

Marlowe, D., and D. Crown. 1960. *The approval motive.* New York: Wiley.

Medini, G., and E. H. Rosenberg. 1976. Gossip and psychotherapy. *American Journal of Psychotherapy* 30:452–62.

Meir, E. I., and A. Barak. 1974. A simple instrument for measuring vocational interests based on Roe's classification of occupations. *Journal of Vocational Behavior* 4:33–42.

Melvin v. Reid. 1931. 297 P. 91, 93 Cal.

Meyer, D., H. Leventhal, and M. Gutmann. 1985. Common sense models of illness: The example of hypertension. *Health Psychology* 4:115–35.

Midgeley, M. 1978. The objection to systematic Humbug. In *Heart and mind.* London: Methuen.

Mierrow, C., trans. 1962. Jerome, *Letters.* Ancient writers: The works of the fathers in translation 33. New York: Franklin.

Mintzberg, H. 1973. *The nature of managerial work.* Englewood Cliffs, N.J.: Prentice-Hall.

Mitchell, J. C. 1969. *Social networks in urban situations.* Manchester: Manchester University Press.

Mitford, N. 1978. *Love in a cold climate.* Harmondsworth, Eng.: Penguin.

Morreall, J. 1983a. Humor and emotion. *American Philosophical Quarterly* 20:297–304. Reprinted in Morreall, ed., 1987, ch. 22.

———. 1983b. *Taking laughter seriously.* Albany: State University of New York Press.

———. 1984. Humor and philosophy. *Metaphilosophy* 15:305–17.

———. 1989a. Enjoying incongruity. *Humor: International Journal of Humor Research* 2:1–18.

———. 1989b. The rejection of humor in western thought. *Philosophy East and West* 39:243–65.

Morreall, J., ed. 1987. *The philosophy of laughter and humor.* Albany: State University of New York Press.

Murdoch, I. 1970. *The sovereignty of good.* London: Routledge and Kegan.

Nagel, T. 1979. Death. In *Mortal questions.* Cambridge: Cambridge University Press.

Neustadt, R. E. 1990. *Presidential power and the modern presidents: The politics of leadership from Roosevelt to Reagan.* New York: Free Press.

Newcombe, N., and D. B. Arnkoff. 1979. Effects of speech style and sex of speaker on person perception. *Journal of Personality and Social Psychology* 37:1293–1303.

Oakley, A. 1972. *Sex, gender, and society.* London: Temple Smith.

———. 1974. *The sociology of housework.* New York: Pantheon Books.

Osmond, H. 1957. Function as the basis of warf design. *Mental Hospitals,* 23–29.

Parlett, D., trans. 1986. *Selections from the Carmina Burana.* Harmondsworth, Eng.: Penguin Classics.

Pavel, T. 1978. Literary criticism and methodology. *Dispositio* 3:147–48.

Pearson, J. C. 1985. *Gender and communication.* Dubuque, Iowa: Brown.

Peirce, C. S. 1931–1958. *Collected papers,* vols. 1–8, C. Hartshorne, P. Weiss, and A. Burks, eds. Cambridge, Mass.: Harvard University Press.

Peiser, C., and I. E. Meir. 1978. Congruency, consistency, and differentiation of interest predictors of vocational satisfaction and preference stability. *Journal of Vocational Behavior* 12:270–78.

Pitts, B. A., trans. 1985. *The fifteen joys of marriage [Les XV joies du mariage].* New York: Peter Lang.

Post, R. 1989. Foundations of privacy: Community and self in the common law tort. *California Law Review* 77:957.

———. 1990. The constitutional concept of public discourse: Outrageous opinion, democratic deliberation, and *Hustler Magazine v. Falwell. Harvard Law Review* 103:601.

Power, E. 1964. *Medieval English nunneries.* New York: Biblo and Tannen.

Radice, B., trans. 1981. *The letters of Abelard and Heloise.* Harmondsworth, Eng.: Penguin.

Reiss, H. T., and L. Wheeler. 1991. Studying social interaction with the Rochester Interaction Record. *Advances in Experimental Social Psychology* 24:269–318.

Restatement (Second) of Torts. 1977. Section 652D.

Robbins, H. W., trans. 1962. Guillaume de Lorris and Jean Le Meun, *The romance of the rose*. New York: E. P. Dutton.

Roe, A. 1956. *The psychology of occupations*. New York: Wiley.

Rogers, E. M. 1983. *Diffusion of innovations*. 3d ed. New York: Free Press.

Rosch, E. 1977. Human categorization. In N. Warren, ed., *Advance in cross-cultural psychology*. London: Academic Press.

————. 1978. Principles of categorization. In E. Rosch and B. B. Lloyd, eds., *Cognition and categorization*. Hillsdale, N.J.: Erlbaum.

Rosenbaum, J. B., and M. Subrin. 1975. The psychology of gossip. *American Journal of Psychotherapy* 29:263–70.

Rosenberg, M. J. 1965. *Society and the adolescent self-image*. Princeton, N.J.: Princeton University Press.

Rosenthal, R., and R. L. Rosnow. 1985. *Essentials of behavioral research: Methods and data analysis*. New York: McGraw Hill.

————. 1991. *Essentials of behavioral research: Methods and data analysis*. 2d ed. New York: McGraw Hill.

Rosnow, R. L. 1977. Gossip and marketplace psychology. *Journal of Communication* 27:158–63.

————. In press. Inside rumor: A personal journey. *American Psychologist*.

Rosnow, R. L., and G. A. Fine. 1976a. Inside rumors. *Human Behavior* 3(8):64–68.

————. 1976b. *Rumor and gossip: The social psychology of hearsay*. New York: Elsevier.

Rosnow, R. L., and M. Georgoudi. 1985. Killed by idle gossip: The psychology of small talk. In B. Rubin, ed., *When information counts*, pp. 59–73. Lexington, Mass.: Heath.

Rosnow, R. L., and R. Rosenthal. 1989. Statistical procedures and the justification of knowledge in psychological science. *American Psychologist* 44:1276–84.

Rosnow, R. L., H. Wainer, and R. L. Arms. 1969. Anderson's personality-trait words rated by men and women as a function of stimulus sex. *Psychological Reports* 24:787–90.

Rowbotham, S. 1983. Women's liberation and the new politics. In *Dreams and dilemmas*. London: Virago.

Ryle, G. 1954. *Dilemmas*. Cambridge: Cambridge University Press.

Rysman, A. R. 1976. Gossip and occupational ideology. *Journal of Communication* 26:64–68.

————. 1977. How the "gossip" became a woman. *Journal of Communication* 27:176–80.

Sabini, J., and M. Silver. 1982. *Moralities of everyday life*. New York: Oxford University Press.

Sahlins, M. 1972. *Stone age economics*. Chicago: Aldine.

Samora, J., L. Saunders, and R. F. Larson. 1961. Medical vocabulary among hospital patients. *Journal of Health and Social Behavior* 2:83–89.

SAS. 1985. User guide. Cary, N.C.

Scambler, A., G. Scambler, and D. Craig. 1981. Kinship and friendship networks and women's demand for primary care. *Journal of the Royal College of General Practitioners* 26:746–50.

Scambler, G., and A. Scambler. 1985. The illness iceberg and aspects of consulting behavior. In R. Fitzpatrick and J. Hinton, eds., *The experience of illness*, pp. 32–50. London: Tavistock.

Schachter, S., and H. Burdick. 1955. A field experiment on rumor transmission and distortion. *Journal of Abnormal and Social Psychology* 50:363–71.

Schoeman, F. 1984. Privacy and intimate information. In F. Schoeman, ed., *Philosophical dimensions of privacy*. New York: Cambridge University Press.

Shakespeare, W. 1911. *The merry wives of Windsor*. In W. G. Clark and W. A. Wright, eds., *The Complete Works of William Shakespeare*. New York: Cumberland.

Shapersteen, D. J. 1987. Personality and motivation to gossip. Paper presented at the ninety-fifth meeting of the American Psychological Association, New York.

Shaw, M. R. B., trans. 1963. Joinville and Villehardouin, *Chronicles of the Crusades*. Harmondsworth, Eng.: Penguin.

Sheridan, R. B. 1966. *The school for scandal*, ed. J. Loftis. Arlington Heights, Ill.: AHM Publishing Corporation.

Shotter, J. 1989. Rhetoric and the recovery of civil society. *Economy and Society* 18:150.

Skipper, J., and R. Leonard, eds. 1965. *Social interaction and patient care*. Philadelphia: Lippincott.

Skowronski, J. J., and D. E. Carlston. 1987. Social judgment and social memory: The role of cue diagnosticity in negativity, positivity, and extremity biases. *Journal of Personality and Social Psychology* 52:689–99.

Spacks, P. M. 1985. *Gossip*. New York: Knopf.

Starkie, T. 1826. *A treatise on the law of slander, libel*, scandalum magnatur, *and false rumours*. New York.

Stephan, F. F., and E. G. Mischler. 1952. The distribution of participation in small groups: An exponential approximation. *American Sociological Review* 17:482–86.

Stone, B., trans. 1983. Geoffrey Chaucer, *Love visions*. Harmondsworth, Eng.: Penguin.

Suchman, E. A. 1974. Sociomedical variations among ethnic groups. *American Journal of Sociology* 70:319–31.

Suls, J. M. 1977. Gossip as social comparison. *Journal of Communication* 27:164–68.

Suls, J. M., and R. L. Miller, eds. 1977. *Social comparison processes: Theoretical and empirical perspectives*. Washington D.C.: Hemisphere.

Swan, C., and W. Hooper, trans. 1959. *Gesta Romanorum; or, Entertaining moral stories*. New York: Dover.

Szalai, A. 1972. *The use of time: Daily activities of urban and suburban populations in twelve countries*. The Hague: Mouton.

Tannen, D. 1990. *You just don't understand*. New York: Ballantine Books.

Taylor, J. A. 1953. A personality scale of manifest anxiety. *Journal of Abnormal and Social Psychology* 48:285–90.

Taylor, H. J. S. 1977. Teach your pupils to gossip. *English Language Teaching Journal* 31:222–26.

Taylor, R. B., C. B. De Soto, and R. Lieb. 1979. Sharing secrets: Disclosure and discretion in dyads and triads. *Journal of Personality and Social Psychology* 37:1196–1203.

Taylor, S. E., and M. Lobel. 1989. Social comparison activity under threat: Downward evaluation and upward contacts. *Psychological Review* 96: 569–75.

Taylor, S. E., J. V. Wood, and R. R. Lichtman. 1983. It could be worse: Selective evaluation as a response to victimization. *Journal of Social Issues* 39:19–40.

Tiller, T., trans. 1963. John Gover, *Confessio Amantis*. Harmondsworth, Eng.: Penguin.

Tonnies, F. 1957. *Community and society.* New York: Harper. Originally published 1887.

Trofimenkoff, S. M. 1985. Gossip in history. In *Historical Papers/Communications Historiques.* Ottawa: Canadian Historical Association.

Warren, S., and L. Brandeis. 1890. The right to privacy. *Harvard Law Review* 4:193.

Watson, D., and L. A. Clark. 1984. Negative affectivity: The disposition to experience aversive emotional states. *Psychological Bulletin* 96:465–90.

Watson, D., and J. W. Pennebaker. 1989. Health complaints, stress, and distress: Exploring the central role of negative affectivity. *Psychological Review* 96:234–54.

Webb, E. J., D. T. Campbell, R. D. Schwart, and L. Sechrest. 1966. *Unobtrusive measures: Non-reactive research in the social sciences.* Chicago: Rand McNally.

Weber, M. 1947. *The theory of social and economic organisations,* trans. A. M. Henderson and T. Parsons, ed. T. Parsons. New York: Free Press.

Wellman, B. 1978. The community question: the intimate networks of East Yorkers. *American Journal of Sociology* 84:1201–31.

Wharton, E. 1922. *The house of mirth.* London: Macmillan.

Wheeler, L., and J. Nezlek. 1977. Sex differences in social participation. *Journal of Personality and Social Psychology* 35:742–54.

Wills, T. A. 1981. Downward comparison principles in social psychology. *Psychological Bulletin* 90:245–71.

Wilson, E. O. 1974. *Sociobiology: The new synthesis.* Cambridge, Mass.: Harvard/Belknap.

Windeatt, B. A., trans. 1985. *The book of Margery Kempe.* Harmondsworth, Eng.: Penguin.

Wirth, L. 1938. Urbanism as a way of life. *American Journal of Sociology* 44:3–24.

Wood, J. V., S. E. Taylor, and R. R. Lichtman. 1985. Social comparison in adjustment to breast cancer. *Journal of Personality and Social Psychology* 49:1169–83.

Zimmerman, D. 1983. Requiem for a heavyweight: A Farewell to Warren and Brandeis's privacy tort. *Cornell Law Review* 68:292–367.

About the Contributors

Maryann Ayim is a member of the Faculty of Education, The University of Western Ontario, Canada.

Aaron Ben-Ze'ev is a member of the Department of Philosophy, University of Haifa, Israel.

Lorraine Code is a member of the Department of Philosophy, York University, Canada.

Louise Collins is presently residing in England.

Anat Derech-Zahavi was a graduate student at the Department of Psychology, University of Haifa, Israel.

Ronald de Sousa is a member of the Department of Philosophy, University of Toronto, Canada.

Nicholas Emler is a member of the Department of Experimental Psychology, University of Oxford, England.

Franklin Goodkin is at Castleton State College, Vermont, USA.

Robert F. Goodman is associated with the Department of Philosophy, University of Haifa, Israel.

Marianne E. Jaeger is a member of the Department of Psychology, Temple University, Pennsylvania, USA.

John Morreall is a member of the Department of Philosophy, Rochester Institute of Technology, New York, USA.

Ofra Nevo and **Baruch Nevo** are members of the Department of Psychology, University of Haifa, Israel.

Robert Post is a member of the faculty of the School of Law, University of California at Berkeley, USA.

Bruce Rind is a member of the Department of Psychology, Miami University of Ohio, USA.

Ralph L. Rosnow is a member of the Department of Psychology, Temple University, Pennsylvania, USA.

Sylvia Schein is a member of the Department of History, University of Haifa, Israel.

Ferdinand Schoeman passed away before the publication of this book. He was a member of the Department of Philosophy, University of South Carolina, USA.

Anne A. Skleder is a member of the Department of Psychology, Temple University, Pennsylvania, USA.

Jerry Suls is a member of the Department of Psychology, University of Iowa, USA.

Gabriele Taylor is a member of St. Anne's College, Oxford, England.

Laurence Thomas is a member of the Department of Philosophy, Syracuse University, USA.

Index

Abelard and Heloise, 148
Acute illness, 178
Allen, S., 60
Allport, G., 174
Anthropology, 18, 32, 66, 88, 154
  philosophical, 106, 109, 114
Anxiety, 160, 161, 163(table), 166, 173,
  174, 176, 178, 182
Arendt, H., 75
Aristotle, 24, 95, 109
Arluke, A., 17, 23, 139, 154, 156, 183, 188
Art of Courtly Love (Capellanus), 140
Ayim, M., 6, 25, 33, 102–3

Baboons, 121
Back, K. W., 176
Bales, R. F., 130
Barbour, J. S., 178
Belgians, 121–22
Benn, S., 75
Ben-Ze'ev, A., 1, 3, 4, 5, 56, 57, 61, 154,
  188
Bergson, H., 62
Berne, E., 129
Binary categories, 11
Bishop of Lincoln, 147
Boccaccio, G., 139, 143, 144, 149
Borge, V., 62
Brandeis, L., 67
"Branks," 119
Breviari d'amor (Ernengaud), 150
Burns, T., 126
Business managers, 128–29
Butcher of Abbeville, The (Eustache of
  Amiens), 143

California Supreme Court, 67
Canterbury Tales (Chaucer), 139, 140–41
Capellanus, A., 140, 148, 149
Carmina Burana, 146
Chatelaine of Vergy, 152
Chaucer, G., 139, 141, 145
Chimpanzees, 132
Chronic illness, 178
Civil law, 6, 67–71
Code, L., 1, 3, 6, 7
Cohen, J., 160
Coke, E., 121, 123

Collins, L., 7, 25
Commonsensible judgments, 3, 8
"Community lost" social life, 127
Community norms, 65, 66, 67, 69, 70,
  183
Company presidents, 125, 126
Concerning Famous Women (Boccaccio),
  149
Confessio Amantis (Gower), 140
Conversation. See Spoken interaction;
  under Gossip
Conzaga, C., 146
Coolidge, C., 61
Correr, G., 146
Courtesy books for women, 149–50
Crown, D., 158, 185, 187
Cuckold, 146

Decameron (Boccaccio), 139, 143, 146, 147
Defamation law, 65, 67
Dennett, D., 95
Desirade (island), 118
De Soto, C. B., 137
de Sousa, R., 1, 3, 7, 13
de Waal, F., 133
Doings, 131
Ducking stools, 1, 119
Dunbar, R.I.M., 129

Eavesdropping, 130
Efficiency, 12
Egypt, 176–77
Eliot, G., 118
Emler, N., 1, 7·
Empathy, 112–13
Envy, 21, 26, 42, 59
Erikson, K., 67
Ernengaud, M., 150
Eustache of Amiens, 143
Excessive nongossips, 19–20
"Exploratory Analysis of Sex Differences
  in Gossip, An" (Levin and Arluke),
  139
Extrinsically valuable action, 12–13, 14
  and gossip, 13, 38, 107, 195(n2)

Feminism, 3, 5, 7, 105, 106, 114
Festinger, L., 182

Fifteen Joys of Marriage, 142
Fine, G. A., 181, 182
Fines, 1
First Amendment, 68, 69, 70
Flogging, 1
Florida Star v. B.J.F. (1989), 68, 70, 195(n2)
Florida Statutes Section 794.03 (1987), 68
Folkway standards, 23
France, 176
Fraternities, 167
Freidson, E., 171
Fresne, Le (Mary of France), 152
Freud, S., 28
Friendship. *See under* Gossip; Gossipers

Garin lo Brun, 149
Gender inequalities, 138
Georgoudi, M., 154, 156, 167
Gesta Romanorum, 149
Gilligan, C., 114
Glaspell, S., 100
Gloating, 21, 22, 63
Gluckman, M., 66, 80, 134
Godkin, E. L., 69
Goffman, E., 65
Goodkin, F., 8
Good Wife Taught Her Daughter, The, 150
Gossip
  and adaptation, 138
  "backyard," 68–69
  celebrity, 17, 23, 55, 58, 69, 70, 93, 155, 175, 184
  characterization of, 11–12, 13, 18, 21, 23, 24, 47–55, 57–59, 72, 80, 92, 96, 100–101, 104–5, 106–8, 135–37, 154, 156, 166–67, 174, 175, 182
  and children, 21, 143
  and civil law, 6, 67–71
  as communication, 3, 4, 6–7, 8, 15, 16–17, 22–23, 48–49, 52, 53, 66, 79–80, 106, 107, 108, 112, 135, 138, 154, 156, 167, 183–84
  as conversation, 58, 59, 64, 86, 98, 106, 107, 136 (*see also* Slander)
  critics of, 108–9, 111, 181
  and cultures, 20–21, 33, 118 (*see also* Medieval society)
  and curiosity, 15, 18, 38, 42, 133
  as defense mechanism, 182
  defined, 4, 5, 13, 34, 65–66, 131, 139, 181, 183
  effect of, 22, 27, 38, 56, 81, 86–87, 96, 101, 113, 114, 118, 119–20, 154, 169, 181, 182
  as egalitarian, 107
  emotional content of, 6, 16, 40, 59, 79
  and feminism, 3, 5, 7, 105, 106, 114
  and friendship, 15–16, 38, 45, 62, 86, 137
  functional role, 1–2, 3, 4, 69, 71, 117, 132, 133–35, 138, 154–55, 181, 182, 183
  and gender, 5, 8, 20, 25, 86, 94–95, 96, 98–99, 100–102, 111, 114, 118–19, 120, 138, 167, 181, 184, 187, 188 (*see also* Medieval society, gossipers)
  good, 89–90
  and humor, 5, 56–57, 59–64, 107, 144–45
  as inquiry, 86–88, 90–93, 94–99, 100, 102–4, 133, 136, 154, 156, 181, 182
  investigative, 87
  malicious, 13, 19, 21, 25–27, 32, 38–39, 45, 48, 49, 51, 55, 63, 108, 109, 118, 145, 167
  meaning, original, 59
  medical, 8, 169–79
  modern, 1, 4, 5, 118, 181
  moral content of, 2, 101–2, 112, 134, 135, 137
  moral view of, 1, 2–3, 4, 5, 7, 21, 23, 24, 27, 29, 43–46, 59, 66, 106, 109, 112, 113
  motives, 54
  norms, 80–82
  and occupations, 184, 185, 187, 188–89
  as pleasurable, 16, 18, 21, 22, 36, 38, 39, 57, 60, 61, 62, 106, 144–45, 154, 167
  as power, 25, 94, 99, 104, 108, 133–34, 139, 151–53
  professional, 48, 51
  and psychotherapy, 182, 187–88, 189
  punishment for, 1, 118–19
  and reciprocity, 16, 50
  reputation of, 117–20, 137–38, 183, 184–85, 187, 188
  and rumor, 14, 59, 155, 169
  and science (*see* Peirce, C. S.)
  and sensibilities, 29
  settings, 4, 6, 7, 37, 86, 88, 156, 167, 180, 181, 183
  social science approach to, 181
  studies, 4, 7–8, 156–68, 169–70, 183–84
  and subcultures, 33
  tendency to, measure of, 180, 183, 184–89
  topics of, 17, 18, 20, 22, 25, 26, 35–36, 58–59, 86, 90, 96–97, 98–99, 109, 184, 186, 187, 188, 189
  traditional, 1, 2, 4, 8

and truth, 23, 26, 40, 57, 86, 88, 92,
    101, 112, 133, 136, 154
virtues, 1, 2, 3, 5, 7, 11, 15–16, 23, 24,
    27, 30–31, 66
See also Gossipers; Literature, gossip
    in
Gossipers
    characteristics, 19, 37, 42, 90–91, 93,
        111, 112, 118, 134, 138, 139, 155, 158,
        160–62, 189
    child, 21, 143
    detachment, 37, 41, 45–46
    and friendship, 162–64, 165(fig.)
    and gender, 5, 8, 20, 25, 96, 98
    and gossipee, 4, 5, 7, 17, 18, 21–22, 36,
        39–40, 41–44, 45–46, 88, 99, 108,
        114, 155, 157, 159–60, 163–64,
        165(fig.), 181, 182, 194(n7)
    as gossipees, 162–63, 164, 166
    high, 160–62, 163, 166, 182, 184
    insiders and outsiders, 94
    low, 160–62, 163, 166, 184
    moderate, 160–62, 163, 184
    popularity, 160, 161, 165–66
    punishment, 1, 119
    quality of, 57
    relationship between, 4, 5, 39, 40, 41,
        108–9, 182
    topics, 2, 8, 15, 38
    See also under Medieval society
Gossipmongers, 18–19, 155
Gossip Tendency Questionnaire (GTQ),
    184–89, 191–92
Gouldner, A., 70
Gower, J., 140
Great Britain, 1, 15, 119, 170
Gregory IX (pope), 149
Group cohesion, 3, 15, 17, 40, 66, 80, 154,
    181, 183
GTQ (Gossip Tendency Questionnaire),
    184–89, 191–92
Guillaume de Lorris, 140

Hannerz, U., 181
Health care, use of, 169–70, 171
Heidegger, M., 14
House of Fame (Chaucer), 145–46
Hull, D. L., 6, 90
Humor, and gossip, 5, 56–57, 59–64, 107,
    144–45
Humphrey, N., 138
Hunter-gatherers, 122
Hurka, T., 28, 29
Huxley, A., 17

"Illness iceberg," 170

Imagination, 57, 113
Incongruity, 60, 61
Interaction Process Analysis, 130–31
Intimate information, 15, 16, 17, 20, 22,
    25, 26, 32–33, 34, 58–59, 72, 97, 154,
    180, 182
Intrinsically valuable activity, 12–13, 15
Iron mask, 119

Jackson (Miss.), 122
Jacques of Vitry, 143, 149
Jaeger, M. E., 7
Jealousy, 59
Jean de Meun, 139, 141
Jewish law, 1, 181
John of Joinville, 146
Joking, 14, 56–57, 59–60, 61, 144–45
Jones, D., 94
Jourard, S. M., 131
"June Bug" episode, 116
"Jury of Her Peers, A" (film), 100–102,
    104

Kant, I., 22, 26, 30, 31, 43–44, 109
Kempe, M., 146–47
Kerckhoff, A. C., 176
Kibbutz, 185
Kierkegaard, S., 18
Kinsey reports, 31
Knowledge acquisition and transmission,
    3, 4, 6–7, 15, 17, 18, 22–23, 31–32,
    54, 58, 80, 85–88, 112, 131–32, 134,
    135, 181, 183
    and women, 93–94
See also Gossip, as communication;
    Gossip, as inquiry
Kuhn, T., 6

Laetrile, 177, 178
Langland, W., 140, 145, 149
Language, 122–23, 129, 132, 133
    and gender, 96
La Rochefoucauld, F., 31
Lasakow, P., 131
Laughter, 62
Lay medical advice, 169, 171–78
Leventhal, H., 170
Levin, J., 17, 23, 139, 154, 156, 183, 188
Leviticus, 140
Libel, 6, 67, 68
Liberalism, 109–10
Lieb, R., 137
Life of Saint Louis (John of Joinville), 146
Listeners, 123–24, 187
Literacy, 124

Literature, gossip in, 15, 18, 25, 118, 139, 140–42, 143–44, 145–46, 147–48, 152
Lobel, M., 174
Louis XII (king of France), 150
Love, 146. *See also* Medieval society, courtly love

Macaques, 121, 122
Male-dominated work, 110
Malinowski, B., 129, 130
Manifest Anxiety Scale (MAS), 158, 182
Marlowe, D., 158, 185, 187
Mary of France, 152
MAS. *See* Manifest Anxiety Scale
Masculine philosophy. *See* Gossip, critics of; Gossip, and gender
Media, 16, 17, 23, 24, 52, 58, 80, 123–24
and defamation law, 67–71
gossipy, 57, 66 (*see also* Gossip, celebrity)
and medical gossip and rumor, 172–73, 175, 178
Medical folklore, 173
Medieval society
as "close" society, 139, 151, 152
courtesy books, 149–50
courtly love, 140–41, 148, 152
gossip, power of, 151–53
gossip censured, 140–41
gossipers, 141–44, 148–51, 153
gossip motives, 144–45, 151
gossip role, 139, 142
gossip subject matter, 145–48
misogyny, 148–49, 150
oral communication, 151
religion, 140
women's status in, 150–51, 153
Medini, G., 182
Melvin v. Reid (1931), 67
Meyer, D., 170
Mintzberg, H., 125, 126
Mitchell, J. C., 127
Moral codes, 1, 2, 110, 111, 113
Morally neutral characterization, 26, 41–42
Moral theory, 2–3, 105
Moral value, 29
Morreall, J., 5

NA (negatively affective), 175–76
Need-satisfying activities, 16
Negatively affective (NA), 175–76
Nerenz, D., 170
Neustadt, R. E., 86
Nevo, O., 5, 8
Nezlek, J., 125, 126

Nonverbal communication, 130
Nuns, 147–48, 149

Occupational interest inventory (Ramak), 185

Parker, D., 61
Particularistic personal reference, 131–32
Passive resistance, 5
Pavel, T., 89–90
Peirce, C. S., 87, 88, 89, 90, 92, 93, 103
Phatic communication, 129, 130
Piers the Ploughman (Langland), 145, 148
Pisan, C. de, 143–44, 150, 151
Plato, 109
Pornography, 26
Post, R., 6
Postman, L., 174
Preferences, 131
Privacy, 4, 5, 6, 27–30, 32, 46, 51, 54, 65, 72, 109–10, 156
expressive role, 77–78
normative and descriptive, 72–73
role, 74–77
scope, 77–78, 81–82
tort of invasion of, 67–68, 69, 70–71
Private conversation, 16–17, 58
Prototypical categories, 11–12, 13
Psychogenic illness, 176
Public information, 16, 52, 54–55
Publicity, 68
Public shaming, 119

"Quossip," 108

Ramak. *See* Occupational interest inventory
Reiss, H. T., 125, 128
Reputational information, 133–34, 135
"Right to Privacy, The" (Warren and Brandeis), 67
Roe, A., 185
Rogers, E. M., 131
Rogers, W., 60
Romance of the Rose (Guillaume de Lorris), 140
Romance of the Rose (Jean de Meun), 139, 141
Rosenberg, E. H., 182
Rosenberg, M. J., 158
Rosenberg's Self-Esteem Scale, 158
Rosnow, R. L., 154, 155, 156, 158, 167, 181, 182
Rumor, 14, 59, 155, 158, 169, 174, 175
defined, 173
Rysman, A. R., 181

Sabini, J., 135, 156
St. Jerome, 148
St. Paul, 148
Salinger, J. D., 28
Sartre, J. P., 109
Schein, S., 8, 181
Scheler, M., 76, 77
Schoeman, F., 6
Scold's bridle, 119
Secrets, 16, 28, 39, 94, 156, 182
Self-assessment, 173, 174, 182, 183
Self-disclosure, 131
Self-enhancement, 173, 174, 181
Self-esteem, 3, 44, 154, 158, 160, 161, 162, 163(table), 166, 173, 174, 182, 183
Self-understanding, 112, 114, 183
Seminar/small class settings, 88–89
Shame, 76, 119
Shapersteen, D. J., 183
Shotter, J., 100
Silver, M., 135, 156
Slander, 6, 67, 68
"Sleeper effect," 178
Soap operas, 40–41
Sociability, 121–22, 156
Social approval, 160, 161, 162, 163(table), 166
Social communication, 16. *See also* Spoken interaction
Social comparison activity, 174–75, 181–82, 183
Social control, 6, 32–33, 65, 72–73, 75, 76, 194(n8)
Social Desirability Questionnaire, 158, 185, 187, 188
Social norms, 72, 74–77, 80, 82, 94. *See also* Community norms
Social organization, 121, 124, 127–28, 132–33
Social psychological approach, 181
Sociolinguistics, 130
Sociological-anthropological approach, 181
Solidarity, 62, 100–101. *See also* Group cohesion
Sororities, 156, 157, 158–59, 163, 167
Spacks, P. M., 25
Speakers, 123
Spoken interaction, 123–32
    content of, 129–32
    diary record, 128, 130
    as dyadic, 126, 129

group, 126
studies, 125, 128–29, 131–32
triadic, 137
and workplace, 126
Starkie, T., 65
Status, 3, 19, 45, 154, 181, 182
Stocks, 1, 119
"Stroking," 129
Structure of Scientific Revolutions, The (Kuhn), 6
Students, 125, 128, 185
Suchman, E. A., 169
Suls, J. M., 8, 181
Supreme Court, U.S., 68–69, 70, 195(n2)
Surprise, 56, 61
Suzanne of Bourboun (Anne of France), 150
Szalai, A., 121, 122, 123, 124

Taboo topics, 56
Tannen, D., 16, 18
Task-oriented speech, 129–30
Taylor, G., 2, 4, 5
Taylor, J. A., 158
Taylor, R. B., 137
Taylor, S. E., 174
Technology, 124
Thomas, L., 2, 4–5
Time, 69, 70
Time, use of, 121–22, 123. *See also* Spoken interaction
Treasure of the City of Ladies (Pisan), 143–44, 150
"Trifles" (Glaspell), 100–102

Utilitarianism, 29

Valloire (France), 118
Varimax factor analysis, 186
Voyeurism, 182, 184

Warren, S., 67
Weber, M., 124
Wheeler, L., 125, 126, 128
Wilde, O., 14
Wirth, L., 127
Witch burning, 119
Women. *See* Gossip, and gender; Gossipers, and gender; *under* Knowledge acquisition and transmission

J